The State & Agricultural Development in Egypt since 1973

The State &
Agricultural Development
in Egypt since 1973

Simon Commander

Published for the Overseas Development Institute, London
by Ithaca Press, London & Atlantic Highlands NJ
1987

Middle East Science Policy Studies No 11

© 1987 The Overseas Development Institute, London

First published in 1987 by
Ithaca Press
13 Southwark Street London SE 1 1RQ
&
171 First Avenue Atlantic Highlands NJ 07716

Printed & bound in England by
Biddles Ltd Guildford & Kings Lynn

British Library Cataloguing in Publication Data

Commander, Simon
    The state and agricultural development in
    Egypt since 1973.——(Middle East science
    policy studies series; no. 11).
    1. Agriculture——Economic aspects——Egypt
    —— History——20th century
    I. Title II. Overseas Development
    Institute III. Series
    338.1'0962   HD2123

Library of Congress Cataloging-in-Publication Data

Commander, Simon.
    The state and agricultural development in Egypt
since 1973.

    (Middle East science policy studies ; no. 11)
    Bibliography: p.
    Includes index.
    1. Agriculture and state--Egypt. I. Overseas
Development Institute (London, England) II. Title.
III. Series.
HD2123.Z8C66 1987   338.1'862   87-3616
ISBN 0-86372-080-3
ISBN 0-86372-079-X (pbk.)

CONTENTS

iv

List of Tables

Appendix Tables

List of Graphs

GLOSSARY

1 qirat = 1/24 feddan = 175.03m^2
1 feddan = 1.038 acres = 0.42 hectares = 4200.83m^2
1 qantar = 99.05lb = 44.92kg
1 metric qantar = 346.5lb = 157.5kg

1 ardab (wheat) = 330.4lb = 150kg
1 ardab (maize) = 308.4lb = 140kg
1 ardab (lentils)= 352.42lb = 160kg
1 ardab (beans) = 341.41lb = 155kg
1 ardab (barley) = 264.32lb = 120kg
1 dariba (rice) = 2081.5lb = 945 kg

gamiya = cooperative
marwa   = small distributor, irrigation ditch
mesqa   = small canal feeding from 10-40 farms
saqia   = animal drawn water wheel
iltizam = tax-farming
ezba   = hamlet

x

PREFACE

Work on this study started in earnest at the beginning of 1984
after a short preparatory visit to Cairo in the latter part of
the previous year. The entire experience of working in Egypt
proved to be immensely enjoyable, let alone educative. I went
to Egypt imagining it to be moderately similar to some parts
of India where I had previous experience and familial ties.
It rapidly transpired that this was far from being the case
and, at least from my viewpoint, thankfully so. I say this
with no sense of judgement, merely in appreciation of the
pleasures of difference. The most memorable aspect of working
in Egypt proved to be the hospitality, kindness and friendship
that I so regularly encountered. A measly preface cannot give
adequate thanks to those who helped.

Such qualms aside, my greatest debt, but partially redeemed,
is to Ahmed Goueli. His consistent help, encouragement and
participation in the project, despite a wide range of other
commitments, was in fact the critical factor. I am truly grateful for his help and friendship and for having, in effect,
created the conditions and means by which this study could be
undertaken. He was also instrumental in setting up a further
visit to Egypt at the end of 1986 during which a number of
seminars and talks were given in an attempt to achieve a
rather wider dissemination of the study's conclusions.

John Gerhart, formerly the head of the Ford Foundation in
Cairo, played a crucial role by agreeing to the Foundation
funding the research costs. His successor, Lee Travers, was
generous in his comments on drafts of the report and in
agreeing to fund the later trip to Egypt to present the main
conclusions. In London, the Overseas Development
Administration, through its ESCOR research fund, kindly provided the financial support for travel and other costs,
including computing, which were incurred in England. The
British Council and the Ford Foundation supplied the means for
Aly Abdullah Hadhoud my Egyptian collaborator on the original
report, to visit England for a short period in early 1985. I
am grateful to these institutions for their invaluable
assistance.

In Egypt, I should like to thank the inhabitants of the three
villages that were selected for the study for their truly
generous hospitality, let alone their agreement in being asked
all sorts of nosey questions. The Mashour family made me feel
a member of their clan and I should most especially like to
thank the head of the family and omda, Abdul Hamid Mashour, as
also Mohammed Mashour and his immediate family, for their
exceptional kindness and friendship. I learnt more from them
about the intricacies of contemporary Egyptian life than from
anyone, let alone benefiting from the culinary treats to which

I was so frequently invited. Ahmed Mashour, aside from this excellent work, was a true friend and companion.

I am also exceedingly grateful to the families of Aly Abdullah Hadhoud, El Sayed Mahdy, Mohammed Ghabir and Sayed Sanhouti for their hospitality and help in their respective homes and villages.

In the largest village of all - Cairo - Harold Lubell allowed me the run of his most fine apartment in Garden City, as well as offering a great amount of other help, advice and friendship. Cynthia Myntti was a good friend and always encouraging.

This work was done while based at ODI. The Institute provided a relaxed but stimulating environment. I would most particularly like to thank John Howell for his encouragement. Peter Gee gave considerable assistance in editing the manuscript for publication.

In Egypt the Department of Agricultural Economics at the University of Zagazig provided a welcoming base. I am very grateful to the current Head of Department, Professor El Mallahy El Dessouki, as well as Professors Ibrahim Soliman, Shawky Imam, Sonia Aly, Mohammed Radwan and Sayed Sanhouti for their assistance. I would like particularly to thank Aly Abdullah Hadhoud for his collaboration on the original project. I much enjoyed our frequent conversations, generally conducted over an excellent coffee brewed in the byzantine recesses of the Department with unrivalled skill by Azouz and Khalil.

Amongst the many other people who assisted me in Egypt I should like to mention Drs. M.K. Hindy, A. El-Hossary, Yehya Mohie-eldin and A. El-Sahrigy at the Ministry of Agriculture in Cairo; Ismael Bedawi Mahmoud Abdel Fadil, Heba Handoussa and Nicholas Hopkins at AUC; the staff of ADS, particularly Amal Ibrahim and Ibrahim Youssef; Mme Atemed at the FAO building; David Gaiser and Stephen Shepley of the Agricultural Mechanization Project; Ibrahim El-Issawi at INP, as also Nader Fergany, Adrian Davis and Elizabeth Taylor-Awny. At various times and in various ways, Bent Hansen, Carl Gotsch, James Fitch, Roger Owen, Lee Travers, Tony Addison, Paul Howell, Barbara Ibrahim, Andrea Siemsen, S.K. Rao, Terry Byres, Lionel Demery, Jayati Ghosh and John Commander have given most useful advice or criticism.

The three enumerators - Ahmed Mashour, Mohammed Gabir and Abdel Menam Yusuf - undertook their work energetically and efficiently. I could not have hoped for a better team. They were also a pleasure to work with; Rowan Smillie gave excellent computational assistance.

At ODI, Ramila Mistry and Fiona Harris have had, periodically, to transform my foul hand into machine processed prose. They did it awfully well. Barbara Tilbury not only had to do that but, as always, was immensely helpful and efficient, particularly when putting the final study together. Jennifer Dudley had however to bear most of the brunt and did a splendid job. I am truly grateful to her for helping me out so very kindly and efficiently, particularly in the final preparation of the manuscript. Last and most, I thank Nemat Shafik for advice, friendship and much more besides.

Having - with much pleasure - acknowledged and thanked all these friends and colleagues, how very expedient it would be if I could blame them all for the errors, omissions and howling blunders that must litter this study?

Simon Commander
February, 1987

CHAPTER ONE

Introduction

Forty years ago in a pioneering work of social enquiry, Abbas
Ammar spelt out the stark realities of Egyptian rural life.[1]
Land hunger, inequality in the distribution of assets and
income, chronic underemployment and lack of diversification in
the sources of income were the principal features of the rural
economy.   With land monopolised by a very small number of
large estate holders, the discrepancy between the demand for
and supply of hired labour was sufficient to make agricultural
employment the critical factor in determining the level of
welfare amongst the expanded, joint families of the Nile
Delta.   With the limited introduction of agricultural machinery in the 1930s and 1940s, Ammar noted that the demand for
labour had fallen yet further, moreover,

'most of the labourers are not employed all the time and their
already marginal income has been greatly affected. This may
be counted amongst the factors stimulating the rural exodus,
but its serious effect is revealed in the great pressure on
the small holdings and the very low acreage exploited per per-
son in each household'.[2]

Contemporary economic conditions in rural Egypt seem to have
been subject to a dramatic and apparently conclusive transformation.   No longer is the <u>fellah</u> viewed as the deprived and
exploited drudge of productive life but, the supposed scarcity
of labour in rural areas, rather than its super-abundance, has
become the theme of much recent writing on the Egyptian rural
economy and labour market.[3]   While this dramatic change is
commonly attributed to employment opportunities created by the
rapid growth of the oil-producing economies of the Near East,
closer inspection of the basic issues reveals that, superficially at least, much that existed in the 1940s remains relevant today.   The population has sustained a growth rate of
around 2.5% per annum over the last three decades, with urban
demographic growth rates surpassing 3.6% per annum. Migration
from rural areas to Cairo, Alexandria and the other Delta
towns remains a major feature of the economy, but despite this
continuing outflow, the land has to support directly an ever
higher number of humans.[4]   Between 1947 and 1976 the cultivated acreage per head of rural population fell from 0.44 to
0.27 and if the limited availability of land necessarily remains a constant feature, it also should be noted that high

dependency ratios, and relatively low levels of material
advancement still characterise much of Egyptian rural life.
Moreover, the discrepancy in income levels between town and
countryside remains substantial. By the mid-1970s per capita
income levels in the towns were double those for rural
inhabitants.[5]

Nevertheless, a number of very significant changes have occurred in the last decades. Not least of these has been the
phenomenon of land reform and the effective eradication of the
former landed estates. The growth of an industrial and services sector in the towns has also led to the expansion of
employment opportunities, and the establishment of a state-
subsidised educational system has had major implications for
the development of domestic human capital and the structure of
the labour market. With the undeniable increase in employment
possibilities in the Arab and Gulf states since the mid-1970s,
the combined result has been to weaken the historically substantial reservoir of labour in the rural areas.
Consequently, earlier attempts at mechanising Egyptian agriculture have been supplanted by a heavily subsidised and
promoted campaign for further mechanisation. With the population likely to double within 25 years and a widening shortfall in the domestic supply of food relative to current
demand, recent government policy has hinged on, in theory,
promoting greater food self-sufficiency through productivity
increments in agriculture. One substantive barrier - in the
view of many, including the government - has been the lack of
available labour for agriculture. Moreover, this declining
availability has been seen not merely as a compacted, seasonal
phenomenon but as a quasi-structural constraint.

This book is an attempt to understand the changes in the
Egyptian economy of the last decade. In particular, it examines the nature of shifts in the labour market, in employment
patterns and earnings and in the availability and use of mechanical energy in agricultural production. Most of the
analysis is based directly on data collected by means of a
random, stratified sample survey in three Delta villages in
1984. However, it is argued that these villages are broadly
representative of the production and technical conditions
operating in the Delta. As this comprises over 90% of the
cultivated area in the country it can be assumed, by extension, that the results from the survey would be largely

applicable for the economy as a whole. The distribution of land titles and operated holdings, cropping patterns and their intensity, and the nature of the local labour markets do not vary widely in the Delta. For these reasons, a number of broader conclusions regarding recent changes in the Egyptian rural economy have been hazarded on the basis of a relatively restricted sampling frame.

The principal concern of this study is to develop a coherent understanding of recent shifts in the Egyptian labour market. Government policy towards the sector in recent years has been based on the proposition that a shortage of labour now exists in agriculture and that this has manifested itself in falling productivity and constrained production.[6] To overcome this apparent bottleneck, a range of policies has been developed to ease these constraints through the substitution of human and animal energy by mechanical means. Although not the first such attempt to introduce mechanical technology, recent measures have been the most intensive and sustained. Moreover, they have aimed not only to put in place the elements of a primary mechanisation process but also, in the last two years, to go beyond the use of basic agricultural technology - tractors, threshers and winnowers - to implant a more diversified set of technologies. Indicative of the intentions of both the government and a number of major donor agencies has been the trial introduction of small rice combines, as well as a range of harvesting technologies. At present, the shift beyond primary mechanisation has made only tentative progress, restrained by the high levels of plot fragmentation and ownership in Egyptian agriculture and by the substantial investment costs associated with the introduction of such machinery.

Yet the limited progress achieved in transforming the technical framework of Egyptian agriculture cannot simply be explained as a function of farm size and capital investment. There continues to exist a significant technical barrier to mechanisation for the most intensive task - cotton picking. For example, machinery suitable for the short and medium staple varieties grown in North America would not work efficiently on Egyptian cotton. This constraint exists alongside the broader issue of the relative availability and cost of labour. Although it is commonly assumed that labour shortages are now endemic, far-reaching policy decisions have been based both on a very limited amount of reliable data and on highly questionable assumptions. One such assumption has been that past levels of out-migration to the neighbouring Arab and Gulf states will be sustained indefinitely. Thus, a major project - the Second Agricultural Development project - approved by the World Bank in 1985 with an allocation of US$139m, the majority of which would be spent on agricultural machinery, was justified on the assumption of a 'serious and growing shortage of adult farm labour with a rising level of wages for available labour'.[7] If such labour scarcities are in fact strongly associated with an external demand for labour then recent expulsions of Egyptian labour from Libya and a significant reverse flow of labour from Iraq serve warning that this may be an unwarranted assumption. At the same time, current rates of growth in the population and labour force, combined with the fact that over 45% of the population is currently below the age of 15 years, suggest that labour substituting policies may have potentially disastrous longer-term consequences.

At the heart of the current policy choices facing the Egyptian government remain two basic issues. Firstly, there is the question as to whether a labour shortage actually exists and, assuming that the answer is in the affirmative, whether such a shortage is likely to be permanent. Secondly, there is the parallel issue of the level and structure of costs likely to be engendered by maintaining the present policy of promoting and subsidising the cost of capital for machine use and purchase. Although most economic prognoses demand the adoption of contractionary policies and a stabilisation programme, the resilience of the economy and the relative immobility of domestic policies have somewhat belied these expectations. Nevertheless, continuing disequilibrium in the balance of payments and fluctuating or declining sources of resource flows to the economy suggest that a more constrained policy framework will characterise the coming period. With programmes such as farm mechanisation heavily reliant on donor credits or direct imports, their longer run viability will be dependent on the general condition of the external account and the level of overall economic performance.

The book is organised as follows. Chapter 2 contains both a brief historical introduction and a macro-economic overview of developments in the economy in the post-1973 period, paying particular attention to the set of price and investment

signals transmitted to rural producers through the sustained
and entrenched intervention in markets by the state. Chapter
3 sets out the methodology of the study and the means by which
the basic data was collected and organised, and some prelim-
inary information regarding the sample villages is presented.
Then a set of chapters address the key issues of the study,
the demand for labour in Egyptian agriculture and the structure and trend of wages. The latter are then related to recent
developments in the supply of labour to agriculture and to the
distribution of employment that has emerged. While all these
sections draw on other data, most of the conclusions are derived from detailed analysis of the survey results.

Having isolated the basic framework of the agricultural labour
market, subsequent sections look at the implications for
household decision making and resource allocation, paying specific attention to the consequences of machine introduction.
The market for agricultural technology is examined in detail
and close attention paid to the intentions and likely outcome
of the state's recent interventions in the market for agricultural machinery. The final section attempts to draw
together these various strands and presents a critique of
current policies towards the agricultural sector.

Footnotes

1.   Ammar, 1944
2.   ibid., p290
3.   Richards, 1983; Abdel-Khalek and Tignor, 1982.
4.   Kelley, Khalifa and El-Khorazaty, 1982 pp34-42
5.   Waterbury, 1983 p42.
6.   See, for instance, Egyptian Agricultural Mechanization
     Five Year Development Plan, 1982.
7.   World Bank, Staff Appraisal Report: Arab Republic of
     Egypt - Second Agricultural Development Project
     (5342a-EGT), Washington 1985, p24.

CHAPTER TWO

A Macro-Economic Survey of Recent Developments
in the Egyptian Economy

An Historical Introduction

Stretched out along the narrow lifeline between and beside the
Nile, Egyptian society has been, since the early part of the
nineteenth century, both a remarkably homogenous and a
tightly-controlled system. Unlike most other regions of the
Fertile Crescent, the problem of the beduin was solved in
Egypt relatively early by military and economic means. The
granting of private property rights and the abolition of the
iltizam system were factors of the greatest long-term significance.[1] While the characteristic centralism of the Egyptian
state was readily discernible at the time of the Mamluk
Sultanate, let alone in earlier periods, the particular combination of private tenure, state direct taxation, forced
deliveries of cotton (a consequence of growing reliance on
European markets), enhanced public investment in agriculture
and irrigation and an insistent upward trend in the urban
population were all features that emerged most sharply in the
first half of the nineteenth century. British occupation led
to some modification of the role of the state and the legal
conditions determining property, but the substance of colonial
policy, apart from increasing the level of financial and economic dependence on European markets, was the logical development of earlier traits.

By the turn of the century, the Egyptian rural economy was
characterised not only by severe inequalities in land
ownership but also by a truly substantive technical change in
the sphere of irrigation. The completion of a series of
barrages and the first Aswan dam by 1902 enabled perennial
irrigation to supplant the hitherto predominant basin system.
Apart from enabling a far higher proportion of the cultivated
area to remain under cotton, perennial irrigation led to
significant productivity gains.[2] So the basic framework
within which agricultural production and taxation was to develop had been established by the first decade of the twentieth

century.

Yet, if there appears to be striking continuity in the development of productive resources between the period of Muhammad
Ali's dominance and the colonial phase[3], two crucial features
which emerged as the predominant traits of the system were
subsequently to lead to its radical restructuring.   In the
first instance, the rights to private property had been very
unequally spread.   Even as early as 1844 nearly 44% of the
land area was held by grant holders rather than as peasant
land.   By 1896 nearly 80% of landholders owned less than five
feddans but controlled barely 20% of the total area.[4]   Indeed,
using a Gini measure for inequality, it would appear that between 1900 and 1952 the coefficient rose from 0.67 to 0.76.[5]
Secondly, colonial rule exercised a strong negative effect on
domestic industrial growth, despite the attempts of Talaat
Harb and others to remedy this imbalance.   Thus, at the time
of the fall of the ancien regime in 1952, the industrial sector accounted for barely 15% of GDP and employed around 8% of
the labour force.   In addition, the range of products was very
narrow.   With a limited domestic market and low external competitiveness, such industry that had emerged was highly concentrated.[6]

Despite the political rhetoric surrounding their seizure of
power, the substantive measures used by the Free Officers bore
a striking resemblance to the procedures adopted by Muhammed
Ali more than a century before. While land reform whittled
down the maximum legal holding to fifty feddans and thereby
gravely weakened the estate structure of Egyptian agriculture
(see Table 2.1), the domestic financing of industrial-sector
development implied continuing high real rates of taxation on
agriculture.   In particular, the system of forced deliveries
and implicit taxation, through a wedge between border and
farmgate prices, became a corner-stone of policy towards agriculture.

In the industrial sector, the predominant role of the state in
the nationalisation of existing plant or the establishment of
new enterprises was a major characteristic of the growth of
industrial diversity and output.   To that extent, it could be
said that the Nasserist period saw the 'political decapita-
tion' of the large landed gentry and the urban commercial and
industrial class.   In the countryside a class of largely

village-based notables emerged in the place of the landed
gentry, controlling land in a personal or familial capacity in
holdings rarely exceeding 50 feddans. They maintained close
links with the agents of local government and the ruling
party.[7]   As will become clear in one of the village case-
studies included in this book, these rural notables differed
from the largely absentee estate owners who had dominated the
political economy of the countryside before 1952. Most were
resident in their villages, and involved in the direct supervision of cultivation and marketing. Their political allegiance tended to be as ephemeral as the state-animated
political formations that have been the popular aspect of
state hegemony, in theory at least. Other than in the derivation of local economic advantage, such notables have, for the
most part, been content to manipulate the machinery of the
state for their own ends. Although this has implied a rather
fickle allegiance to the particular manifestations of political representation, the fact remains that the state has continued to be viewed as the basic support structure on and
around which private initiatives could be built. This has, of
course, been less true of the relationship between the state
and the industrial classes. The state's desire to allocate
investments outside a purely market framework led logically to
a whole series of nationalisations in the early 1960s. Only
since 1973 has private industrial capital been re-established
to any extent.

Common to both agricultural and industrial sector experiences
in the period following 1952 has been the continuing and pervasive involvement of the state in decision making about
investment and production. At the same time, the role of the
state as the major investor in infrastructure has been coupled
to a wider involvement in the provision of basic welfare
needs. A simple indicator of the profile of the public sector
in Egyptian economic life is the fact that by 1973 between 50%
and 60% of value-added was generated by that sector. While in
1947 government employment accounted for around 13% of total
non-agricultural employment, by 1960 this share had risen to
nearly 27%.[8] This was not only the result of growth in
public-sector economic enterprises, but also the consequence
of substantially-augmented investment in health, housing and
education.

Changes in Egyptian society and economy in the period since

Table 2.1: Distribution of Landholdings by Size, 1950-1977/78

Farm Size (Feddans)	Number of Holdings	%	Area (000 Feddans)	%
		1 9 5 0		
0-1	214.3	21.4	111.8	1.8
1-3	410.0	40.9	709.6	11.6
3-5	162.4	16.2	601.4	9.8
5-10	122.4	12.2	818.4	13.3
> 10	93.9	9.3	3902.8	63.5
Total	1003.0	100.0	6144.0	100.0
		1 9 6 1		
0-1	434.2	26.4	211.2	3.4
1-3	672.7	41.0	1153.2	18.5
3-5	274.3	16.7	990.0	15.9
5-10	170.0	10.4	1100.7	17.7
> 10	90.9	5.5	2767.7	44.5
Total	1642.1	100.0	6222.8	100.0
		1 9 7 4 / 7 5		
0-1	1124.3	42.6	739.0	12.4
1-3	949.2	35.9	2023.5	33.6
3-5	354.8	13.4	1185.6	19.8
5-10	148.5	5.6	944.4	15.8
> 10	65.2	2.5	1091.2	18.2
Total	2642.0	100.0	5983.7	100.0
		1 9 7 7 / 7 8		
0-1	1458.8	48.8	919.9	15.0
1-3	984.3	32.9	2017.4	33.0
3-5	348.7	11.7	1165.6	19.1
5-10	127.6	4.2	785.9	12.9
> 10	69.9	2.3	1226.9	20.0
Total	2989.3	100.0	6118.7	100.0

Source: Abdel Fadil, 1975, p.14: Zaytoun, in Abdel Khalek and Tignor, 1982, p.277. (for 1977/78 figures)

1952 have now been closely analysed and little purpose would
be served by recapitulating the main trends during that
period.[9] However, a number of critical factors should be born
in mind. Firstly, the long tradition of acute centralisation
has been almost unimpaired, and has, of course, been consolidated by the parallel growth in the demographic, let alone
political, importance of Cairo.[10]   Secondly, state intervention, especially in the economic sphere, has remained a
constant feature from 1952 to the present day. Although the
apparent point of difference between the Sadat and Mubarak
regimes and that of Nasser before them has been the extent of
the involvement of government in the direction of the economy,
on closer examination,this distinction turns out to have been
far less pronounced than might initially have been imagined.
Thirdly, despite the pervasive influence of the state, the
lack of a civil politics, satisfactorily articulated to the
system of dirigisme, has meant that the state has effectively
usurped the political stage irrespective of the nomenclature
of the dominant party. This may have permitted relative stability and direct control, but it has meant that the enactment
of policies which might undermine the position of the
bureaucracy, or the proposal of policies requiring some degree
of general consent has proved to be beyond the capacities of
the dominant regime. This has had particular, potentially
explosive, contemporary relevance as substantial state commitments and national welfare pledges made in earlier, more dyna-
mic periods are proving increasingly unsustainable. The
absence of a genuine consultative structure within the
system, coupled to a political and economic 'culture' of diri-
giste welfare provision, appears to prevent the enactment of
policies having direct and economically deleterious implications for sections of the society. By being above politics,
the state has, paradoxically, ensured that it cannot muster,
the genuine support of major segments of society.

Having exhausted the populist political vein through the
expropriation of the larger landowners and industrialists,
management of society thus increasingly presupposed the management of the interests and behaviour of the new political
classes that have been spawned. While it could be argued that
in the countryside this class has tended to be the larger
landholders, rather than the mass of small farmers, the
decreasing relevance of the urban/rural distinction - at least
in Lower Egypt - has been accompanied by a common cross-sector

development: the growth of public employment and direct
dependence on the state for the provision of a wage and a subsidised level of consumption.

If the level of public intervention has tended to increase
over the period from 1952 onwards, there have been several,
often strident, changes in the political rhetoric used to
justify a range of policy shifts.   Perhaps the two most
striking examples have been the phases of 'Arab socialism'
from 1959/60 through to the mid-1960s and the Open Door policy
- Infitah-el-Iqtissad - ushered in by Sadat in 1973.   Apart
from their different foreign policy implications, these political shifts have involved different trade and financial regimes and approaches to the relative public/private balance in
domestic production. Yet, even here the degree of dissimi-
larity has often been over-stated, if only because of the
relatively poor response of foreign capital to liberalisation
of investment conditions (eg Law 43 of 1974) as well as the
pronounced preference of domestic capital for seeking out
investment largely in non-manufacturing sectors.[11] This has
been conditioned in part by the structure of domestic relative
prices which, at least since 1973/74, accelerated a shift of
resources away from the production of tradables to the expansion of services.   Thus, although economic liberalisation has
undoubtedly unleashed a wide set of initiatives from within
the private sector - initiatives in marked contrast to the
severely resource-constrained years between 1967 and 1973 -
the scale of departure from previous practice - particularly
with regard to the state's role, should not be overestimated.

A crude periodisation of the range of critical policy decisions taken in the last three decades can be made.   From 1952
to the early 1960s, the main focus was on the reconstitution
of land holdings and power in the countryside.   High priority
was given to consolidation and diversification of the
industrial sector along standard import substituting lines.
This was, initially, envisaged within a mixed economy framework with private capital playing a leading role.

This policy was then radically modified and from the early
1960s until 1967 a series of measures were passed which not
only resulted in major nationalisation of banking and
industrial houses, but also nationalisation of foreign trade
and, post-1964, the imposition of quantity controls on

imports.[12] At the same time the economy was made – at least
formally – subject to centralised and planned allocations.
However, the five year plan projections proved to be largely
unrealistic in terms of their targets. Of more consequence
was the allocation system within the domestic economy that
resulted from such a control regime. This was naturally associated with the growth in public ownership. By 1973 not far
short of 75% of manufacturing output originated from the
public sector, whose rapid growth was largely a product of the
political stance adopted in the early and mid 1960s.[13]
Although these policies were associated with falling productivity levels and increased wage shares in the manufacturing
sector, relatively high levels of domestic investment coupled
to strict regulation of export and import trade flows, yielded
– until 1964 – GDP growth rates of over 5% per annum.
However, this level of economic activity was substantially
sustained by the growth in public sector consumption.
Domestic savings, as expected, failed to grow and this
resulted in recourse to increased external borrowing.
Dependent on the cotton harvest and with poor additional
export prospects – partly the consequence of under-investment
and excessive taxation of agriculture – the financing of
planned expenditures already posed major problems by 1964/5.
The disastrous war with Israel – combined with the substantial
channelling of resources to non-productive sectors of the economy, including, of course, the military – resulted in a major
domestic recession. With much private capital either
expropriated or taken out of the country and with restricted
access to international capital markets, the period between
1967 and 1973/4 was severely deflationary.

The shift in economic strategy known as <u>Infitah</u> thus followed
a period of contraction in the economy including a severe
repression of consumption. Linked to the release of a series
of very substantial concessional capital flows, liberalisation
of certain trade barriers, the lowering of taxation on the
agricultural sector and the encouragement of joint
foreign/domestic industrial and commercial ventures, the new
policy stance sought to free the economy from the dual
constraints exercised by low domestic productivity – particularly in the public sector – and the balance of payments.
While GDP had commonly registered annual growth rates of
below 2% between 1967 and 1973, in the subsequent period from
1973 through to 1982 real GDP at factor cost grew by around 9%

per annum.[14] Although this phase was marked by an apparent
dismantling of the range of State interventions in the economy, much of this was merely political rhetoric.
Consequently, as Egypt currently finds itself under increasing
economic pressure the basic problem that faced the regime in
the mid-1960s has resurfaced, albeit in a somewhat different
guise. At the heart of the problem remains the question of
the level of public expenditure commitments and economic performance in the public sector, while, at the same time, there
is considerable evidence that under present conditions agriculture is incapable of fulfilling the tasks required of the
sector. With food production lagging substantially behind the
rate of growth in domestic consumption and cotton exports subject to flat world market demand, the net trade contribution
of the sector has turned negative.[15]

The Egyptian Economy since 1973

Whatever the original intentions behind the Open Door Policy,
the actual consequences of the shift in economic priorities
have been both varied and at times exceedingly confusing. For
despite the undoubted loosening of a number of key controls
and a retreat from a materials-balance plan framework, the
resulting economic and social configuration has only very partially acquired the traits of market capitalism. Although
economic liberalisation measures have been of some significance, the fact remains that over the last decade the level of
state involvement in the economy has stayed very high.
Moreover, the variety of interventionist instruments used by
the state have not markedly diminished. In agriculture, for
example, the state intervenes not only through the usual
fiscal measures, but also through output quotas, price fixing
and the monopoly supply of inputs and organised credit. If
the net weight of the measures on agriculture may have
declined when compared with the Nasserist period, it is still
important to note that the measures themselves remain
operable.

Perhaps what demarcates the ten years following Infitah from
the two previous decades has been the actual performance of
the economy. Between 1973/4 and 1982 GDP grew at around 9-10%
per annum.[16] However, after such accelerated growth through
the 1970s, the rate of growth of real GDP began to decline
sharply after 1982/83, falling below the 8% growth rate

projected in the Development Plan for 1982/83 - 1986/87.   In
1984/85 real GDP grew at around 7.1%, declining to 5.9% in
1985/86.   Since 1973, sectoral performance has been patchy
with   agriculture,   in   particular,   performing   poorly.
Nevertheless, the rate of growth in economic activity has
substantially exceeded levels attained in the two decades
following the 1952 revolution.

Yet, it is important to note that the factors behind this
acceleration have, for the most part, lain outside the real
economy.   It is now abundantly clear that the combination of
substantial concessional capital inflows, petroleum earnings,
remittances from Egyptian migrant workers, Suez Canal revenues
and earnings from tourism has provided the key to these higher
levels of growth.   Indeed, a recent estimate suggests that the
share of such exogenous resources (barring concessional capital flows) in GDP rose from a mere 6% in 1974 to 45% in
1980/81.   Growth in petroleum output and Suez Canal revenues
alone accounted for a quarter of total GDP growth in this
period.   In addition, by 1985 aid transfers to Egypt by the
USA exceeded $2.5bn, making the country the second largest
recipient of American aid.[17]

The components of Egyptian economic growth since _Infitah_
suggest that growth has been most marked outside the commodity
producing sectors.   Indeed, between 1977 and 1982 while the
latter grew at an annual rate of 5.8%, the distribution and
service sectors registered growth rates of 12.1% and 9.6%
respectively (see Table 2:2).   Moreover, the major components
of commodity sector growth were in petroleum and construction.
Industry managed to grow at around 6% while agricultural output grew at 2.3% p.a.   in the same period.   Clearly, the rapid
expansion in exogenously generated resources has fed through
into the economy in a way that has mainly benefited non-
commodity producing sectors.   This has followed logically from
a domestic price structure which has encouraged a shift of
resources away from the production of tradables to the expansion of services.   While gross investment as a share of GDP
has grown from around 22% in 1974 to over 30% by 1982, it is
important to note that the direction of investment has shown a
marked shift to service sectors.[18]   This can be seen in Table
2:3 where gross fixed investment in services comprised around
14% of gross fixed investment; by 1981/82 this had risen to
over 29%.   Indeed, despite the intention to encourage the

Table 2.2: Egypt: Growth Rate of Real Gross Domestic Product by Sector: 1977-1985/86
(Annual rate in percent)

	1977-81/2	1982/3	1983/4	1984/5	1985/86	Plan 1982/3-86/7	As Proportion of GDP 1977	1982/3
Commodity Sectors	5.8	7.6	8.3	7.2	5.1	8.5	50.1	52.7
Agriculture	2.3	3.0	2.9	3.4	3.5	3.7	22.7	18.7
Industry and Mining	6.0	7.2	9.3	9.9	10.3	9.1	15.4	13.9
Petroleum	12.8	4.5	4.5	10.6	2.3	12.2	5.8	14.8
Electricity	4.8	2.5	9.7	9.2	10.1	10.7	1.3	0.7
Construction	11.3	7.0	7.4	2.3	3.5	8.3	4.9	n.a
Distribution Sectors	12.1	6.4	6.1	6.0	5.6	7.2	30.3	28.7
Transportation, Communication and Storage	8.3	6.2	6.5	6.2	6.0	9.7	6.8	6.0
Suez Canal	21.1	1.6	2.5	-8.5	3.0	5.4	2.5	3.1
Trade, Finance & Insurance	12.5	5.0	1.9	9.7	6.9	6.9	19.3	18.4
Hotels and Restaurants	5.8	7.5	8.2	n.a.	n.a.	7.0	1.7	1.2
Other								
Services Sector	9.6	5.8	5.9	8.2	8.4	8.1	19.6	18.6
Housing	7.7	7.0	7.8	8.5	7.8	9.0	3.7	1.9
Public Utilities	7.2	9.3	8.5	n.a.	n.a.	13.9	0.3	0.3
Social services and Social Security	8.5	2.2	1.5	n.a.	n.a.	6.9	4.2	4.3
Government services	10.6	5.8	5.9	n.a.	n.a.	8.3	11.4	12.1
Gross Domestic Product At Factor Cost	8.6	7.0	7.2	7.1	5.9	8.1	100.0	100.0

Table 2.3:   Egypt: Gross Fixed Investment at Current Prices, 1974-1984/85
             (in millions of Egyptian pounds)

Sector	1974	1975	1976	1977	1978	1979	1980/1	1981/2	1982/3	1983/4	1984/5
Commodity Sectors	361	594	802	1070	1492	2111	2423	2112	2476	2546	2676
Agriculture	54	94	98	146	191	258	375	293	305	369	416
Industry and Mining	192	287	379	561	769	1010	1005	977	1204	1239	1261
Petroleum	74	122	186	206	201	448	593	272	264	291	374
Electricity	30	60	59	109	203	234	325	365	539	497	480
Construction	11	31	80	48	132	160	125	205	164	150	145
Distribution Sectors	198	399	399	473	729	974	1019	1366	1705	1736	1834
Transportation, Communications and Storage	190	384	373	443	692	904	911	1200	1590	1615	1706
Trade and Finance	8	15	26	30	37	70	108	210	159	172	132
Services Sectors	126	289	270	330	444	679	1051	1206	857	1088	1209
Housing	53	177	128	126	136	221	451	90	63	51	56
Public Utilities	29	39	45	66	96	165	276	374	366	532	562
Other	44	73	97	138	212	293	324	742	428	505	420
Less: Expenditure for Land Purchases	5	17	21	35	47	58	79	n.a.	n.a.	n.a.	n.a.
Gross Fixed Investment	680	1265	1450	1838	2618	3705	4414	4684	5038	5370	5719
Public Sector	598	852	966	1477	2179	2803	3158	3527	3577	3918	4130
Private Sector	102	413	484	361	439	902	1256	1157	1461	1452	1589
Foreign Investment	34	88	182	204	218	497	550	n.a.	n.a.	n.a.	n.a.
Oil companies	32	81	155	155	136	371	609	n.a.	n.a.	n.a.	n.a.
Law 43 companies	2	7	27	49	82	126	341	n.a.	n.a.	n.a.	n.a.

Source: Ministry of Planning

inflow of foreign capital into the economy, particularly through Law 43 of 1974, the experience so far has suggested that most joint enterprises established within the framework of the Law have largely financed their operations from local sources. The foreign investment component has been weak, while strong preference for capital-intensive technology has minimised the level of employment gain. In addition, few of these enterprises have been export oriented and thus by having recourse to the free market to purchase foreign exchange to pay for inputs and dividends, the net effect may actually have been a drain on foreign exchange reserves. Although Law 43 companies' investment may have reached a billion dollars by 1985, all available evidence suggests that these enterprises have largely steered clear of the commodity-producing sectors.

In terms of aggregate fixed investment, moreover, while private sector investment has increased as a share of total investment over the last decade, the private sector's share remained roughly constant between 1977 and 1981/2 at 20-21%. When private investment is disaggregated, it further emerges that the share of non-oil investment has risen rather gradually, from around 10% of total private investment in 1976 to 17% by 1982. Thus, all available indicators point to the fact that despite a relatively high domestic investment rate, the direction of this investment and its composition has led to a movement away from the core commodity sectors and a very high continuing share of public investment in total investment.

Accompanying the growth in investment since 1973/74 has been the sharp rise in domestic consumption. Indeed, while private and government consumption amounted to 81% of expenditure on GDP in 1977, by 1982 this had risen to over 88%, largely at the expense of domestic savings. All the increase came through the growth in private consumption, with government consumption falling slightly in this period. At the same time, the composition of effective demand has been closely associated with the overall balance of payments situation. Thus, the ratio of net imports of goods and services to GDP rose from under 10% in 1977 to 13% in 1981/82. By 1982/3 current account payments exceeded half of GDP.[19] However, the inflow of resources from external earnings allied to access to concessional capital meant that up to 1983/84 the current account deficit had declined (save in 1981/82) as a proportion of GDP. As foreign exchange availability has been high in the

period from 1973/74, the result has been a substantial growth
in domestic consumption and the share of imports. This can
partly be explained by pent-up demand from the pre-1973 period
and liberalisation of import controls. As non-oil exports have
performed relatively poorly, with unit values falling for the
traditional major export item - cotton - this has naturally
resulted in a deteriorating trade balance.[20]   By 1985 the
trade deficit exceeded $6bn with a current account shortfall
of around $1.8bn.

Falling oil prices, declining remittances and tourist receipts
over the last two years have combined to weaken the overall
balance of payments position. Export earnings have continued
to fall since 1981/82. External borrowing is presently in
excess of 105% of GNP and debt servicing alone amounts to 42%
of current account receipts.[21]   Growing balance of payments
constraints have not only raised the level of foreign debt but
also necessitated the re-introduction of import restrictions
coupled to some credit restraint. Since late 1985 one consequence has been that the government of Egypt entered into
protracted negotiations with the International Monetary Fund
for a stand-by facility. These negotiations finally resulted
in May 1987, in the government securing such a facility for
$300m.

If the ten years following the introduction of the Open Door
economic strategy were principally characterised by the very
substantial inflow of foreign exchange and a sharp rise in
domestic demand for goods and services, the utilisation of
these incremental resources does not appear to have provided a
solid basis for a more sustainable growth path. In the first
place, the return on domestic investment has been relatively
low particularly in the commodity sector. Incremental
capital-output ratios for agriculture and manufacturing have
been high (at around four for agriculture and five for manufacturing) while the framework of relative prices and controls
has meant, as Bruton has pointed out, that new investment has
not substantially contributed to the reduction of the structural features giving rise to low productivity.[22] With movement towards constrained foreign exchange availability, the
failure to raise productivity domestically in the years of
foreign exchange plenty are likely to have severely detrimen-
tal longer-run implications.

While it is still too early to say whether the present
contraction in external earnings will be of a more permanent
nature, it is obvious that growth strategies based simply on
fortuitous combinations of exogenous resource inflows and
political rents are unlikely to provide a sufficiently stable
basis for maintaining a strong growth path. This appears to
have particular relevance in the Egyptian case. Firstly,
although oil exports accounted at their peak in 1981/82 for
over 19% of GDP, Egypt has been subject to the general downward pressure on the price level. Secondly, with current
domestic petroleum product prices at a quarter of the international equivalent price this has obviously accelerated the
rate of depletion, while also squeezing the export share. At
present rates of depletion and known stocks, Egyptian reserves
would be exhausted by the end of this century with peak production being reached by the end of the 1980s.[23] Thereafter,
higher production costs and cost-recovery transfers to foreign
companies would markedly reduce the benefit to the Egyptian
economy. In addition, the level of export earnings will
obviously depend on price trends largely determined outside of
the Egyptian economy.

The second external resource made available to the economy
since 1974 has been remittances (see Table 2.4). By 1980
these amounted to more than 12% of GDP. During the period
1970-1984, remittances through official channels grew at an
annual rate of over 40%. The real rate has been higher given
the reluctance of most migrants to transmit all their earnings
through official channels at discriminatory exchange rates.
Yet, reliance on demand for Egyptian labour from other Arab
countries carries with it a number of potentially destabi-
lising implications. In the first place, migration has been
almost entirely to neighbouring Arab states and to the Gulf
countries. Estimates of the number of migrants involved are
exceedingly hard to come by. From what evidence is available
it seems that from between 0.8m and 1m migrants in Arab
countries in 1980, the figure had risen to around 3m by 1985.
Much of this increase has been a direct consequence of manpower shortages in Iraq caused by the Iran-Iraq war. Clearly,
long-term dependence on the demand for Egyptian labour holding
up at present levels involves great risk. As in the case of
oil exports, the revenues from this source are likely to be
subject to continued downward pressure in the foreseeable
future. Remittances for both 1985 and 1986 appear to be below

Table 2.4: Workers' Remittances, 1973-1984

Year	$m	Year	$m
1973	86	1979	2445
1974	189	1980	2912
1975	366	1981	2855
1976	755	1982	2082
1977	897	1983	3166
1978	1761	1984	3900
		1985*	3750
		1986*	2900

*estimate

Source: Ministry of Finance

Table 2.5: Public Finance as a Share of GDP

	1974	1979	1980/1	1981/2	1982/3	1983/4
Public Sector Revenues	27.3	29.0	42.6	40.2	38.4	36.2
Oil and Suez Canal	(11.9)	(5.4)	(13.8)	(9.9)		
Public Sector Expenditure	47.8	56.0	60.9	62.9	56.4	55.9
Current Expenses	(26.4)	(25.2)	(26.7)	(29.4)		
Subsidies	(9.4)	(10.8)	(12.5)	(10.7)		
Investment	(13.8)	(20.0)	(21.7)	(22.8)		
Public Sector Deficit	20.5	27.0	18.4	22.7	17.9	19.7

Source: IBRD, 1983 p4.

the peak in 1984 and exhibit a strong downward trend. This appears to hold even now for the other principal exogenous earnings. Tourism earnings have declined in recent years while high tariffs levied by the Suez Canal Authority have deterred custom. Even if both these revenue sources held up at peak levels this would not compensate for major declines in oil or remittance income.

The Role of the State

If the apparent aim of the government is no longer to establish control of the 'commanding heights' of the economy, and subsequently to control that economy through physical planning, the fact remains that the profile of the state is strongly imprinted in all crucial spheres. As Table 2.5 shows, public sector revenues and expenditures have increased their share of GDP.

Oil revenue taxes and Suez canal tariffs were a major element in the rise in government revenues. By 1983/84 these, combined with surpluses generated by publicly-owned enterprises, accounted for nearly 37% of total government revenue. On the expenditure side it emerges that the share of investment in total government expenditure rose substantially between 1974/75 from around 35% to over 45% at its peak in 1978. Thereafter, the investment share declined so that by 1983/84, at 32%, investment was a lower proportion of state outlays than in the first years of Infitah. Further decomposition of government allocations shows that the structure of the investment budget has itself undergone substantial modification. Most marked has been the increased share of general public services investment expenditure. From 2.5% of total public sector investment in 1974, this share has risen to nearly 10% by 1983/84.

Table 2.6 also shows that investment allocations to economic services have declined somewhat. From a peak of 82% of total public sector investment in 1975 their share had fallen back to around 70% by 1983/84. Public investment in the agricultural sector has shown the sharpest rate of decline, being kept at roughly half the peak share of 1975 for the next eight years. Thus, in the last decade public expenditures have apparently been increasingly geared towards non directly-productive activities.

Table 2.6:   Egypt: Public Sector Investment Expenditure: Shares by Title, 1974-1983/84

	1974	1975	1976	1977	1978	1979	1980/1	1981/2	1982/3	1983/4*
General Public Services	2.5%	2.6%	5.5%	6.4%	4.4%	5.7%	9.8%	12.3%	8.8%	9.8%
Education	3.8	4.4	3.0	2.5	3.6	3.2	2.8	3.5	2.7	5.2
Health	1.2	1.6	0.2	0.7	1.0	0.9	0.5	0.8	0.7	1.5
Housing and Social Services	8.0	8.1	16.2	9.5	9.0	12.4	9.8	11.5	10.8	12.5
Economic Services	77.4	82.1	33.9	38.0	42.4	41.7	33.4	29.2	39.5	33.7
(Agriculture)	9.1	10.2	5.2	4.8	5.1	6.8	5.3	4.6	5.1	8.4
(Mining, Petroleum and Manufactures)	41.7	39.5	10.8	4.7	4.4	3.9	3.9	3.1	4.4	3.4
(Electricity)	5.5	5.2	4.2	6.6	9.1	7.9	10.2	6.4	9.3	8.0
Other public investment**	7.1	1.2	41.3	43.0	40.0	36.2	43.7	42.7	37.4	37.3
Total (£ million)	597	913	1375	1549	2311	2614	3766	4671	4682	4520

*   Estimate
** Since abolition of public economic organisations at the end of 1975 no functional classification of public
    sector company investment has been available.

Source: Ministry of Finance

Although the investment budget has grown very slightly in terms of its share in total government expenditure, total expenditure as a proportion of GDP has increased quite significantly. In 1974 this stood at 48%, and by 1981/82 it had exceeded 63% before falling back in 1983/84 to 56%. This trajectory was sustainable because of the parallel increase in government revenues. These in turn were strongly associated with the overall level of external earnings to the economy.

Table 2.7 provides an estimate of the share of external resources in total government revenues. It can be seen that such revenues had climbed from 11% in 1976 to around 35% by 1980/81. Despite a post-1982 fall in oil sector revenues the share of external revenues exceeded 25% of total revenues in 1982/83.

This inflow of resources to the economy and to the state, both directly and indirectly, allowed the deficit to remain broadly constant between 1974 and 1984, when measured as a proportion of GDP (see Table 2:5). However, this was achieved at the expense of more structural measures to correct the inherent weaknesses in public finance. Thus, in recent years, taxes on domestic goods and services have been highly inelastic and have only amounted to between 4–5% of GDP. Likewise, personal income taxation has remained pitifully weak. In 1982/83, for instance, personal income tax accounted for just over 1% of total public revenue and direct taxes as a whole amounted to a quarter of total revenues.[24] This represents, in the latter case, a slight improvement over the position in the early 1970s but in the case of personal income tax the share has actually been halved in the intervening decade. Clearly, the growth of external resources has detracted from the pressing need for domestic tax reform and a more efficient use of available tax instruments. With agricultural land taxation now limited to holdings of above three feddans and charged at a basic rate of 14% of the highly deflated annual rental value, direct taxation of the sector remains desultory, while the effective incidence of personal taxation remains confined to the urban and rural salariat.

The rather precarious equilibrium in public finance stabilised by the growth in co-opted revenues has allowed for sustained deficitary financing to be maintained. This has been done through a combination of foreign borrowing and recourse to the

Table 2.7: External Revenue as a Share of Total Government Revenues
            (£E millions)

	1976	1977	1978	1979	1980	1981/2	1982/3
Total Government Revenue	2015	2755	3306	3684	7373	8231	9391
External revenues	217	398	497	690	2588	2250	2335
External/Total Revenues	.11	.14	.15	.19	.35	.27	.25

Source: Sadiq Ahmed, Public Finance in Egypt, World Bank Staff
Working Paper No.639, 1984, Washington, p.13.

domestic capital market. However, the limited development of
the latter has meant that borrowing from the Central Bank has
been the dominant feature in the growth of domestic liquidity.
With the various measures of money supply growing at between
three and six times the rate of growth in real output up to
1982/83, this has resulted in the usual inflationary pressure.
Bruton points out, however, that given the rate of growth in
domestic liquidity the actual inflation rate has been surprisingly low.   This is attributed to savers' preference for
holding foreign exchange as a store of value because of the
differential in real interest rates and medium-term downward
pressure on the exchange rate for local currency.[25] Thus,
while this may have forced down the rate of inflation it also
implied an effective forswearing of investible resources for
the domestic economy. In addition, it is also important to
note that the reduction of inflation - particularly prior to
1983 - had been achieved by extensive use of price and quantity controls. But these interventions have themselves been
increasingly determined by the availability of resources, and
a contraction in resource availability would not only imply a
higher cost to the economy in maintaining existing expenditure
commitments but would also have substantial inflationary consequences through increased deficit financing.

Three major areas of public expenditure present particularly
intractable management problems. Most striking has been the
enormous growth in public allocations to food subsidies in the
last decade. From a mere 0.1% of GDP in 1970/71, such expenditures now account for over 8% of GDP and nearly 13% of total
public expenditure. As Table 2.8 shows, this is principally
the result of provision of subsidised wheat flour and bread.
In addition, monthly quotas of rice, sugar, oil and tea are
provided to ration card holders.

Although this subsidised provisioning was initially largely
confined to urban areas, there has been a very significant
expansion in the range of such services in the last five
years. A recent study found that although coverage was better
developed in urban areas (largely as a function of the availability of bakeries) almost all villages had ration shops and
over 50% had co-operative shops distributing a wide range of
subsidised items.[26] In the survey villages included in this
study, all villages had ration shops and one also maintained a
co-operative shop. This growth in the availability of ration

or subsidised food items has been reflected in the expansion of costs associated with the food subsidy system. The net losses incurred by the General Authority for Supply Commodities through the administration of the scheme (Table 2.8) are not simply domestic resource costs. For reasons that will be touched on in more detail later, an increasing proportion of the Authority's demand, for wheat in particular, have had to be satisfied through imports, thereby invoking a direct foreign exchange cost. In the conditions of relative foreign exchange plenty that have operated since 1974 the scale of the overall subsidy structure has been correspondingly inflated and progressively dissociated from the capacities of the state to sustain such expenditures in the longer term. Attempts to raise the price of basic subsidised goods have met with considerable, and violent, political opposition.[27] Although the share of subsidies in current expenditure has fallen quite considerably since the peak year of 1979, this has principally reflected the movement in international prices for purchased commodities rather than a narrowing down of the actual domestic commitment itself. Clearly, further real reductions in the scale of expenditure pledged through subsidies will demand politically unpalatable policies. This poses very real problems for a state where the mechanisms for arriving at political convergence on key issues are either non-existent or inchoate.

Although growth in subsidy expenditure has been the most notable feature in the evolution of public finances over the last decade, of possibly greater overall significance has been the continuing growth in public-sector employment. This emerged as a major feature of the labour market in the Nasser period, in particular after 1961 and the spate of nationalisation measures. In the early 1960s state employment may have accounted for 9% of the total labour force (excluding the army).[28] By 1976 this share exceeded 27% of the labour force. Since then, the trend has been consistently upwards. The latest Labour Force Sample Survey (1981) estimates government and public sector employment at nearly 32% of the labour force.[29] Although the majority of these jobs were located in urban areas, it is important - particularly in the context of this study - to note that 30% of government sector jobs in 1980/81 were in rural areas.

Despite growing pressure on government resources, employment

Table 2.8: Trading Operations of General Authority for Supply Commodities, 1970/1 - 1983/4

	1970/1	1972	1973	1974	1975	1976	1977	1978	1979	1980/1	1981/2	1982/3	1983/4
Subsidies	41.8	41.9	136.2	393.2	423.7	281.4	343.2	452.4	996.8	1665.4	1828	1684.5	na
Wheat and Flour	20.9	15.1	79	216.4	260.9	171.6	149.1	222.8	588.3	776	736	760.9	743.8
Maize	0.8	0.4	4.4	16.5	31.1	23.1	40.6	53.8	38.5	104	141	154.7	235.8
Edible fats and oils (rationed)	10.4	15.8	16.8	55.3	72.2	43.2	54.6	137.4	200.2	133.4	125	243	156.9
Sugar "	8	6	19	68.9	20.8	6.1				224	132	112.5	23.2
Tea							18.3	12.8	54.6	26.5	29	31.2	47.3
Coffee							5.6						
Other	1.7	4.6	17	36.1	38.7	37.4	75	25.6	115.2	401.5	665	382.3	na
Profits	38.6	30.5	47.2	63.1	15	31.2	12.6	29.3	44.5	0.7	2.8	2.4	na
Total Net Losses	3.2	11.3	89	330.1	408.7	250.2	330.6	423.1	952.3	1664.7	1825.2	1682.1	na
Subsidies as % of total Current Expenditure	0.4	1.1	7.6	23.3	23.9	14.0	17.6	20.8	27.0	26.8	24.0	19.5	na
% of total Public Exp.	0.2	0.7	5.5	16.5	16.9	9.8	10.9	11.9	16.2	16.7	14.9	12.7	na
Share of GDP	0.1	0.3	2.3	7.6	9.4	4.8	5.3	6.6	8.1	10.0	9.4	8.1	na

Source: General Authority for Supply Commodities and Alderman (et al), October 1982, p.16.

in the public sector has grown by around 7.5% per annum between 1980/81 and 1985/86 and this reflects the continuing
demand for government employment generated by the University
Graduate Employment Guarantee Scheme and, to a lesser extent,
the hiring of discharged army personnel. As a result of this
expansion the government's wage bill rose by over 25% in this
latter period, while wages as a share of current government
expenditure rose from 23.4% in 1979 to 27.2% in 1983/84.[30]

Three principal features of the employment issue stand out.
Firstly, there has been a relatively rapid rise in the share
of total employment accounted for by the public sector. By
the end of 1985 over a third of the civilian labour force were
in the public sector. In addition, the strength of the armed
forces was put at 367,000 in 1980/81; some 10% larger than in
1973 but roughly smaller by the same proportion than in the
peak year of 1978/79.[31] With the labour force growing in
recent years at 2.5% per annum, it is obvious that government
employment has grown well in excess of the rate of growth in
the labour force. Secondly, the bulk of jobs generated in the
government sector have been non-productive. At the end of the
1970s nearly 75% of state sector work was apparently in administrative departments.[32] Economic organisations accounted
for only 16% of total state employment. Thirdly, although
public-sector salaries are low by comparison with the private
sector, a complex system of bonuses and additional payments
has meant that over the last five years the implicit rate of
compensation for government workers has not declined as dramatically in real terms as would appear from the trend in basic
salaries.

However, the structure of government employment leads to
inflationary pressures not only through enhanced demand for
market-sector output from non-producers but also by virtue of
the discrepancy in wage increments and productivity in the
public sector industrial concerns.[33] In 1983/84, for example,
average payments to these workers increased by 12.8% while the
nominal value of output grew by only 10.6%. Thus, if chronically high levels of over-employment are acknowledged to be a
feature of the administrative sector (a 1979 survey put the
number of civil servants in Cairo with no real work at
240,000),[34] studies of public-sector enterprises reveal very
high levels of surplus labour, mostly in the clerical categories. Handoussa shows, for example, that while for

textiles, clothing and leather manufactures, skilled workers
accounted for 93% of employment in private-sector enterprises,
in the public sector this proportion dropped to 64%.[35]
Moreover, even amongst skilled workers in the public sector
there was found to be a very high level of underemployment.
Such deep inefficiencies in the productive system obviously
have economy-wide implications as the public sector currently
accounts for around 68% of the gross value of industrial production.

The third area of government expenditure to resist any major
attempts at pruning has been defence. Despite the fall in
budgeting allocations following the 1973 war and, subsequently, the Camp David agreement, defence which accounted
for between 36-45% of current expenditure between 1974-1976,
appropriated around 29/30% in 1983/84. However, when measured
in relation to GDP it is instructive to note that defence
expenditures in the two years 1982/83-1983/84 amounted to
around 9% of GDP, the same proportion that existed in
1974-1975.[36] When it is remembered that this level of expenditure exceeds current allocations to health, housing, education and social services by over 50% and that defence
expenditure sums to almost half the total investment budget
for the public sector, it is obvious that more productive use
of these resources could be made. Despite the present peace
with Israel it seems unlikely that these commitments will be
reduced substantially.

Developments in the Agricultural Sector, 1973-1985

In the recent past the agricultural sector has been subject to
a number of profound changes. In the mid-1960s the sector
accounted for 30% of GDP and over 56% of the labour force. By
1984/85 it generated around 17% of GDP and accommodated 36% of
the labour force.[37] At the same time, many - including the
government - have argued that the sector has moved away from
its traditional condition of acute labour surplus to one in
which there is actually a scarcity of labour. This supposed
transition provides one of the main themes of this text. At
this stage, however, the aim is to give a broad picture of
recent developments in the sector preparatory to a more
detailed examination of these labour market issues.

State intervention in Egyptian agriculture has had a long

history. Public investment in irrigation and more recently in
drainage, has been a major component in sustaining the relatively high levels of land productivity, particularly in the
core Delta region. At the same time the state has maintained
a long established variety of taxation instruments for the
sector. Apart from a tax levied on all arable land owned by
households with more than three feddans and based on annual
(institutional) rental values, the principal means of
extracting surplus from the countryside remain output controls
and administered pricing.

These policies were initially devised for cotton and it is
with this crop that they still have maximum impact. As monopoly purchaser of cotton output at fixed prices, the state
derives considerable benefit from the wedge between export
prices and farm-gate prices. In 1981 the accounting ratio for
the cotton price was 2.13, with producers gaining roughly 40%
of international prices over the most recent period. In addition to cotton, a range of other crops are subject to forced
deliveries and price controls. Wheat prices in particular are
substantially below international prices (see Table 2.9).
Rice is currently subject to a 40% compulsory levy. State
rice procurement prices in the 1984 survey were found to be
between 60-75% of the open market price. Other crops subject
to controls include sugarcane, soyabeans, groundnuts, beans,
lentils and a variety of vegetables.

The major winter season crops grown in the Delta - birseem
(clover) and wheat - are not subject to direct controls,
although in the case of the latter, administered procurement
prices for flour, coupled to the market profile, allow the
state de facto regulation of the price. Of the principal
summer season crops, only maize is entirely unregulated. The
substantial differential in the rate of increase in producer
prices for controlled and non-controlled crops has meant a
consistent switching into the latter. This has also been closely associated with the expanded domestic demand for
livestock products. In recent years, only for meat - both red
and poultry - have domestic prices remained consistently above
their border price levels. This protection has not only had
implications for livestock holdings but has also resulted in
increased area allocations to fodder crops, which may have
been further facilitated by the relatively weak enforcement of
area controls since the mid-1970s.[38]

Table 2.9: Ratio of Domestic Farmgate and Procurement Prices
            to International Prices 1970-1984

	--Rice--		-Wheat--		Cotton	Maize	Sugarcane
	A	B	A	B	B	A	B
1970	1.00	0.96	1.50	1.27	0.83	1.06	0.60
1971	1.09	1.07	1.21	1.14	0.70	1.03	0.51
1972	0.94	0.94	1.09	1.03	0.71	1.19	0.35
1973	0.41	0.39	0.59	0.52	0.40	0.62	0.46
1974	0.34	0.30	0.57	0.52	0.47	0.71	0.18
1975	0.55	0.55	0.77	0.76	0.62	0.76	0.30
1976	0.97	0.97	0.80	0.85	0.52	0.78	0.58
1977	0.96	0.85	1.06	0.98	0.56	1.31	0.78
1978	0.74	0.73	0.86	0.69	0.50	1.03	0.81
1979	0.63	0.63	0.55	0.57	0.48	0.73	0.71
1980	0.57	0.52	0.66	0.60	0.38	1.05	0.28
1981	0.59	0.51	0.72	0.63	0.40	0.73	0.46
1982	1.19	0.87	0.69	0.68	0.43	1.09	0.98
1983	1.14	0.95	0.84	0.75	0.34	1.10	1.02
1984	n.a.	0.95	n.a.	0.82	0.41	n.a.	1.59

A = Farmgate to International Price calculated at weighted average
    exchange rate

B = Procurement

Source: IBRD, 1986 p22.

The implicit taxation of the sector through forced deliveries
and administered prices has been offset to some extent since
the mid-1970s by the growth in subsidies on fertilisers and
pesticides.   These are exclusively distributed through the
village co-operative gamiya system.   In the case of cotton
pesticides, the subsidy per feddan has risen sharply since
1974 from £E7.91 to £E65.14 in 1983.[39] Total input subsidies
have likewise experienced a rapid rate of increase.   When
deflated by the consumer price index, input subsidies rose
from around £E15m in 1972 to £E92.5m in 1980.[40] At the latter
date this comprised about 2% of total government expenditures
and just over 1.1% of the total value of commodity imports.

Apart from input subsidies, agricultural producers have also
benefited from the highly subsidised cost of capital. Short-
term crop loans have been made available, at 3% interest
rates, either through the gamiya or the Principal Bank for
Development and Credit (PBDAC).   Likewise, loans under the
food security title for poultry farming and livestock attract
interest rates of 7%; mechanisation loans are currently
offered at 8% p.a.   This contrasts with the commercial bank
rate of 13/14% and, perhaps more significantly, the rate of
inflation in the economy which, since 1982, has exceeded 17%
p.a., at a conservative estimate.   Nevertheless, although the
rate of effective implicit taxation of agriculture has undoubtedly fallen over the last two decades, Cuddihy estimated that
for 1974/75 agricultural producers' incomes were reduced by
£E1.2bn, with consumers - principally urban consumers -
gaining £E1.02bn and the state deriving a transfer of £E179m.
This suggests that the transfer of resources away from the
agricultural sector has not generally been associated with
enhanced allocations to industry.

Since 1974/75, however, the overall level of implicit taxation
on the sector has apparently fallen. It has been estimated
that by 1980 the total burden on agriculture was less than 20%
of the peak level of 1974 (when measured in constant 1975
prices).   This would yield an indirect tax of around 17%.[41]
Other computations place the figure at a slightly lower level
- 14% in 1981.[42]

The widespread use of administered prices and area controls
has historically led not only to severe domestic price distor-
tions but also to suboptimal land allocations.   Hansen and

Table 2.10: Consumer and Producer Transfers on Major Crops, Egypt, 1974/75 (£E millions at parallel exchange rates: Net of Input Subsidies

Crop	Producer Transfer	Consumer Transfer	Transfer to State
Rice	-562	+518	+44
Wheat	-78	+334	-256
Cotton	-254	+122	+132
Sugar	-400	+40	+360
Maize	-120	-242	+28
Meat	+214	-242	+28
TOTAL	-1200	+1021	+ 179

Source: Cuddihy, 1980, p.17.

Table 2.11: Ratio of Economic to Private Returns per Feddan, 1965-81

Crop	1965	1971	1975	1981
Cotton	1.47	1.41	2.21	2.72
Wheat	.69	.61	1.21	1.27
Barley	1.01	.66	1.12	1.30
Beans	1.34	1.85	1.63	.82
Onions	1.54	4.85	3.86	15.53
Lentils	1.48	1.58	1.26	.46
Maize	.68	.82	1.32	.61
Rice	2.25	.26	2.38	2.88
Groundnuts	1.08	1.11	1.67	2.89
Sugarcane	.41	.53	1.88	1.37
Tomatoes	.05	.28	.70	1.58
Oranges	1.00	.48	.11	2.27
Birseem	*	*	*	*

* Negative Economic Return

Source: IBRD, 1983(a), p.161.

Nashashibi, for example, estimated that misallocation of acreage between 1962-68 may have been as high as 7.9%, with over 4.4% being attributable to government interventions. This may have engendered a loss of output sufficient to have covered the foreign exchange gap of the 1960s.[43]

In the present period, the structure of relative prices, allied to the overall level of control over particular crops, has led to a 'split' market. Producers clearly aim to maximise the area under non-controlled crops principally at the expense of cotton, rice and beans. Indeed, many larger farmers have in recent years been prepared to part with fines of up to £E100 per feddan (1984) for failure to cultivate cotton. This is not surprising considering that, (using 1970 as the base year), by 1984 controlled crop prices had risen by around 3.4 times, fruit and vegetable prices by 3.8 times and birseem by over 5.7 times. The strong shift in relative profitability in favour of livestock products has accounted for the shift towards fodder crops, such as birseem. Indeed, the growth in the introduction of HYVs (high yielding varieties) for wheat in the early 1970s was abruptly reversed because of the new varieties' low straw yield. Table 2.11 provides some information on the effect of current price signals on the ratio between economic and private returns. Maize, lentils and beans all offer economic returns that fall below the private return. In the case of birseem, the economic rate of return is strongly negative. With nearly 25% of the cultivated area under birseem between 1978/81 and a further 15% under maize, lentils and beans this implies a continuing high level of land misallocation.[44] Area allocations to rice and cotton, which have relatively high societal returns but are controlled crops, have declined in the recent period.

If the rate of taxation on agricultural producers has been falling since 1976, the fact remains that the sectoral growth rate has been a rather weak one, averaging under 2% through the 1970s. Between 1975 and 1982 agricultural output grew at around 2.3% p.a., rising to just under 3% between 1982-84. This contrasts with the planned growth rate of 3.7% for the period 1982/83-1986/87. A variety of explanations for this low level of growth can be adduced. In the first place, there is the simple fact of land shortage. Barely 3% of the land area is available for production and by 1976 the cultivated acreage per caput for the rural population had fallen to 0.27.

Although as much as 63% of the agricultural investment budget was allocated to reclamation of new lands between 1965 and 1980, results to date have been disappointing. Since the early 1960s around 1.1m acres have been brought into production but only a third of this area has managed to cover variable costs of production.[45] At the same time, current estimates place the amount of land lost to production through urban encroachment and other factors (eg. brick factories) at around 50,000 acres a year. This implies that in the recent past 0.45% of the total cultivated area has been sacrificed each year. Overall output response has been limited, even though current cropping intensity averages around 200% and crop yields are relatively high by ldc standards and have been rising over the last 15 years.

The weak rate of growth in agriculture can partly be explained by shifts in the sectoral allocations of investment. Thus, between 1952/53 and 1959/60, agriculture attracted between 12-13% of total investment in the economy.[46] This rose sharply between 1960 and 1965 to over 23%, falling to 20.4% for the rest of the decade. Part of this steep increase was attributable to the Aswan Dam project. After 1970 the share of agriculture fell sharply so that by 1975/76 it attracted around 8% of total investment. Throughout this period public investment accounted for nearly 94% of total agricultural investment.[47]

Although total expenditure for agriculture began to rise again in 1979, it is important to note that the agricultural investment budget for most of the 1970s was at less than half its mid-1960s level in terms of the total budget. Between 1980 and 1983 allocations to agriculture appear to have remained broadly constant in terms of total government expenditure. Clearly, over the last two decades agriculture has suffered from the state's emphasis on industrial and urban investment as well as an increased commitment to welfare expenditures, such as food subsidies. However, this has not manifested itself in terms of relative prices, or more exactly the intersectoral terms of trade. The latter may have moved slightly in favour of agriculture (Figure 2.1). Rather, it has been manifested through marked intersectoral income disparities and a failure to circumvent infrastructural bottlenecks to raising production, such as investment in drainage and agricultural services.

The current scale of the problems facing Egyptian agriculture can most vividly be seen in domestic food production. From the early 1970s onwards Egypt has had to import an increasing share of its requirements. This has been a function not only of a weak producer response, but also a consequence of current land allocation and relative prices as well as the growth in domestic consumption levels consequent on the inflow of external resources to the economy post-1973/74. Food deficits have led to increased imports - financed by the easy availability of foreign exchange - and by 1981/82 the cost of food imports exceeded by some five times the sum of export revenues from the traditional staple - cotton - and other agricultural exports. Wheat alone comprised around 6.5% of the total cost of commodity imports between 1978 and 1983.

Between 1975 and 1981 the import prices of wheat and flour - the major imported food commodities - increased by around 60%, as did the price of other agricultural commodities. However, the export price for cotton increased by 38% and prices for other agricultural exports by 49%.[48] With domestic selling prices for wheat and wheat flour averaging between 27-37% of the import price (1980/81-1981/82) the result, as previously mentioned, has been a sharply growing burden on government expenditure, as well as an increased foreign exchange cost. The overall trade balance - previously in surplus in 1970 - had turned negative to the tune of $800m by 1977 and around $2.5bn by 1980/81. Agricultural exports fell back from 25% of total exports to 9% in the same period.

By 1980 the gap between domestic food production and actual consumption had grown to over 8m metric tons and at current consumption levels this deficit would rise by the end of the century to around 40m tons. At present, food aid, mostly wheat from North America, meets half the import requirements on concessional terms.[49] This level of food aid and its share in total wheat imports is likely to fall in the near future.

Using a crude index of food self-sufficiency it is clear that for most major food items, except rice, fruit and vegetables, there has been a significant decline in domestic supply capacity relative to demand. While there has been some growth in the area and export volume of fruits and vegetables consequent upon the relatively fast increase in world prices since the

GRAPH 2.1

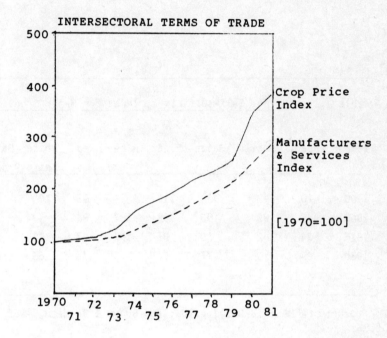

INTERSECTORAL TERMS OF TRADE

Crop Price
Index

Manufacturers
& Services
Index

[1970=100]

Table 2.12: Egypt, Self-sufficiency Index for Major Crops, 1960-80 (%)

Year	Wheat	Lentils	Maize	Sugar	Rice	Red Meat	White Meat	Dairy Products	Fish
1960	70	92	94	114	-	95	100	93	95
1965	35	93	93	99	137	81	-	-	-
1975	34	42	86	81	107	87	99	92	92
1980	25	10	77	57	75	75	65	62	54

Source: CAPMAS: IBRD(a), p.103: Von Braun & De Haen, 1983, p.21.

mid-1970s, the longer term prospects are clouded by the expansion of the EEC southwards.[50] In the case of rice, domestic supply has barely run ahead of demand and this has resulted in a substantial contraction in the share of output for the export market.

Conclusion

Any assessment of developments in the agricultural sector since 1952 must take note of the major gains in output and productivity that have occurred despite relatively heavy taxation of producers. However, in the last decade despite an enormous increase in the use of fertilisers and pesticides, because of the subsidised distribution of inputs through the gamiyas, a number of less positive features have come to light. In the first place, the extension service has almost ceased to function. Hardly any of the farmers interviewed in the 1984 survey had had any recent dealings with the village extension officer and this pattern has been widely reported by other surveys and enquiries. Secondly, inadequate investment has been directed towards improvement of the irrigation system and, in particular, the development of more adequate drainage to combat the growing salinity problem. Although increased allocations to drainage work were made in the 1970s, the pace of implementation has been rather slow.[51] Thirdly, the structure of relative prices, indissociable from the system of administered prices and forced deliveries, has diverted resources away from food production towards fodder cultivation. This has had high private returns and has been a major factor in boosting farm household incomes in the last decade but it has implied heavy, wider costs being incurred by the society, particularly through grain purchases. Fourthly, the forced delivery system has retarded movement towards a greater level of regional specialisation in the cropping pattern.[52] Fifthly, output increments have been restrained by the more general problem of farm fragmentation. This has acquired possibly greater significance in the recent past because of the incompatibility of mechanical technology with the level of fragmentation that exists for most farms. As it is commonly believed that labour shortages now impose a genuine constraint on production, strategies for substituting machine energy for human labour will increasingly have to contend with this problem.

A shortage of labour in the agricultural sector would not only
mark an abrupt change from earlier conditions but would imply
truly substantial shifts in both the structure of the labour
market and the framework of agriculture. At present, between
53-56% of the Egyptian population can be classed as rural.
This amounts to between 24-25m people. The most recent estimates suggest that around 4.4m are employed in agriculture,
approximately 35-36% of the entire labour force. Given the
size of the agricultural labour force, the longer-term impact
on employment in agriculture of the current emphasis on mechanisation is a critical issue facing Egyptian policy makers.

Footnotes

1.   Baer, 1962 and 1969, pp.210-229.
2.   Richards, 1982(a), pp.55-99.
3.   Rivlin, 1961.
4.   Issawi, 1963, p.156.
5.   Richards, 1982(a), p.153.
6.   Hansen & Marzouk, 1965 pp.113-170; Issawi, 1963
      pp.169-198; Davis, 1983.
7.   Waterbury, 1983 pp.263-306; Springborg, 1982.
8.   Mabro, 1974 pp.141-2; Mead, 1967 pp.99-130.
9.   The reader is referred to: Mead, 1967; Abdel Fadil, 1975
      and 1980; Issawi, 1965; Mabro & Radwan, 1976; Saab,
      1967; Waterbury, 1983; amongst others.
10.   Waterbury, in Abdel Khalek & Tignor, 1982, pp.307-350.
11.   Hansen & Radwan, 1982, p.65; Abdel-Fadil & Salah, 1984,
      p.117ff.
12.   Hansen, 1975, pp.201-211.
13.   Ikram, 1980, pp.233-239.
14.   IBRD, 1983(a), pp.408-409.
15.   Commander, 1984, pp.3-6.
16.   Ministry of Planning figures.
17.   The composition of the aid programme for FY 1985 was;
      $1.3bn military, $815m economic, $222m food aid (PL480)
      plus half of $500m for balance of payments support (the
      latter to be spread over two years)
18.   IBRD, 1983(b), Statistical Appendix.

19. Ministry of Finance data.
20. International Financial Statistics, Vol.38, No.8, August
     1985, pp.184-85.
21. IBRD, 1986
22. Bruton, 1983, pp.688-89.
23. Dervis et al, 1984.
24. Ahmed, 1984; M. Reda A El-Edel, 'The impact of taxation
     on income distribution: an explanatory attempt to esti-
     mate tax/income in Egypt', in Abdel-Khalek & Tignor,
     1982, pp.132-164.
25. Bruton, 1983, pp.696.698; Abdel Fadil & Salah, pp.150ff.
26. Alderman & Von Braun, 1984, pp.14-15; Alderman et al.,
     1982; Scobie, 1983.
27. As in January 1977 or, on a more minor scale, in 1984
     when a bout of rioting in Kafr Dawar, an industrial town
     in the vicinity of Alexandria, led to immediate can-
     cellation of the proposed price changes for bread.
28. Hansen & Radwan, 1982, pp.62-3.
29. CAPMAS,   Labour   Force   Sample   Survey,   1981.
30. Ministry of Planning figures: See also Hansen & Radwan,
     1982, for a description of the employment schemes.
31. Sternberger, 1983.
32. El-Issawi, 1983(b), p.68.
33. Gemmell, 1982, pp.207-222.
34. Bruton, 1983, p.690.
35. Handoussa, 1983, p.6ff.
36. Ministry of Finance data. See also Sternberger, 1983.
     It has been estimated that between 1979 and 1983
     Egyptian purchases of arms amounted to $5645 million;
     42.5% of which accrued to the US. MEED, 19 October 1985
     p.6.
37. IBRD, 1983(a), p.97.
38. Habashy & Fitch, p.13ff.
39. Hebbelthwaite, 1985, p.12.
40. Von Braun & De Haen, 1983, p.28.
41. Ibid, p.72.
42. IBRD, 1983(a), p.144.
43. Hansen & Nashashibi, 1975, p.193.
44. Ministry of Agriculture data.
45. Gotsch & Dyer, 1982, pp.129-147.
46. Hansen & Marzouk, 1969, p.46ff.
47. El-Issawi, 'Interconnectons between Income Distribution
     and Economic Growth', in Abdel-Khalek & Tignor, 1982,
     pp.116-7.

48.   IBRD, 1983(a), p.432.
49.   Presidential Mission, 1982; Thomson, 1983, pp.178-186.
50.   Von Braun & De Haen, 1982, pp.46-56.
51.   Ikram, 1980, pp.229-232.
52.   De Janvry, Siam & Gad, 1983, pp.493-500.

CHAPTER THREE

A Profile of the Sample Villages

Surveying the Labour Market: Some Basic Issues and Hypotheses

The nature of the changes in the Egyptian rural economy over the last decade are, as yet, poorly understood. Until the publication of the 1981/2 Agricultural Census results the only available national set of statistics relating to the agricultural sector date back to 1961.[1] Yet despite the absence of an organised and regular system of data collection a series of major, far-reaching policy and planning decisions have been taken in recent years. These have not involved simple modifications to the existing set of interventions in markets made by the state, but have instead extended or initiated a range of interventionist measures. In response to an apparent scarcity of labour in agriculture, government policy has been to subsidise capital, machine imports and most recently, to establish machinery hire stations in rural areas.

The exact nature and degree of this labour scarcity has been poorly mapped. Rather, substantive conclusions have been arrived at on the basis of simple observation and reliance on officially collected rural wage data. This latter time-series, collected annually by the Ministry of Agriculture, has, however, been restricted to adult male and child (male) labour. Apart from a high level of aggregation - where the information is presented in terms of Governorate averages - there are further reasons for supposing that the official series may disguise substantial variations in the wage trend both within and across regions.

Thus, although the wage statistics unequivocally point to a post-1974 wage spiral their coverage has been partial. At the same time, such wage information alone by itself does not necessarily reflect the shifts in the supply function of labour that tend to be assumed. Thus, rather than reflecting contraction in the supply of labour, the wage spiral could, hypothetically, be explained either in terms of a standard Ricardian paradigm[2] or else be viewed as a function of the shifts in the supply of labour in other sectors of the economy where the effects of an internationalised labour market have been felt most strongly. Clearly, skilled labour and construction work would be the sectors of activity most strongly affected.[3] In other words, such interference in the functioning of the non-agricultural labour market could have wider implications both for the general price level and indirectly for the level of wages in agriculture.

While the price of labour must to some extent reflect supply conditions in the particular labour market, the nature of the agricultural labour market, with its continuing regional variation and segmentation by sex, suggests that simple abstraction from the wage trend may not necessarily give a coherent picture. This is particularly true in the case of agriculture where sharp seasonal variations in the demand for labour remain a constant feature.

The household survey on which the bulk of this study's conclusions are based was designed to provide accurate, village-level information on the demand for and supply of labour. In addition, wage information was collected on a monthly basis and also, by task. Rather than being confined to male and boy labour, specific attention was given to the role of women in production and processing and the wage levels commanded by women for such tasks. The data collected in this way, despite the limited number of sampled villages and households, complement other available survey generated data, as well as providing a higher degree of accuracy and detail than the limited information customarily collected by official sources.[4]

The primary focus of the survey was on the question of the availability of labour to agriculture and the degree to which this had determined a shift in the production technique. The survey was designed to address five main issues. Firstly, it aimed to estimate the level and distribution of labour demand in agriculture, paying particular attention to the variation in seasonal requirements and the type of labour used for specific tasks. Secondly, the survey was to provide data from which could be estimated the supply function of labour to agriculture. This was largely posed in terms of farm household supply and was correspondingly related to the distribution of available farm labour across activities. Information was collected both on the allocation of labour by sector, with particular emphasis being placed on mapping the role of female labour and the degree of labour market participation by female household members, as well as the time distribution of that labour. Data were also collected regarding the returns to labour by type of activity as well as by agricultural task. Thirdly, emphasis was placed on estimating the degree and variation in the levels of off-farm employment for household members. This involved classification by type of non-farm work and distribution of time by category of work. Fourthly, data were collected regarding the structure of farm production costs and, in particular, the labour factor share. Lastly, the questionnaire was designed to elicit detailed information concerning the degree, type and cost of labour substitution in agriculture.

Apart from gathering a reliable - if limited - database with which to address the issue of labour availability in agri- culture and, hence, the appropriate technology for production, the survey was designed to provide some answers to a number of key hypotheses:

(i)   that the level of non-farm employment had grown substantially and that this had initiated a higher level of on-farm labour activity by female members of the labour force;

(ii)   that diversion of male labour into non-farm work had resulted in a growth in the level of female labour market participation;

(iii)   that the continuing predominance of small farm holdings resulted not only in limiting the level of possible mechanisation but that such small farms acted as a constraining factor on the release of family labour - particularly household heads - into the labour market;

(iv)   that mechanisation in Egyptian agriculture had attained almost complete introduction for power inten- sive tasks but that the substantial harvesting labour requirement had not been affected by the use of mecha- nical energy;

(v)   that substitution of mechanical energy inputs had

largely supplanted animal power and that until now the
labour substitution effect had been weak; and

(vi)   that tightness in the agricultural labour market had
led to, on the one hand, the emergence of inter-
seasonally linked labour contracts and, secondly, that
large farmers had responded either by paying wage premia or else by recourse to sharecropping contracts.

Survey Design and Application

The survey was carried out in three Delta villages in 1984.
One village was selected from each of the following
Governorates, Sharkiya, Gharbiya and Dakhaliya.[5] Although
each Governorate possesses a variety of ecological zones, the
greatest part of the Delta remains remarkably homogenous. The
major differences have been expressed through variation in the
distribution of landholdings. Thus, Gharbiya (and neighbouring Menoufiya) are characterised by high levels of farm
fragmentation and the overwhelming predominance of small
farms, the majority falling below one feddan in size. In
general, both these Governorates have been marked by intensive, commercialised, small-farm production. In Menoufiya and
Qalyubiya, in particular, the proximity of the Cairo market
has led to a notable shift into vegetable and fruit production. By contrast, Dakhaliya and Sharkiya were historically
characterised by the predominance of large estates. At the
end of the 1930s, for example, 0.3% of the total landholders
in Sharkiya controlled just under 30% of the total area in
units of over 100 feddans. Indeed, 22% of the land area was
held by estates of over 2000 feddans each.[6] A comparable
degree of inequality in land distribution could be found in
Dakhaliya - at the time of the first land reform measures,
around 105,000 of the total requisitioned area of circa
131,000 feddans, were controlled by only 45 landowners.[7]
Although land reform ultimately succeeded in reducing the
average size of holding and consolidated the predominance of
the smallholder, in both Sharkiya and Dakhaliya the larger
farms have retained relatively more importance than in most
other parts of the Delta (see Table 3.1).

In the first instance, basic data were collected from the
gamiya regarding the distribution of landholdings and cropping
patterns in six villages. These were villages in pre-selected

Table 3.1:   Distribution of Landholdings:
             Sharkiya, Dakhaliya and Gharbiya Governorates, 1974/5

Farm Size (feddans)	Number of holders	% Total holders	Area (feddans)	% Total Area	
0-1	119984	38.7	72902	11.5	
1-3	145824	47.2	263664	41.8	
3-5	24419	7.9	87367	13.8	SHARKIYA
5-10	11291	3.7	81133	12.9	Governorate
>10	7613	2.5	126066	20.0	
TOTAL	309131	100.0	631132	100.0	
0-1	109909	38.5	70280	9.9	
1-3	122336	42.8	228277	32.3	
3-5	34051	11.9	115577	16.4	DAKHALIYA
5-10	12945	4.5	85221	12.1	Governorate
>10	6728	2.3	207366	29.3	
TOTAL	285969	100.0	706721	100.0	
0-1	105190	44.5	73498	17.2	
1-3	97498	41.2	173176	40.4	
3-5	25651	10.9	91445	21.4	GHARBIYA
5-10	5835	2.5	42071	9.8	Governorate
>10	2127	0.9	47471	11.2	
TOTAL	236301	100.0	427661	100.0	

Source: Ministry of Agriculture, Agricultural Economics Bulletin, 1979
        (in Arabic)

clusters and the final selection was made in terms of variation in size, population, access to services and the cropping pattern. The common inclusion of rice in the sifi crop was one factor guiding the final selection. Although, such a limited sample could not hope to include the complete range of ecologies and production systems in the Delta, it can reasonably be argued that the sampled villages were broadly representative of the main production and labour conditions holding in the core areas of Egyptian agriculture. However, it is important to note that the survey revealed very signifi- cant variations in the level of labour commitment to agri- culture, the degree of female labour market participation and the structure and level of rural wage rates. Thus, while the villages sampled can be taken as generally representative of conditions in Egyptian agriculture, the prevalence of such variation cautions against the adoption of conclusions and policies that are derived from a highly uniform and undif- ferentiated view of developments in the rural economy.

Once the Governorates and villages had been selected, full tabulation of the register of land rights (hiyaza) was made. This not only provided details of the extent and type of land holding (owned or rented) but also gave an indication of the cropping pattern of each household. This register provided the basic sampling frame. In each village, 55-60 households were sampled from this original frame. The size of the sample was thus a given but the actual sampled households were selected by the usual random, stratified procedure. Households were classed by size of holding before being ran- domly selected. However, as can be seen from Table 3.2, the limited range of large households within these sampled villa- ges severely reduced the sample size from the larger farm-size classes.

Following a systematic pre-test in each of the three villages, administration of the questionnaire to each of the selected households was carried out in two stages. The first stage occurred between August and September, with a further round completed after the sifi harvest in November and early December. Sampling was carried out by one enumerator per village. Although more time-consuming, this allowed for greater consistency in data collection and minimised the problems of supervision. All three enumerators either lived or worked in the selected village or a neighbouring village.

All were graduates and two were MSc students in the Department
of Agricultural Economics at Zagazig University. The third
enumerator worked for the government extension service.

The final sample comprised 171 households, all of which either
owned or rented land. Although it would have been desirable
to include landless households in the sampling frame, this did
not prove possible, largely because satisfactory basic
listings were absent - such as the hiyaza records - for non-
landholders. While the head of household was generally the
principal source of information, enumerators were encouraged
to maximise the number of household members present at each
enumeration. This condition was normally fulfilled since each
questionnaire demanded multiple visits to sampled households.
However, the usual problems were encountered in trying to
construct profiles of female labour force activity. Thus,
while on-farm female labour inputs were very satisfactorily
estimated, the degree of hired agricultural labour done by
female members of the sampled households may have been
underestimated. Likewise, the data collected probably
underestimated household income, although close attention was
generally paid by the enumerators to eliciting accurate information.

Village Characteristics

All the sampled villages showed a similar cropping pattern.
Despite some variation in area under fruit trees and vegetables, the homogeneity of production and rotational cycles
was very clear. In other respects, the villages displayed
very different characteristics. This was true simply in terms
of their basic attributes, with the Gharbiya village having a
population of under 2,500 inhabitants compared with the Sharkiya
and Dakhaliya villages with populations of between 14-21,000
inhabitants. Table 3.2 provides some summary characteristics
of the three villages. Apart from substantial differences in
the number of households and the size of the village's cultivated area, it can also be seen that the number and proportion
of landless households to total landholding households varies
widely. In the case of the Sharkiya village, where average
landholdings were significantly higher than in the other two
villages, landless households comprised over 22% of the total
of landless and landholding units. This proportion fell to

Table 3.2: Summary Characteristics of Sample Villages (classified by Governorate)

Village	Sharkiya	Dakhaliya	Gharbiya
Population	14000	21000	2500
Haizin/landholders	1297	1644	234
Total Area (feddans)	1851.7	1753.8	203.4
Average holdings (feddans)	1.43	1.07	0.87
Number of Landless Households	370	235	25
Nearest Town and Distance	Minyet-el-Qam - 8km	Aga - 11km	El Santa - 6km
Markets	Minyet-el-Qam	Daily meat market Twice weekly general market	Shirshaba - 2km (Mon/Fri Santa - Thursday
Retail Shops in village	8	23	6
Cooperative: Consumer Type Agrarian Reform Credit	Yes No Yes	Yes No Yes	Yes No Yes
Agricultural Credit Bank	Yes	No (nearest 2km)	No (nearest 3km)
Agricultural Extension Officer	No (in Minyet)	No (in Aga)	No (in Santa)

Table 3.2 Summary Characteristics of Sample Villages (cont'd)

Available Facilities and Services

	Sharkiya	Dakhaliya	Gharbiya
Hospital	Yes	Yes	No
Medical Centre	No	Yes	No
Primary School	Yes	Yes	No
Preparatory School	Yes	Yes	No
Secondary School	Yes	Yes	No
Veterinary Station	Yes	No	No
Paved Road	Yes	Yes	No
Bakery	Yes	Yes	No
Government Machinery Station	Yes	No (at Aga)	No (at Santa)
Machinery Repair Shops	1 (full facilities available at Minyet)	No	No (nearest at Santa)
Number of Households in which one or more family members have worked in Arab States in last 5 years	150	170	30

between 10-13% in the case of the Gharbiya and Dakhaliya villages.   In terms of access to services and facilities both the Sharkiya and Dakhaliya villages were better served than Gharbiya village.   However, all were closely linked to neighbouring hamlets, villages and towns by well frequented paved or dust roads.   In all cases, public transportation, either by bus or by pick-up, was relatively easily available.   While the Dakhaliya village was on the main Mansoura to Benha road, the Sharkiya village was situated beside a secondary road to Cairo and in the Gharbiya case there were direct bus and taxi services to Cairo from Santa, as well as railway links to Tanta and Mohalla-el-Qobra.   In none of the sampled villages could transportation be viewed as a constraint on mobility, either of produce or humans.

Although Table 3.2 demonstrates some variation in the average size of holding across village, it is clearly the case that the vast majority of landholding units, whether rented or owned, are small, with the bulk comprising less than one feddan.   The predominance of small holdings was especially pronounced in the Gharbiya case.   This was consistent with the general characteristics of villages in Gharbiya and Menoufiya where village size and operated units are relatively small. More striking was the general absence of the formerly dominant large estates.   Save in the Sharkiya example, farms of over 10 feddans were extremely rare.   Table 3.3 presents some basic information about the distribution of land rights and the tenurial basis on which land is controlled.   While in all cases between 93-97% of farm units fell below three feddans the proportion of the total area controlled by these units varied from 70% in the Sharkiya case to between 79-83% in the two other cases.   It is important to note that in the Sharkiya village this distribution was associated with a higher level of land concentration, so that although farms of over ten feddans comprised less than 1% of total landholding units, they nevertheless controlled about 9.4% of the total area.

When this distributional spread is compared with the most recent data for the respective governorates as a whole, it can be seen (Tables 3.1 and 3.3) that the sampled villages have a lower degree of skewedness in land distribution.   Thus, in Sharkiya and Dakhaliya the 1974/75 evidence suggested that around 2.4% of landholders controlled between 20-29% of the total area.

Table 3.3: Distribution of Landholdings, 1984 Sample Villages

Farm Size (feddans)	Total Units	% of Total Units	Area Controlled (feddans/qirats)	Area as % of Total	Owned Area	Rented Area	Rented Area as % of Total
SHARKIYA							
0-1	721	55.6	405.22	21.9	207.12	198.10	48.9
1-3	487	37.5	891.05	48.1	601.17	289.12	32.5
3-5	43	3.3	143.19	7.8	139.21	3.22	2.7
5-10	34	2.6	236.09	12.8	234.09	2.00	0.8
>10	12	1.0	174.11	9.4	174.11	-	-
TOTAL	1297	100.0	1851.18	100.0	1357.22	493.20	26.07
DAKHALIYA (*)							
0-1	592(1066)	64.3(64.9)	264.19(481.13)	29.0(27.5)	229.12 (416.6)	35.07 (65.07	13.3(13.7)
1-3	288(494)	31.3(30.0)	457.09(798.06)	50.1(45.5)	347.10 (679.9)	109.23(118.17)	24.0(14.8)
3-5	28(48)	3.0(2.9)	99.19(168.02)	10.9(9.6)	87.07 (135.8)	12.14 (32.04	12.6(19.1)
5-10	11(27)	1.2(1.6)	65.18(163.11)	7.2(9.3)	57.06 (82.4)	8.12 (81.07	12.9(49.7)
>10	2(9)	0.2(0.5)	24.22(141.11)	2.8(8.1)	24.22 (94.22)	- (46.13	- (32.9)
TOTAL	921(1644)	100.0(100)	912.15(1753.19)	100.0(100)	746.07(1409.19)	166.08 (344.00)	18.2(19.6)
GHARBIYA							
0-1	158	70.5	79.09	39.1	78.05	1.04	1.5
1-3	59	26.3	88.19	43.7	85.14	3.05	3.6
3-5	4	1.8	13.17	6.7	13.17	-	-
5-10	3	1.4	21.04	10.5	21.04	-	-
>10	-	-	-	-	-	-	-
TOTAL	224	100.0	203.01	100.0	198.16	4.09	2.1

*Figures in brackets are for entire village – figures out of brackets are for the section of the village in which sampling was taken.

Sources: Village Agricultural Cooperatives

The degree of concentration in landholdings is likely to be understated in official records, although not dramatically. While in two of the sampled villages large farms were either absent or of marginal significance, in the case of the Sharkiya village the hiyaza records only began to hint at the degree of concentration of economic and political power in the village. In fact, this village was effectively dominated by one major family, although there were a number of other substantial families resident in the ezbas (hamlets). The recent history of this family provides a fascinating insight into the evolution of local power during the various regimes which have ruled the country since the Free Officers' revolt of 1952.

As one of the six influential families of Minyet-el-Qam markaz, the dominant village family's interests ran from extensive land ownership, through to ownership of the village's brick factory, carpet and plastic pipe manufactories as well as to substantial interests in dairy and poultry farming. Apart from the land and plant they owned in the village, family members also controlled a marble factory in Zagazig and had major commercial interests in the Gulf. As importantly, the head of the family remained the village omda (headman) while other family relations represented the area in the Majis-el-Shaab or on local representative councils. With its characteristically flexible allegiance to the political requirements of the moment, the family has been able to withstand, even benefit, from the Nasserist restructuring of land ownership while, through its political patronage, ensuring that the village derived substantial benefits from state resources. With a large hospital, veterinary service, significant investment in irrigation drainage and pumping, as well as the recent addition of a government Agricultural Mechanization Centre, the access to services in the village far surpasses the norm. Much of this is directly attributable to the combined effect of political patronage and the high level of investment in infrastructure and productive activity by family members.

With about a hundred family members resident in the village and a further thirty members working in the Gulf, the economic interests of these households have been truly diversified. While such interests are spread over a substantial number of nuclear households, the family appears to act coherently as an organised clan interest in the village.

Although it was not possible to measure the size of the family's landholdings exactly, it can be estimated that between
400-475 feddans are owned and worked by its members. This
comprises between 22-26% of the total land of the village.
One of the more powerful family members, living in an _ezba_,
annually farms over 150 feddans as a consolidated estate.
Although the estate is legally owned by his brothers and
remains in their name, the farm functions as a consolidated
entity, but with some profit-sharing. Thus, despite the legal
ceiling of fifty feddans, registration of land in family members' names can circumvent these restrictions.

The dominance of one extended family or clan in the village
was not only reflected in the range of material benefits and
the flow of state resources to the village but also in relation to the labour market and the production technology.
Thus, the relatively high demand for seasonal labour on the
larger farms in the village was directly reflected in the wage
rate. Larger farmers - as will be seen in Chapter 5 - paid
significant wage premia to ensure an adequate supply of
labour. This suggests that with a tightened labour market,
larger landholders were prepared to pay wage increments as a
means of securing adequate labour at the optimal period.
There was no evidence that sharecropping had been used as a
means for securing labour on an incentive basis and it appears
that share contracts have generally declined over the last
five years. Despite the presence of a large set of landless
households in the village, the growth of non-farm employment
and the easy availability of transportation has resulted in a
very widespread diversification in employment. This may
account for the absence of share contracts.

In addition to the competitive structure of the labour market
within the village, it was also striking to note the degree of
investment in agricultural machinery. Apart from the machine
stock of the Mechanization Centre and those owned by individual farmers (see Chapter 9) there was also an enterprise,
based in the village, which specialised in hiring out machine
services. This particular entrepreneur owned five tractors,
as well as a number of irrigation pumps and threshers. The
combined result of this relative abundance of agricultural
machinery was that the use of mechanical energy was widely

diffused for power-intensive activities. The establishment of
the Mechanization Centre just outside the village was seen, by
the larger farm households, as potentially offering mechanical
solutions to the customary harvest season labour bottlenecks.

If the Sharkiya example offers an interesting fusion of political and economic interests, structured around the concerns
of a defined, dominant clan, the same conditions, let alone
material results, cannot be found in the other two case studies. Yet, while the level of inequality in asset distribution was most pronounced in the Sharkiya case, two particular
features remain common to all selected examples. In the first
place, the small farm sector remains the backbone of the production system. However, as will become clear, this sector no
longer functions as a set of quasi-subsistence producers
(after accounting for forced deliveries) reliant on limited
material inputs and household labour. Rather, small farms
enter the labour market both to hire in labour and,
increasingly importantly, to hire out their labour. Whereas
the Egyptian rural labour market of the 1950s or 1960s was
largely characterised by the restrictive nature of its
unskilled labour market and by the relatively low access to
education, that of the 1980s has been marked by increasing
mobility and a growing retention of children in education. To
that extent, the entire structure of expectations appears to
have undergone a profound change. Even if the constriction on
the supply of labour to agriculture remains less tight than
commonly imagined, or planned for, possibly the most striking
continuity across a number of diverse village types was the
importance of non-agricultural work and income. As will
become clear, this phenomenon appears to be de-linked from the
nature of the landholding structure and the distribution of
assets.

To understand the nature of this change and its implications
for the agricultural sector, it is first necessary to look, in
detail, at the production system itself and, in particular, at
the labour requirements generated by that system. The
following chapter therefore concentrates on the demand for
labour in agriculture and its distribution, both temporally
and by type of labour.

Footnotes

1. Fourth Agricultural Census 1961, 1967.
2. Ricardo, 1951 p93ff.
3. Hansen and Radwan, 1982 pp139-160.
4. Other survey generated data include, inter alia: Egyptian
    Farm Management Survey, 1980: Richards and Martin, 1982:
    Youssef, 1983: Reiss, Lutfi et al., 1982.
5. In the Dakhaliya case the village selected was split into
    two administrative zones - east and west. Sampling only
    occurred in the western section.
6. Ammar, 1944, p289.
7. Abdel-Khalek, 1971.

CHAPTER FOUR

The Demand for Labour in Egyptian Agriculture

Introduction

Two principal sources of demand for labour can be identified
in the agricultural sector; the first derives from crop production, the second from work associated with livestock
raising. While the two activities are hardly distinct, there
are, in the Egyptian context, some important differences in
the composition of the labour force involved in each branch of
activity. At the same time, the balance between crop and
livestock work has been modified substantially over the last
decade. As crop production provides 'intermediate goods' for
livestock production such shifts in balance have major implications across the sector as a whole.

Historically, crop production has constituted the principal
source of demand for labour. This demand has been satisfied
variously by the combination of hired and family labour
inputs; a combination that has undergone major changes in the
recent past. To this extent, it is clear that land redistribution since 1952 has had the effect of raising the proportion
of family to hired labour in crop production. This has
reflected the predominance of small-holdings in the agrarian
regime of the Nasser period. Before then, dwarf holdings predominated and a sizeable share of the agricultural lacked
lacking access to land. The skewedness of land distribution
obviously implied that the major demand for labour
(particularly, hired labour) originated from the large-farm
sector. In Sharkiya, for example, around 3.4% of total landowners held nearly 60% of the total area; by contrast 93% of
farms fell below 1½ feddans and constituted barely 31% of the
total area. As the overwhelming proportion - 75% - of these
small farms were less than half a feddan, the on-farm
employment potential was clearly seriously constrained.[1] The
later reconstitution of land rights, while not completely
changing the framework of the demand for labour, naturally had
major implications for the derivation of labour demand. At
the same time, developments outside the agricultural sector in
the past decade have also affected the configuration of

labour-use patterns in Egyptian agriculture.

While particular regions of the country are known for their
concentration on certain crops - eg. sugar cane in Qena - the
Delta as a whole has historically concentrated on the production of basic cereals and, of course, cotton. At the height
of the two-year cotton rotational system adopted between 1890
and 1910, the proportion of the cultivated area under cotton
approached a third. The principal food crops then comprised
maize, rice, wheat, beans and millet. At the same time, about
a fifth of the cultivated area was habitually allocated to
fodder cropping and to birseem in particular.[2] By the 1950s
the major food crops - wheat, maize, rice, beans and sorghum -
accounted for just under half of the total area allocations
with birseem occupying around 23% and cotton 18% of the total
cropped area.[3] As Table 4.1 demonstrates, the area under
fodder crops has tended to grow at a steady rate while the
area under cotton and wheat has undergone a significant long-
term decline. When it is remembered that wheat is grown principally for its straw and maize is commonly used as fodder,
actual allocations to animal feed have been far more substantial than the area under birseem would suggest. Indeed, birseem being a <u>shitwi</u> crop, the fodder requirements for the
period from September through to February are largely provided
by maize, cotton stalks and by such stocks of straw and birseem that households can maintain.

Apart from the obvious implications for the domestic supply of
food grains, the shift in the distribution of the cropped area
has had substantial implications for the patterns of labour
use, the timing of those labour inputs and the structure of
production costs. At the same time, it is important to note
that the nature of the irrigation system has changed substantially with the installation of the High Dam and the consequent importance of the <u>sifi</u> as against the <u>nili</u> crop.

The three sampled villages display cropping patterns and
intensities broadly in line with the national distribution.
However, it should be born in mind that these villages were
selected for sampling partly because of their cropping patterns and, in particular, the cultivation of rice alongside
maize in the <u>sifi</u> crop. While rice dominates in the more
northerly parts of the Delta, maize remains a more important
crop in the areas from which the villages were selected.

Table 4.1: <u>Egypt: Proportion of Cropped Area Under Major Crops, 1950-1981</u>

	1950/54	1960/64	1970/74	1978/81
Winter (<u>Shitwi</u>) Crops				
Birseem	23.2	23.8	25.8	24.9
Wheat	16.7	13.5	11.7	12.4
Beans	3.5	3.5	3.2	2.2
Barley	1.3	1.2	0.7	0.9
Lentils	0.8	0.7	0.6	0.2
Vegetables	0.4	0.5	1.7	2.3
Other	1.4	2	1.7	1.8
Summer (<u>Sifi</u>)Crops				
Cotton	18.8	17	14.3	10.7
Rice	5.4	7.7	10.1	9.0
Maize	0.3	2.6	11.5	12.8
Sorghum	4.1	4	4.3	3.6
Vegetables	1.3	2.5	3.3	4.4
Sugarcane	1	1.2	1.8	2.2
Other	0.8	1.3	1.5	2.3
<u>Nili</u> Crops				
Maize	18.2	14.2	3.2	4.3
Vegetables	0.7	1.3	2	2.3
Other	0.8	0.7	0.6	0.4
Orchards	1.0	1.4	2.3	3.1
Total Cropped Area	9412	10289	10855	11092
(feddans '000s)	100	109	115	118

Except for a relatively small area under beans and vegetables, and a very limited land area devoted to fruit production, the predominance of the five major crops; wheat and birseem in the shitwi harvest and cotton, maize and rice in the sifi crop is most striking.   There was no nili cultivation in any of the sampled villages.

If the cropping pattern in the sampled villages broadly corresponds to the national trend, with heavy weight being given to the cultivation of fodder crops, the general trend towards a declining allocation to cotton is also visible. Most particularly, credence seems to be given to the view that cotton area allocations are evaded by larger farms and that the main burden of growing cotton has been shifted onto the small farms.   Table 4.2 shows a sharp decline in the proportion of cotton in the cultivated area as farm size increases. Nearly 40% of households with farms of over 5 feddans did not grow cotton at all; either preferring to pay the fine levied through the gamiya or else avoiding the penalty by one means or another.   Amongst other consequences, this results in a diminished demand for labour on the larger farms, given the high level of labour inputs in cotton production relative to other crops.   In general, larger farms substitute maize for cotton, not only because of the higher rate of return from the non-administered crop but also because of its role as fodder.

The Demand for Labour in Crop Production

The long-run movement out of traditional cereal food crops has had implications for labour requirements in crop production and to some extent, for the seasonal distribution of those labour requirements.   Thus, the strong preference for maize cultivation across all sampled villages is not unconnected with the fact that it matures and can be harvested prior to both the rice and cotton crops.   As the great bulk of farms are composed of between two and three fragments, in which different crops are sown, the cultivation of maize alongside cotton and rice is made more attractive by the staged labour requirements that this cycle sets up.   Although obviously connected to the relatively tight agricultural labour market that has developed during the last decade, this is not a sharp departure from past practice in itself in so far as seasonal and harvesting peaks have always generated a sharp upturn in

Graph 4.1

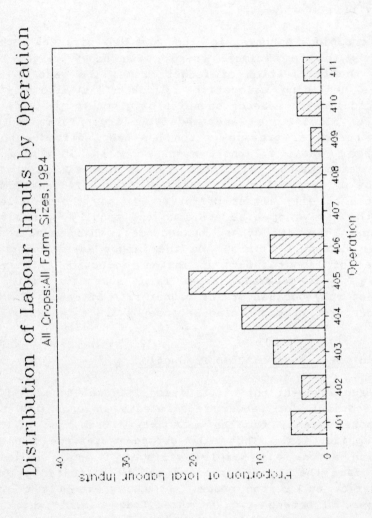

GRAPH 4:1 Codes: 401=Manuring: 402= Bed Preparation: 403=Cultivation:404=Weeding:
405=Irrigation: 406=Chemical Fertilizer:407=Pest Control: 408=Harvesting:409=Threshing
and Winmowing :410= Transportation: 411=Other

the demand for labour. For _all_ crop production, it was found
that harvesting - which included both cotton picking and
cutting - accounted for as much as 35% of total labour inputs
(see Graph 4.1). In the case of cotton alone, the proportion
rose to over 54%.

As significant in determining the volume of labour inputs is
the actual crop mix. A distinct rotational system operates,
organised around a two-crop structure and, in particular, the
role of cotton. This is not only because cotton remains a
forced cultivation but also because it remains longer on the
land and places a relatively heavy toll on land fertility. In
the regions selected for this study a rotational cycle exists
as follows:

Rotation

Long	Rice	Beans	Cotton	Wheat	Maize
Birseem		Short		&/or	&/or
		Birseem		Vegetables	Vegetables

Indicative of the variation in labour requirements is the fact
that cotton generates a pattern of labour use on average between three and four times greater than that commonly employed
in the cultivation of the principal _shitwi_ crops, wheat and
birseem. The average labour use for rice and maize, the other
sifi crops, varies between half and two-thirds of that for
cotton.

In addition - and this is a point that will be returned to
later - the quantum of labour used in production varies
substantially across each village even if the ratios of labour
use between crops remain broadly similar. In the case of the
Gharbiya village, cotton labour inputs were just about half of
those of the other two villages. The same disparity was evident for the other major crops, except for long birseem.

Looking at Table 4.3 it is evident that, in the first instance, the winter season customary crop mix sets up a labour
requirement roughly a third of that generated in the _sifi_
season when a combination of cotton, rice and maize is sown.
Secondly, although the highest levels of labour intensity

Table 4.2: Distribution of Gross Cropped Area: All Sample Villages by Farm Size, 1984

Crop	0 - 1	1 - 3	3 - 5	5 - 10	>10	ALL
	Farm Size					
Shitwi						
Wheat	14.8	16.5	17.9	18.9	11.4	16.2
Long Birseem	14.6	11.5	12.8	15.7	17.5	13.8
Beans	0.7	0.7	1.9	1.4	7.9	2.1
Vegetables	0.4	0.8	-	-	-	0.3
Short Birseem	18.9	20.1	16.5	15.3	4.3	16.1
Sifi						
Cotton	19.1	18.8	14.0	11.9	4.2	14.8
Rice	13.0	11.0	10.9	12.0	12.1	11.6
Maize	18.0	19.5	24.7	24.7	37.9	23.8
Vegetables	0.5	0.9	1.3	-	4.7	1.3
Total Area:	99.1	222.1	139.8	92.5	94.8	648.3 Feddans
	15.3	34.2	21.6	14.3	14.6	100%

Table 4.3: Total Labour Inputs: Hours per Feddan in Equalised Man-Hours: by Farm Size.

Farm Size	Wheat	Beans	Long Birseem	Short Birseem	Cotton	Rice	Maize
0 - 1	155	339	211	93	622	420	368
1 - 3	153	139	203	96.5	699	456	320
3 - 5	131	206	234	95	604	366	340
5 - 10	122	296	153	76	683	319	321
>10	244	197	125	78	1009	350	396
All	150	220	204	94	658	419	341
Village a	196	343	194	128	746	592	545
Village b	130	-	196	40	398	285	178
Village c	122	152	218	109	814	434	277

Village a = Sharkiya
Village b = Gharbiya
Village c = Dakhaliya

Table 4.4: Average Labour Inputs per Feddan in Crop Production for 1983/4 (standardized man-hours)

Farm Size (feddans)	Sharkiya Village a	Gharbiya Village b	Dakhalia Village c	All Villages	All Villages
	------ Man-Hours ----------------------				Man-Days
0 -1	2214	961	1378	1384	261
1 - 3	1745	1073	1668	1566	295
3 - 5	1395	988	1808	1557	294
5 - 10	1039	1112	1815	1434	270
> 10	1302	-	2027	1544	291

were reported for farms of between 1-3 feddans, the variation across farm size was possibly smaller than expected. This suggests that the traditional distinction between family labour-intensive small farms and the less intensive larger farms, reliant more on hired labour, has less relevance now than it did in the comparatively recent past. The absence of a significant degree of variation, such as was reported in a 1978 survey, where small farms utilised over double the labour inputs of farms above five feddans, can be directly related to the increased participation in the non-agricultural labour market by male family members in small farm households.[4] This has tended to equalise the average quantum of labour inputs across farm size. However the discrepancy, still holds strongly in the Sharkiya village, from which governorate the earlier data were generated.

Although a number of basic tasks associated with crop production are now relatively fully mechanised (see Chapter 9) the overwhelming predominance of labour as an input in the production process is clear. On average, it constitutes around three-quarters of total inputs, when measured in hours. Moreover, it is important to note that labour time appropriates a greater share of total production time on the larger farms than on the small units. For farms of over ten feddans labour accounts for around 90% of the total time allocated to crop production.

As would be expected, the distribution of labour time fluctuates seasonally as also by type of labour. Historically, the two peak periods have been May-June and September-October. The first shitwi harvesting peak has been associated with a much enhanced demand for male labour, while the second sifi peak has, largely by virtue of the importance of cotton, been associated with a much enhanced demand for female and child labour.[5] These features are amply brought out in Graph 4.1, although there was, in the 1984 survey, particularly in the Sharkiya village, a rather earlier peak in April. April and May accounted for nearly 27% of total labour inputs and about 30% of total adult male inputs. In October and November, while the demand for labour accounted for 37.5% of total labour inputs, the share of total male labour time was below 30% but reached 55% for all female and child labour inputs. Although the demand for female and child labour, and particularly for hired female labour, was relatively strong in

Labour Inputs by Month:1984
By Category of Labour

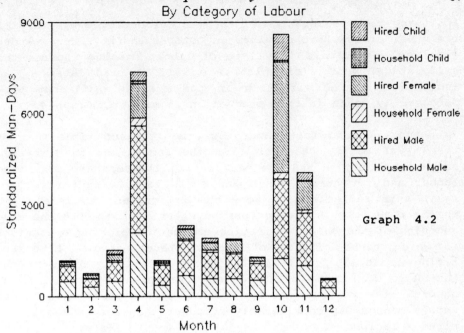

Graph 4.2

Labour Inputs (Equalized):1970
All Farm Sizes

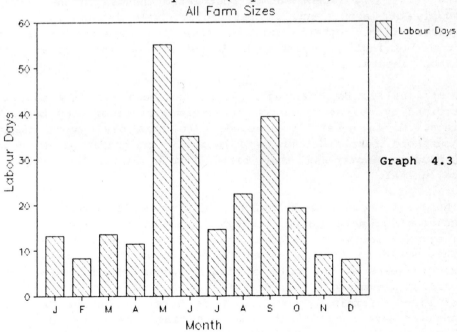

Graph 4.3

April and May, the quantum of such labour deployed was only of
the order of 35% that required in October and November. Apart
from the variation in the type of labour demanded across the
agricultural year - of which more will be said later - an
indication of the variation in the quantum of labour time
embodied by month in crop production is given in Graph 4.2.

In October demand for labour was some fourteen times that of
the trough month, December.   At the same time, the variance
between the trough and the peak is still more sharp for hired
labour and for hired female and child labour, in particular.
Again this reflected the very sharp increment in female and
child labour use in the October/November period, with the con-
junction of the maize separating and cotton picking operations
in which these classes of labour predominated.   Likewise,
hiring of female and child labour is relatively high in June
and July when rice planting and transplanting occurs.   In
general, the variance in the demand for non-adult male labour
across months was considerably stronger than for household and
hired male labour.

The relatively recent set of postulated changes in the actual
supply of labour and, in particular, male labour, to agriculture might, ceteris paribus, have been expected to have a
number of implications for the labour mix and the intensity of
labour inputs.

Historically, Egyptian agriculture has been strongly characterised by sex segmentation vis-a-vis a range of crop tasks.[6]
Thus, it is generally assumed - to this day, even - that
household female labour is relatively insignificant in crop
production work and that hired female labour is likewise
peripheral.

The first assumption holds, but in a crucially modified form.
Household female labour, though important in livestock work,
remains relatively insignificant in crop production even now.
This would be the case even if, as seems likely, the survey
underenumerated the role of family woman labour.   However,
earlier assumptions fall drastically when it comes to the role
of hired female labour and it is here that a set of major
changes have occurred. At the same time, the spread of tasks
undertaken by women, particularly hired female labour, has broadened across all farm size classes.   Female labour provides

between a third and half of the labour time allocated to planting and the application of chemical fertilizer. Women also play, as expected, a major role in harvesting and, to a far more limited extent, in weeding. Irrigation work is overwhelmingly dominated by males, as are the major tasks of ploughing, weeding, threshing and winnowing, and transportation of the crop.

If the spread of tasks undertaken by women has broadened from the traditional concentration on rice planting, pest control, cotton picking and maize separating, the aggregate effect is more noticeable. Table 4.5 suggests that over the last two decades, the proportion of male labour time of total labour time has declined for most crops and across all farm size classes. However, it is significant that the proportion of male labour in cotton and rice production has remained roughly constant. As cotton cultivation alone accounted for over 62% of total female and child labour inputs and rice and cotton accounted for over 75%, the overall weight of male labour in crop production remains very substantial. Although it would be true to say that there has been some degree of substitution of female and child labour for male labour, this level of substitution is less than might be predicted if a severe shortage in adult male labour was the principal characteristic of the agricultural labour market.

A further comparison, using 1978 survey-generated data relating to Sharkiya Governorate, suggests that the intervening six years have not seen a further displacement of male labour by other types of labour. Nor, equally, has there been a marked falling off in the average commitment of labour resources to crop production.

If labour use data collected in the early 1960s[7] is compared with 1984 data (Table 4.7) no noticeable trend towards declining labour inputs in crop production is apparent, even when adjusting for the different average lengths of the working day. Thus, in the early 1960s the normal working day took up between seven and eight hours; but by 1984 it was around 5.3 hours on average in the villages surveyed.

The figures presented here have been confirmed by other recent survey work; indeed some estimates suggest levels of labour commitment to birseem greater than those reported. In any

event, it is clear that labour-use patterns are considerably
dispersed.

In the 1984 survey data, for example, it was found that labour
use levels in the Gharbiya village were, with the exception of
long birseem, between a third and two thirds of the level in
the other sampled villages. In the case of cotton, average
labour time was about half and this was the case across all
farm size classes. As will be seen later, this has to be
associated with the overall employment profile in the village
and, in particular, the relatively high importance of non-farm
work in most households' employment structure. At the same
time, the considerable weight given to livestock rearing in
this village (and the absence of data on the time allocation
to such work) may well be a factor explaining the low levels
of labour absorption in crop cultivation. However, it is
important to note that although the time spent might be lower,
the share of male labour in total crop labour time was, if
anything, slightly higher than the average. This again points
to the lack of a major substitution of female and child labour
for male labour, even under conditions where this would seem
most probable.

Thus, while it seems that there has been no general downward
trend in the last two decades in the quantum of labour committed to crop production - a factor that has obvious implications for any discussion of labour shortages and of the impact
of mechanisation - there have been major shifts in the composition of the demand for labour. On the one hand, the share
of tasks done by women and children has undoubtedly risen to
some extent, but, perhaps more importantly, the share of hired
labour, including hired woman and child labour, has risen in a
very marked manner. This is despite the fact that, as alluded
to earlier, the proportion of the landless labour force in the
rural sector has fallen back considerably. Furthermore,
although the size and proportionate strength of the landless
labour-force in each of the surveyed villages was markedly
different, the weight of hired labour in total labour inputs
was far less dispersed than might have been expected. In the
Gharbiya village the share of hired labour tended to be higher
than elsewhere, pointing to one effect of a wider labour
market.

An indication of the scale of change in the hiring patterns of

Table 4.5: Male Labour Inputs as a Proportion of Total Labour Inputs, 1961 and 1984

Crop	1961	1984	1961	1984	1961	1984
			Farm Size (feddans)			
	5	5	5-20	5-10	20	10
Wheat	84.6	69.5	84.2	71.4	87.2	78.4
Long Birseem	87	71.6	87	56.8	85.2	79.8
Short Birseem	100	67.4	100	74.6	100	91.2
Beans	77	64.3	72	-	70	68.2
Cotton	39.4	43.3	37.7	28.8	37.6	34.1
Maize	80	59.8	80	63.1	80	78.1
Rice	57.3	58.4	58.7	60.5	56.6	65.6

Sources : Mohie-Eldin, 1975 and ODI/Zagazig Survey, 1984

Table 4.6: Distribution of Labour Inputs: By Sex: Sharkiya

Crop	Male		Female		Child		Equalized Man-Days per feddan	
	1978	1984	1978	1984	1978	1984	1978	1984
Cotton	45.3	44.2	13.7	43.4	41	12.4	145.2	141
Rice	74.3	74.8	14.7	19.9	11	5.3	63.4	112
Maize	72.8	75.9	17.6	19.8	9.6	4.3	46.7	103
Wheat	83.0	92.0	12.6	5.9	4.4	2.1	34.1	37

Source : Youssef, 1983: ODI/Zagazig Survey, 1984

Table 4.7: All Farm Sizes: Standardised Man-Hours per Feddan, 1963 - 1984

Crop	Man-Hours	
	1963	1984
Cotton	675	658
Maize	219	341
Rice	420	419
Wheat	206	150
Long Birseem	141	204
Short Birseem	83	94

Table 4.8: Work by Non-Family Members as % of Total Labour Input by Farm Size, Family Size and Sex-Age Group, 1964/65

Farm Size (feddans)	Male	Female	Children	Proportion of Farms Hiring Labour *
0.5 - 2	6.2* - 7.3%**	2* - 9.4%**	4.6* - 26.2%**	24%
2 - 5	13* - 27.8%**	13.6*- 16.3%**	16.2* - 33.5%**	36%
>5	36.1* - 72.2%**	23.1*- 41.1%**	45.3* - 93.2%**	53%
>10	-	-	-	85%

* More than 3 working family members
** 3 and less working family members

Source : Hansen, 1969, p302 and * Mabro, 1971, Table 11.

Egyptian farmers can readily be gauged when comparing data
collected in the mid-1960s with the 1984 data (see Table
4.8). The INP/ILO survey found relatively low hired labour
time in farm production with much of that time being accounted
for by peak season hiring, with the labour-force being drawn
from the landless.[8] In this context, it should be remembered
that most estimates have placed the proportion of landless
households at above 45% of total agricultural households in
this period.[9]

The undisputed decline in the landless labour force has not
resulted in a squeeze on labour hiring. Indeed, all households, irrespective of farm size, hired some labour in crop
production in the course of the 1983/84 crop year. Tables 4.9
and 4.10 demonstrate beyond doubt that labour hiring is
widespread among all farm-size classes and for all crops,
though obviously being positively related to farm size. Only
birseem engenders currently a relatively low hired labour component. This is quite understandable given that birseem tends
to be sown on unploughed land with cutting normally regulated
by daily fodder requirements or browsed in the field by the
livestock. The information presented in Table 4.10 had
further borne out when regressing hired labour hours on the
operated area. This was done both for all crops and by individual crop. The results showed that total hired labour hours
were positively associated with the size of holding; this
relationship being statistically significant in most instances.

On average, across all crops, hired labour accounts for over
40% of labour time allocated to crop production on the
smallest farms and over three-quarters on farms of between
three and five acres. Moreover, female and child labour
accounted for between 27-37% of total labour time and for between 32-34% of hired inputs. Compared with the 1978 Sharkiya
data which put the proportion at between 20-33% of all hired
labour, this would substantiate the point about an increasing
role for women in crop production.[10] At the same time, the
data shows that not only do significant amounts of female
labour power get transacted through the market but that, to a
more limited extent, household women participate in crop production.

The use of female labour has increased in compacted, highly

Table 4.9: Labour Inputs: by Sex and Type

Farm Size (feddans)	Household Female	Hired Female	Household Child	Hired Child	Hired Female and Child	Total Female and Child	Household Male	Hired Male	Total Male
0 - 1	6.8	13	2.7	4.6	17.6	27.1	49	23.9	72.9
1 - 3	4.6	25.5	1.2	5.1	30.6	36.4	33	30.6	63.6
3 - 5	0.5	27.7	0.9	4.9	32.6	34	23	43	66
5 - 10	1.5	31.2	1.1	2.9	34.1	36.7	8.8	54.5	63.3
> 10	-	12.2	1	12.8	25	26	-	74	74
ALL	3.2	22.5	1.4	5.8	28.3	32.9	26	41.1	67.1

Table 4.10: Source of Crop Labour

Farm Size	Hired 1976/7	Hired 1984	Household 1976/77	Household 1984
0 - 1	23	42.5	77	57.5
1 - 3	30	61.4	70	38.6
3 - 5	41	75.6	59	24.4
5 - 10	45	88.5	55	11.5
>10	47	99	53	1.0

Source: Farm Management Survey, 1977 and ODI/Zagazig Survey, 1984

seasonalised tasks - particularly harvesting - where the fall
in the landless labourer population and the availability of
male labour has had most effect.

The substantial expansion in the volume and share of hired
labour time in total crop production appears to be a continuing trend. Comparing 1978 information with 1984 data, it
emerges that the share of hired labour has risen considerably
for almost all tasks. In the case of ploughing, for example,
this can be explained by the growing substitution of tractor
ploughing for the traditional draught-drawn plough. As the
former is almost invariably done by hired-in equipment and
operator, the shift from a 94% share of _family_ labour in this
task in 1978 to a 74% share for _hired_ labour can be readily
understood.

The association between the use of machine and animal inputs
in crop production and the level of labour inputs was further
tested in regression analysis. As hired labour inputs for
machine and animal use were almost entirely male, the functional form adopted was to regress hired male labour hours on,
in the first instance, machine and animal hours and, secondly,
on a number of variables proxying household male endowments as
well as the volume of non-crop income of the household.

In the first case, as Table 4.11 demonstrates, hired male
labour inputs were found to be positively related to machine
and animal inputs and this association was significant at a 1%
level. The second equation aimed at estimating the relationship between the availability of male household labour and
the level of hired male labour use. Four independent
variables were specified. Three were effective proxies for
the amount of non-resident male labour, while the last
variable - total non-crop income - represented the level of
non-farm employment achieved per household. The latter level
was hypothesised to be an accurate proxy for the availability
of labour within the household for own-farm agricultural work.

If non-farm income is accepted as a suitable proxy for household male labour availability, it emerges that, as expected,
hired male labour time is positively associated with the
volume of non-crop income. This relationship was statistically highly significant. This appears to support the dual
argument that the profile of the hired male labour force has

Table 4.11: Log Linear Regression for Determinants of Hired Male Labour
             Use (a12)

(a) Dependent Variable: Hired Male Labour Hours

Mean: 2.1859
C.V.: 14.3485

Independent Variable	Coefficient	Standard Error	Significance Level
Machine Hours	.7524	.06288	0.001
Animal Hours	.3104	.06780	0.001

R^2 = 0.5155   F Value = 77.14   No of Observations = 148

(b) Dependent Variable: Hired Male Labour (a12)

Mean: 337.339
C.V.: 133.599

Independent Variable	Coefficient	Standard Error	Significance Level
Total non-Crop Income	.15356	0.03190	0.0001
Males, 15-60 years Abroad (Dummy)	-759.042	284.814	0.0086
Males Abroad: Proportion Males, 15-60 years	638.836	443.525	0.1519
Males Abroad: Proportion of Total Household	1233.174	1589.027	0.4390
Constant term	178.431	52.4349	0.0009

R^2 = .1678   F Value = 7.412   No of Observations = 152

undergone some change with the hiring of male labour being
associated with the use of machinery and that hired male
labour tends to substitute for household male labour when non-
farm employment is significant.

The growth in the proportion of hired labour is evident for
all major crop activities, if less dramatic. At the same
time, more traditional, quasi-reciprocal, labour transactions
have become increasingly marginal. Mazamlah (reciprocal
labour) was found to be almost non-existent, save in one of
the sampled villages where a modified form operated for maize
separating in which only woman labour was involved.

The Demand for Labour in Livestock Production

Possibly one of the most striking changes in the framework of
agricultural production over the last decade has been the
emergence of animal husbandry as a profitable and widespread
activity. While, in general, this has taken the form of cow
or buffalo rearing, poultry farming, often in modern units,
has also emerged as a significant resource.[11]

The ownership of animals, particularly draught ones, has
always been important in Egyptian agriculture. Aside from
tasks such as ploughing and transportation of the crop, animal
energy has been central to the prevailing irrigation systems.
This has obviously been the case most particularly when saqias
(the Egyptian water wheel) have been employed. Despite an
undoubted trend towards the substitution of diesel or electri-
cally powered pumpsets for the saqia, the latter remains the
major distributor of water in the majority of Delta villages.
Where this is the case, the stock of draught animals maintained on-farm tends to be higher. However, saqia work - commonly one or two hours a day - is not considered by most
farmers to be overly taxing for animals kept largely for their
milk or meat function. To this extent, existing calculations
of the opportunity cost of such livestock have tended to over-
estimate production losses through irrigation work.[12] The
emergence of animal husbandry as a major household industry
can largely be explained by the relative price structure. As
was mentioned earlier, red meat prices have been consistently
above their border price levels, while, partly as a consequence of the elaborate food subsidy programme developed
since 1973, the growth in demand for meat and dairy products

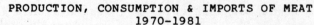

PRODUCTION, CONSUMPTION & IMPORTS OF MEAT
1970-1981

GRAPH 4.4

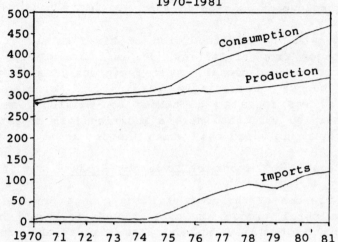

PRODUCTION, CONSUMPTION & IMPORTS OF POULTRY
1970-1981

GRAPH 4.5

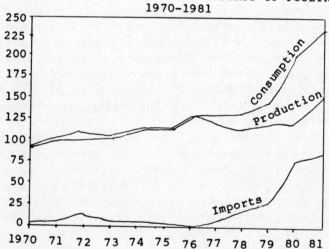

has run substantially ahead of the production capacity.[13]   In
the last decade alone per capita consumption has grown by
nearly 25% and despite an increased volume of imports, both of
meat and milk, their respective prices have increased at a
rate considerably in excess of the price rises for field
crops.   A similar trend in consumption has held for both
chicken meat and egg production. as is clear in Graphs 4.4 and
4.5.

The impact of these shifts in the relative prices of agricultural outputs has been various. On the one hand, the area
under birseem, particularly long birseem, has increased while
maize provides the major source of green fodder in the summer.
One further effect has been to depress the area under HYV
wheat on account of the relatively low straw yield.[14]
Indicative of the premium placed on straw as against the main
grain output is the fact that in 1984 the ratio of the value
of such secondary output to primary output was 1.5:1.

Nevertheless, despite the major redirection of Egyptian agriculture towards the satisfaction of the fodder requirements of
livestock, there is little doubt that fodder scarcity is the
principal constraint on the augmentation of the stock of
animals.[15] Although the availability of processed animal feed
has increased in the last five years, a very definite supply
lag still exists. One consequence has been that a lively
local market for fodder has emerged at the farm level. Most
have hypothesized that this would involve the selling of
fodder by larger farmers to the small, land constrained households. Yet, the 1984 data appear to suggest that this is not
the case, if only because of the substantial livestock
holdings on the larger units. Nevertheless, as Table 4.12
demonstrates, significant proportions of birseem output are
sold across farm size, with that share of marketed output
tending to rise with farm size. On the smallest units, a
significant share of marketed output originates from farms
without livestock and in the Gharbiya village where animal
raising was of particular importance, the proportion of
marketed output was lower than the average.

The significance of livestock in the small farm economy can
clearly be seen in the distribution of livestock holdings and
the proportion of farms with livestock. Over 80% of those sampled held animals (other than poultry), but over five-sixths

Table 4.12:   Proportion of Birseem Output Marketed, By Farm Size, 1984

Farm Size (feddans)	Long Birseem	Short Birseem
0 - 1	20.5	24.3
1 - 3	20.2	41.8
3 - 5	29.7	28.6
5 - 10	39.0	45.6
>10	8.5	0

Table 4.13:   Livestock Ownership 1950-1984

Farm Size (feddans)	Proportion of Households possessing one or more head of cattle	Head of Cattle per Household	Prop-ortion	Head	Prop-ortion	Average per feddan	Head
	------------1950----------		----1961----		----------1984----------		
0 - 1	-	-	-	-	87.3	2.4	1.
0 - 2	68	1.4	69	1.7	-	-	-
1 - 3	-	-	-	-	72	1.1	1.
2 - 5	88	1.9	87	2.4	-	-	-
3 - 5	-	-	-	-	65	0.9	3.
5 - 10	-	-	-	-	66.6	1.02	6.
5 - 20	95	2.9	91	3.7	-	-	-
>10	-	-	-	-	66.6	3.5	45
20 - 50	95	5.8	83	7.5	-	-	-
50 - 100	93	10.4	76	15	-	-	-
>100	92	30	73	34	-	-	-

Source: Abdel-Fadil, 1975 p30 * 1984, ODI/Zagazig Survey (1950 -1961 Figur
          relate to All Egypt)

of those households without livestock were concentrated in one
of the sample villages.   Ironically, this - the Dakhaliya
village - was famous through the Delta for the quality of the
meat sold by the numerous butchers whose stalls line the main
road to Mansoura. Thus, although a considerable proportion of
the crop-related tasks traditionally performed with animal
power have now been superseded by the use of mechanical
energy, the stock of animals does not appear to have declined.
However, whereas in the past animals were commonly shared in
ownership, this hardly exists at all at present.   Rather the
long-term trend has been towards a more widespread household
ownership of cattle and other animals, as can be seen from
Table 4.13.

Probably the most striking development has been the growing
importance of cows and buffaloes on the smallest farms. While
this has manifested itself primarily in the increased proportion of small farms owning cattle, the animal-operated feddan
density index is perhaps more revealing.   On the smallest
farms the density is more than double that for all other farm-
size classes, bar the largest. In addition, around two-thirds
of all households own a donkey. These are for uses ranging
from personal transportation to moving the crop, taking fertiliser to the field, and in some cases, the pulling of the
saqia. Apart from these types of livestock and the very common ownership of poultry, few other animals were in evidence.
Barely an eighth of the sample owned sheep and only three
households maintained the traditional animal used for crop
transportation, the camel.   Indeed the camel traders at the
weekly market at Shoeshalamun, near the Sharkiya village,
complained of a consistently declining recent market for these
beasts of burden. The pick-up truck has in effect substituted
substantially for these animals.

Although the 1984 survey did not explore detailed labour use
patterns in livestock work, there are sufficient recent data
to warrant comparison. Fitch and Soliman, for instance, found
that livestock work was not only more intensive on the smaller
farms, but that it engendered a labour requirement considerably in excess of that used in crop production.[16] Moreover,
this labour requirement was almost entirely satisfied by
family labour, and was concentrated in the relatively slack
winter months when crop requirements were low. Furthermore,
female family labour played a particularly prominent role

contributing, on farms of less than five feddans, as much as
40% of the total time worked in livestock activity. This, it
was argued, was a reflection of social preferences as much as
anything else. On-farm work was deemed acceptable for family
women, but the hiring-out of their labour was still considered
to be somewhat degrading. At the same time, small farm animal
husbandry, with its relatively high returns to labour, was
seen as a particularly efficient soak for the family workforce as a whole.

The relative significance of livestock work can be seen in
Table 4.14. As much as 73% of total labour time on small
farms was absorbed in non-crop work and while the particularly
notable feature was the role of women in this work, it is
important to remember that nearly three-quarters of male
labour time on the smallest farms was directed towards
livestock work. Naturally, this reflected the primary
constraining feature of small farm production: land. On
larger size farms the proportion of male time devoted to animal husbandry fell drastically. With the exception of the
largest farms where nearly two-fifths of livestock labour was
hired, the significance of family work relative to family crop
work was very visible. A positive correlation between family
size and livestock holding was further found to exist. One
consequence, Fitch and Soliman argued, was that entry into the
hired farm labour market was restrained through the additional
on-farm work generated by animal husbandry.[17] The scale of
labour requirements generated in this type of work can be seen
in the crop-livestock ratio across farm size. While for the
smallest units the ratio in 1977 was 2.6:1 for livestock, this
was more than reversed for farms of above five feddans.
However, a weighted average from the Farm Management Survey
data produced a ratio of only 1.25:1 in favour of crop work.

More recent research into this question (although employing a
narrower data base, eight villages in four Delta Governorates)
has confirmed some of the earlier findings but has produced
less univocal conclusions on a number of the issues already
raised. Thus, hired labour was found to be of continuing
marginal importance in livestock work. However, as was found
in the Sharkiya village sampled in 1984, permanent farm labour
is principally employed on the largest farms in animal work.
Nevertheless, the hired labour contribution in general was
estimated to be between 3-4% of total labour time, with only

Table 4.14: Labour use for Livestock and Crop Activity: 1976/77

Farm Size (feddans)	Livestock Labour Inputs as % of Total Labour Inputs	Crop Labour % Hired	Livestock Labour % Hired	Family Labour: % of							
				Crop Labour				Livestock Labour			
				M	F	C	E	M	F	C	E
0 - 1	72.6	23	0	53	2	4	17	46	40	0	13
1 - 3	39.8	30	2	43	2	5	21	30	41	1	27
3 - 5	32.4	41	7	39	1	5	14	37	42	1	13
5 - 10	14.6	45	10	27	1	7	20	50	24	1	16
>10	15.6	47	39	32	1	6	14	37	17	0	7
Weighted Average	44.2	35	2	40	2	5	18	40	40	0	18

Source : Fitch and Soliman, 1983, p65

M = Male
F = Female
C = Child
E = Elder

an eighth of the sampled farm households actually hiring any labour in this branch.[18] When labour was hired, it was mainly confined to cleaning and feeding operations. This would appear to be an established system throughout the Delta and sets off livestock work from other crop associated labour. However, 1981 data suggested that female labour's share was between 20-30% of total labour time, depending on the weight given to milk production.[19] Secondly, and as expected, the role of female labour was inversely associated with farm size, as was the overall volume of labour inputs. Perhaps most importantly in this context, it should be noted that the share of male labour has remained high. At, on average, 70% of total labour time, the male share was somewhat higher than in the 1977 figures.

In the absence of any more recent data, using the 1981 coefficients and combining them with the information regarding the size and type of animal herds, Table 4.16 gives some indication of the relative weights of crop and animal work in the overall employment framework of the farm for the 1984 sample.

The proportion of male and hired labour inputs for the largest farm size class is likely to be severely underestimated. In the 1984 sample, the entire livestock holding was concentrated for this class in the Sharkiya village. In the two sampled cases, it was principally buffaloes that were kept, as well as some Frisians, for their milk producing capacity. As these farms were linked to a milk marketing chain which collected the produce daily and shipped it in refrigerated trucks to Cairo, the scale and nature of the operation was very different from that predominating on most farms. Furthermore, these milk producing units employed almost entirely male labour, most of whom were permanent hands. Secondly, the estimates regarding the share of livestock work in total labour time are likely to be biased upwards as in one of the villages (Dakhaliya) there was little evidence of any significant dairy or meat farming.

Bearing in mind these caveats it would nevertheless seem that there has been a general shift in farm activity towards livestock work. In all cases, bar that of the middle order farms, livestock labour time comprises over half total inputs. Although such activity has tended to be dominated largely by family members, the more substantial holdings employ permanent

Table 4.15: Labour Hours per Animal Unit per Annum, 1981: Sharkiya

	Male	Female	Child	Total
Landless	504.9	324.6(243.5)	36.6(18.3)	866.1(766.9)
0 - 3 Feddans	598.6	167.2(125.4)	133.2(66.6)	848.3(790.6)
>3 Feddans	479.8	133.2(100)	84.9(42.5)	697.9(622.3)

(Figures in brackets are for standardized man-hours)

Source: Soliman and Mahdy, 1984

Table 4.16: Estimated Distribution of Labour Inputs by Activity Per Annum, Crop Year 1983/84

Farm Size (feddans)	Crop Man-Days	Livestock Man-Days	Total Man-Days per Annum	Total Male Labour Input as % of Total Man-Days	Total Hired Labour Inputs as % of Total Man-Days*	Livestock Man-Days as % of Total Man-Days	Crop Man-Days as % of Total Man-Days
0 - 1	82	212	294	74.8%	14.3%	72.1%	27.9%
1 - 3	180	248	428	70.9%	28%	57.9%	42.1%
3 - 5	316	243	559	67.3%	45.8%	43.4%	56.6%
5 - 10	447	462	909	66.0%	49.7%	50.8%	49.2%
>10	1628	3311	4939	70.6%	59.4%	67%	33%

* Hired Livestock Proportions calculated using 1977 and 1981 data

male labour. On smaller farms the importance of household
female labour is clear, even if the actual proportion of total
inputs in livestock work accounted for by women and children
is roughly the same as in crop work; that is, between 25-30%.
However, Soliman and Fitch's finding that there was a strong
positive association between family size and animal holdings
was not substantiated in regression analysis with the 1984
data. But, as expected, a positive correlation existed between densities of humans and livestock, as also between the
value of livestock holdings and the operated area.[20]

Conclusion

This chapter has analysed the distribution of labour time in
agriculture. Taking crop production, it would seem that
despite an undeniable long-term trend away from historically more labour-intensive crops, such as cotton, towards
those demanding less labour in production (principally
birseem), the quantum of labour units habitually committed to
crop cultivation has not fallen substantially. With the
possible exception of wheat, during the last two decades
average labour inputs per feddan have either remained constant
or increased. This result was derived equalising differences
in the length of the normal working day in agriculture.

The relative constancy over time of the volume of labour
inputs employed in crop production belies the substantial set
of changes that have occurred in the composition and distribution of that labour time. Thus, the post-1952 predominance of
the small farm economy has meant that over 77% of the total
man-days used in crop production in the 1983/4 crop year were
generated within the small farm sector where holdings fell
below three feddans (see Table 4.17). Moreover, given the
greatly enhanced role of hired labour in crop production, even
for the smallest farms, these two farm size classes also
accounted for a little under 70% of total hired labour time in
the three sampled villages.

Secondly, the role of female and child labour has undoubtedly
increased, even if the spread of tasks undertaken by such
labour has not grown substantially. Thirdly, and as significantly, the role of hired labour has developed dramatically.
Labour hiring is common to all farm size groups and is spread

Table 4.17:   Land Control, Crop Production and Employment:
              All Villages, 1984 Survey

Farm Size (feddans)	% of total Farms	%of total Area	% of total man-days employment in crop production	Average man-days crop labour generated by farm size per annum	% total hired labour time in crop production per annum
0 - 1	60.1	25.1	27.6	172	18.7
1 - 3	34.2	48.2	49.9	546	49.6
3 - 5	3.1	8.9	8.5	1020	10.5
5 - 10	2.0	11.1	8.3	1538	11.9
>10	0.6	6.7	5.7	3743	9.3

across all crops; though preponderance is found with cotton
and rice cultivation.   By contrast, save for the largest
farms, livestock work, which has grown in importance in the
last decade, has remained almost entirely a family based set
of operations. Extrapolating from earlier survey results, the
overall share of livestock work in total labour time approxi-
mates 60%.

Using these somewhat fragmentary statistics to derive any
conclusions on a national level is obviously a hazardous task.
However, on the basis of constant labour coefficients,
Richards has estimated that, through changes in the cropping
pattern and the area available for cultivation, the total
labour use in crop production had increased by roughly 24%
between 1950/54 and 1970/74.[21] Of this increment some 63% can
be explained by the expansion in the cultivated area. Taking
the period 1969/71 - 1976/78, the period in which it is commonly argued that a shortage of male labour in agriculture had
emerged, it would seem that labour use in Egyptian agriculture
as a whole may have risen by around 5%. Since then, the rate
of increase is likely to have been slacker as the actual area
in cultivation - the principal component of the rate of change
in the volume of labour inputs - may have declined very
slightly. This evidence clearly strongly suggests that an
increase in the demand for labour in crop production cannot be
used as a major explanatory factor for the supposed labour
shortage in agriculture. The fact of a possible, albeit very
limited, rate of increment in the volume of labour inputs in
crop production, coupled to the relatively small diminution in
the proportion of male labour inputs in total crop labour
time, suggests that the scale of labour scarcity may have been
grossly over-estimated.

Footnotes

1. Ammar, 1944; Mohie-eldin, 1975; Baer, 1962;
    Richards, 1982.
2. Baer, 1969, pp62ff.
3. Richards, 1982, p170.
4. Richards and Martin, 1983: Youssef, 1983.
5. The labour coefficient used in the calculations on the
    1984 data were males 1, women 0.75, children 0.5. These
    were not derived from either the wage rate or the marginal.

product but were adopted more as conventional ratios.
Apart from the nature of the judgement involved, it should
be pointed out that where agricultural tasks are to a
significant degree segmented by sex, the differential productivity implied in the assumed ratio may be inapt. If
this was the case, then it would obviously increase
further the share of female and child labour time in the
total labour allocation.

6. Hansen, 1969, pp298-314.
7. See Mohie-eldin, 1975: Hansen and El-Tomy, 1965.
8. Hansen, 1969.
9. Radwan, 1978: Harik, 1979.
10. Youssef, 1983.
11. USDA, Livestock and Poultry Annual, 1984: Goueli and
    Soliman, 1984.
12. For instance, Dyer, 1981 and Dyer and Imam, 1983.
13. Soliman, 1982; Soliman, El-Azim and Habib, 1983; IBRD,
    1983a pp129-132.
14. El-Tobgy, 1976 pp98-100.
15. Fitch and Soliman, 1983 pp45-60.
16. ibid., pp65/66.
17. ibid., p60.
18. Richards and Martin, 1983. See also Soliman and Ragab,
    1983.
19. Soliman and Mahdy, 1984.

20. Linear Regression for Livestock Ownership

Dependent Variable: Total Livestock Value
Mean: 2086.17
C.V.:   150.91

Independent Variable	Coefficient	Standard Error	Confidence Level
Owned Area	69.276	3.6771	.0001
Saqia Ownership	450.186	614.7570	.4650
Constant Term	-12388.670	328.4869	.0002

R^2 = 0.6858;   F Value = 177.93;   No of Observation = 166

21. Richards, 1982, pp231-237.

CHAPTER FIVE

Agricultural Wages and Their Determinants

Recent Wage Trends

The current state of the labour market in Egyptian agriculture
is perhaps best interpreted in terms of the movement in relative factor prices.   Indeed, as will be demonstrated more
fully in Chapter 8, this is precisely what farmers are
complaining about when they speak of labour scarcity.
Although large farmers with ten and more feddans complained of
difficulties in securing enough of the preferred type of
labour at specific times in the 1984 survey, the quantitative
aspect has most relevance in any discussion of the effects of
timely inputs of labour in crop production.   This argument
suggests that the principal effect of constrained labour
supply is a loss in productivity resulting from the inability
to secure sufficient labour at the optimal period.

However, while there is ample evidence to suggest that seasonal labour scarcities are customary, the level of implied
scarcity is discontinuous from the trend over the last decade.
This has been manifested most obviously in the sharp upward
trend in the price of labour, and of male labour in particular.   Most observers assume, logically enough, that the
latter feature represents parametric shifts in the supply
function of labour to agriculture.   The problem is seen
largely as specific to the agricultural sector, although it is
generally recognised that such implied shortages coexist
alongside severe mis-matching and possibly growing
unemployment in other sectors of the Egyptian labour market.[1]
However, there is, as yet little agreement about the factors
behind such shortages; whether, this is an inevitable outcrop
of the process of economic development or whether labour
hiring constraints are the consequence of ill-conceived policies resulting in major misallocations of productive factors.
In addition, most accept that relatively recent short to
medium term movements of labour outside the Egyptian economy
have aggravated the level of shortage, even if this transfer
of labour is not cited as the primary determinant of the
discontinuous trend in real wages.

Yet if the question of labour quantities and their distribution in employment is still an ill-explored terrain, beset by
major lacunae in data, the actual wage trend in the recent
period is also poorly mapped. Thus, the first stage of the
analysis has to commence by setting out the primary indicators. This, given the shortcomings in the available data, is
rather more complicated than might at first sight appear.

The discontinuous rise in the money price of labour in the
past decade can perhaps be best understood when placed in a
rather longer-term perspective. In the thirty years before
1952, wage rates remained broadly constant through the 1920s,
fell drastically in the Depression years, and then rose in the
middle 1940s through to the early part of the 1950s.
Thereafter, real wages declined sharply, only recovering in
the mid-1960s. As a consequence of the general economic slump
after the 1967 war, and the ill-conceived interventions in
Yemen, the late 1960s saw a further period of decline so that
by 1973, the trough year, real wages were about 80% of their
1966 level. All told, it would seem that in the two and a
half decades post-1948, real wages increased by around 1% per
annum.[2] This broad trend emerges from the use of a variety of
indices.

The trend of wages after 1973/4 has not been clear cut. While
there is complete agreement regarding the upward trend of
wages, the rate of increment is still open to dispute as is
the trend in real wages. In addition, there is little
agreement about the spread associated with the upward wage
trend. Some would argue that this has been a general phenomenon across sectors and categories of labour, while others seem
to suggest that the phenomenon has largely been a feature of
the agricultural labour market and has had most impact on male
wage rates.[3]

Using the standard time series wage data collected by the
Ministry of Agriculture, it emerges that between 1973 and
mid-1986 agricultural wages rose seventeen-fold in nominal
terms for adult males and children. The Ministry figures do
not provide any information regarding female hired labour.

Table 5.1 demonstrates that although the rate of growth in
wages has been much slacker in real terms, there has nevertheless been a substantial increase. This increase would be of

Table 5.1: Agricultural Wage Trends, Egypt 1973 - 1986: Official
            Ministry of Agriculture Data

Adult Males

Year	Money Wage	Money Wage Index (1973 = 100)	Consumer Price Index-Rural	Real Wage Index (1973 = 100)
1973	28.5	100	100	100
1974	35.1	123	114	108
1975	46.5	163	128	127
1976	61.6	216	143	151
1977	76.0	267	157	170
1978	90.0	316	181	174
1979	107.0	375	192	195
1980	137.0	481	240	200
1981	181.0	635	273	233
1982	235.0	825	311	265
1983	309.0	1084	386	281
1984	383.0	1344	421	319
1985	443.0	1554	470	331
1986*	477.0	1674	539	311

Boys

Year	Money Wage	Money Wage Index (1973 = 100)	Consumer Price Index-Rural	Real Wage Index (1973 = 100)
1973	13.5	100	100	100
1974	16.7	124	114	109
1975	21.0	156	128	122
1976	28.2	209	143	146
1977	36.3	269	157	171
1978	42.6	316	181	175
1979	47.7	353	192	184
1980	60.6	449	240	187
1981	82.1	608	273	223
1982	107.0	793	311	255
1983	147.0	1088	386	282
1984	192.0	1422	421	338
1985	207.0	1533	470	326
1986*	241.0	1785	539	331

* January-July, 1986

Source: Ministry of Agriculture, A.R.E.

comparable, if more fluctuating, magnitude if a cruder maize price index was used as the deflator.[4] In either case, real wages increased rapidly between 1974 and 1976. In the following year the trends diverge somewhat, as maize producer prices were increased by 50%. However, the overall trend was undoubtedly upwards, so that by 1980 real wages for adult males had doubled since 1973. The rate of increase was even sharper in the following three years, but in 1986, the real wage declined, according to official data, for the first time since 1973. The last entry shows male agricultural wages below their 1984 level.

Two caveats should be noted when referring to official wage data. In the first instance, the information is obviously highly aggregative, yet as we shall see, there are very wide variations in wage rates across relatively proximate areas. Secondly, the price deflator - the official rural consumer price index - appears to estimate rather low inflation rates through the 1970s. Apart from the fact that commodity and regional weights are derived from family budget survey data gathered in the mid-1960s, there is fairly general agreement, though no acceptable alternative time-series, that rural inflation rates have been considerably higher than the average 14% rate estimated for the period 1973-mid-1986. If inflation was assumed to have run at around 20% p.a. for this period then the real rate of increase would, at its peak in 1984, have been only of the order of 80%. However, in the absence of reliable, alternative price data, we have no option but to rely on the official consumer price index.

Official wage data also allow for analysis of the degree of variation in wages across the agricultural year. However, the procedures by which the data have been collected and the problems in aggregation that they tend to spawn suggest that the information they impart should be checked by comparison with survey generated statistics. An indication of the degree to which official and survey data can vary is clearly discernible when standing off the detailed ILO/INP data collected in 1964/5 against the official statistics for that period.[5] In the latter case, the peak and trough wages diverged by only 25-26%. However, the adjusted wage rates distributed monthly showed a far higher rate of variance. The peak-trough divergence can be estimated at c.43% in the case of adult male wages. It was precisely this variance that was used to argue

against the idea of a surplus labour, two-sector model having
applicability in the Egyptian context.[6] Now, of course, few
would suggest that the contemporary agricultural labour market
approximated the stylized conditions of a surplus labour
model.

However, drawing on the somewhat limited non-official statistics for monthly wage rates and adjusting for the upward
trend over the reference period, the characteristic harvest
peaks are visible but the amplitude of the monthly variation
has become somewhat weaker. In the case of the 1984 data, it
was found that the peak-trough divergence for adult male wages
was no higher than 14% (see Graph 5.1). This could be
interpreted in terms of a higher reservation wage for this
category of labour. For, as will become clearer later in the
chapter, variations in the wage rate are principally associated with machine use and skills. Current wage levels for
largely unmechanised agricultural tasks show little variation
when looked at by farm-size class. Given the fact that large
differences in the volume of labour inputs still exist and
that harvest peaks have not been significantly flattened by
the use of mechanical energy, this lack of seasonal fluc-
tuation suggests somewhat altered features for the labour
market in agriculture. The hypothesis that the lack of
variance over the year in the male wage rate can be explained,
in part, as a result of a higher reservation wage is bolstered
by further evidence from the survey.

Household members were asked how many days in each month of
the year they had sought hired work in vain work in the agricultural sector. They were also asked what wage rate they
would expect to command for this work. As expected, the
majority of respondents were male and came from small farm
households. Altogether 43% of sampled households had one or
more respondents and over half the latter came from farm
households with holdings of under one feddan.

With regard to the wage rate expected for hired agricultural
work, it was found that there was a consistent upward variance
of the expected with the actual, going rates in the respective
villages. In a limited number of cases, the reverse was the
case, but this was for students theoretically available for
work in the slack summer months from July through to

GRAPH 5.1

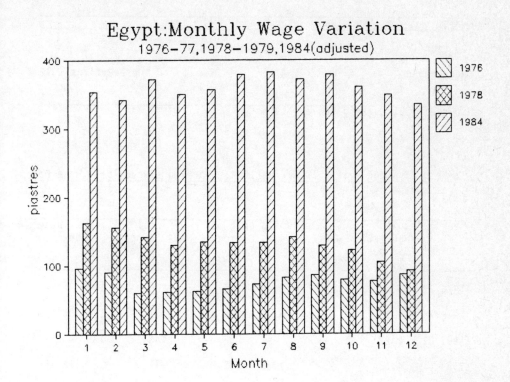

Table 5.2: Wages: Adult Males-Current and Acceptable Rates for
            Hired Agricultural Work: Delta, 1984

Wage	Sharkiya	Gharbiya	Dakhaliya	
Current	4.55	3.65	3.45	
Acceptable	4.78	4.06	3.87	No. of Observations = 72

Source: ODI/Zagazig Survey, 1984

Table 5.3: Wage Rates, 1976/77 - 1984: Sharkiya (Survey Data Wage Rates)

Year	Adult Male Wage (LE) (per day)	Female Wage	Child Wage	Cost of Living Index (1973=100)	Official MOA Sharkiya Real Wage Index	Real Wage Index M F C
1976/77	0.81	--	--	148	100	100 -- --
1978/79	1.53	0.73	0.36	186	117	150 100 100
1981/82	2.22	--	--	292	143	139 -- --
1984	4.55	2.26	1.36	456	217	183 126 154

M = Male   F = Female   C = Child

Sources: 1976/77-FMS: 1978/79 I. Youssef, 1983: 1981/82-Agricultural
          Mechanization Project: 1984-ODI/Zagazig Survey, 1984

September. The expected wage diverged between 5-12% from the current average rate and by between 6-14% if comparison was made with the going wage level for small farms (ie those with less than three feddans).

These features of the wage rate tend to suggest that the primary determinant of the wage rate in agriculture is no longer the exclusive demand for labour <u>within</u> that sector.

If survey-derived results regarding the seasonal wage variation diverge somewhat from the official figures, this is less true in the case of the general trend in wages since 1973. However, piecing together the results of various surveys it is possible to arrive at some conclusion regarding the trend of female wages, about which official statistics are almost entirely absent. As it now appears that female labour accounts for over a quarter of total inputs in crop production generally, it is clearly necessary to have some indication of the development of wages for this category of labour, as also of the differential between male, female and child labour rates. For this, one need have recourse to the figures generated by village surveys and other, non-official sources.[7]

For the Delta Governorate of Sharkiya it is possible to compute the wage trend over the course of much of the last decade. The results, given in Table 5.3, show a real wage increment for adult males of around 83% in the period 1976/7 to 1984. The entries for 1981/2 and 1984, which relate to the same village, further demonstrate that real wages have continued to rise in the most recent past. Using the more reliable 1978/79 data as the benchmark, it can be seen that male and female real wages have climbed by around 22-26% over the last six years. However, the general rate of increase for child labour would appear to be stronger in the same reference period.

The rising trend in male real wages that emerges from the data presented above needs, however, to be complemented by more specific information on the wages offered for the tasks that are principally undertaken in the agricultural production process. Thus, a more accurate method may be to look at wages by crop and by operation, taking account of the specific age and sex-specific characteristics of the labour market. The sense of this is obvious if it is remembered that over three-quarters

of all hired child labour inputs are devoted to just two
operations, harvesting, which basically means cotton picking,
and manuring. Furthermore, as Table 5.4 clearly demonstrates,
the trend in real wages when broken down by crop shows surprisingly divergent paths. More exactly, the rate of increase in
wages for all categories of labour is sharpest in the case of
cotton. For the other principal field crops, bar birseem for
which time series data are not available, real wages have
increased at a rather slow pace and for women and children
have, possibly, declined somewhat.

If hired wage rates are decomposed by task, it emerges that,
in the case of adult male labour, those operations for which
men are the dominant work-force have seen a more significant
rate of increase than for the average. For ploughing,
weeding, irrigation and harvesting work, which accounted for
nearly three-quarters of all hired male labour time, real
wages appear to have increased between 3-19% in this period.
In the case of female labour, the level of increase for their
principal operations has been under 5% and for child labour,
the real wage for cotton picking had fallen by around 20% in
the last six years. This can partly be explained by the fact
that in 1984, as a result of frequent complaints of labour
shortage in the cotton picking season the state regularised
the release of schoolchildren for this work at relatively low
wages (normally £E1 per day).[8]

The evidence presented for the Sharkiya village is broadly
confirmed by that available for the Dakhaliya village surveyed
in 1984. Previously, in 1980/81 data had been gathered on
wage rates in an adjoining village.[9] As wages were closely
replicated in these two villages in 1984, it seems reasonable
to assume that this was also the case in 1980/81. Here, it
was found that while adult male wages had risen by around 40%,
female real wages had risen by around 5% and child wages had
remained constant.

While official survey data therefore agree in estimating a
rising real wage trend for labour, breaking down the available
wage information by crop and by task, a possibly more accurate
representation of the wage movement gives a slightly different
picture. In general, it would seem that male wages have risen
most substantially but that the rate of increase in the last
4-6 years has been rather less spirited than might commonly be

Table 5.4:   <u>Agricultural Real Wages: Sharkiya, 1978/79-1984 (1978/79=100)</u>

Crop	Adult Males	Females	Children
Cotton	135	147	157* (85)
Rice	103	107	80
Maize	112	97	83
Wheat	104	87	-

(* attributable to the low average wage for pest control work reported
for 1978/79 (19 piastres). In 1984 almost all the work of pest
control was done through <u>gamiya</u>-organized aerial spraying. ( )=
for cotton picking and manuring work which comprised over 77%
of all hired child labour inputs.)

Table 5.5:   <u>Dakhalia: Wage Rates: 1980/81-1984</u>

            (Wages in Egyptian Pounds per day)

	Male Wages	Female Wages	Child Wages
1980/81	1.44	1.24	1.02
1984	3.45	2.13	1.68

Source: Hadhoud, 1983 and ODI/Zagazig Survey, 1984

supposed. For female and child hired labour inputs the upward trend has been considerably weaker and in some important cases real wages may not have risen at all.

However, it is as well to remember that while the real wage trend has demonstrated a less sharp rate of increment than has been commonly supposed, the picture changes somewhat when the time-wage relationship is considered. Some forty years ago agricultural labourers normally toiled from sun-rise to sun-set - twelve hours on average, with only an hour's break at midday.[10] By the 1960s the working day had been reduced in most parts of Egypt to around 8-10 hours. The contemporary average working day in the three sample villages was 5.3 hours, although this varied quite considerably by task. Table 5.6 gives an indication of the lengths of the working day for particularly important crop operations. Perhaps the most striking feature is the short working day for tractorised ploughing. As will be made more explicit later, the wage rate for ploughing, without allowance for the length of the working period, is already high relative to other crop tasks, and this disparity would be even greater if the time element was taken into account.

The 1984 survey further allows for analysis of the variation in wages by sex and by task. Table 5.7 presents some of this evidence and also includes information concerning the distribution of hired labour time by particular operations. From this, it can be seen that relatively substantial differentials exist, not only by category of labour, as would be expected, but also to a lesser extent by task. Thus, in the case of adult male labour, it can be seen that the wage for ploughing - a task now almost entirely done with tractors - exceeds the average male wage by around 15%. This could be taken to represent the skill premium associated with the hiring-in of plant and labour that is currently the norm in all the surveyed villages. This feature was further tested using regression analysis (see Table 5.8).

Wage rates for the principal categories of labour were regressed on a series of dummy variables signifying the use or ownership of machinery in crop production. A further independent variable for the cropped area for each household was also included in the equations. In the case of tractor use, there

Table 5.6: <u>Average Working Day; By Operation, 1984</u>

Cotton picking:	6 - 9 hours
Cotton cutting:	3 - 5 hours
Harvesting (Wheat, Maize):	5 hours
Rice Transplanting:	8 - 10 hours
Rice Harvesting:	5 - 6 hours
Ploughing (Tractor):	2 hours per feddan (1 man)
Ploughing (Non-mechanized):	12 hours per feddan (1-2 men)
Threshing:	3 - 7 hours
Weeding:	5 hours
Irrigation:	5 hours
Winnowing:	3 - 6 hours

Average for All Villages, All Operations: 5.3 hours

Source: ODI/Zagazig, 1984

was a positive association with the <u>male</u> hire wage rate that
was significant at the 1% level. Where irrigation pumps were
used, the male wage was negatively associated with their use,
but positively associated where such pumps were owned. As
only 11% of the sampled households were pump owners, this
result is obviously more limited. Interestingly, the
ownership of tractor power, as distinct from its use, was
negatively associated with the male wage rate. This result
would tend to confirm, albeit indirectly, the effect of the
market for machinery, and particularly tractors, on the wage
rate. As the vast majority of farmers rely on the tractor
hire market for their ploughing and threshing requirements and
these demands are bunched temporally, this allows for relatively inflated hiring charges to be levied by tractor owners.
In the case of female and child wage rates, no statistically
significant link with machinery use or ownership was found.
This is as expected, given the dominance of male labour in
tasks where mechanical energy has become important. Table 5.7
further confirms the fact that, unlike in the case of male
labour, female and child rates showed relatively little
variance by task.

Despite the undoubted increments in wages over the last
decade, it should be noted that the differential between male,
female and child labour has not appreciably altered. In the
mid-1960s it was found that, for the Delta, female casual wage
rates were commonly some 60% of the male rate and child wages
were just under half the latter level.[11] By 1984, it appears
that female and child wages had fallen relative to the level
of the adult male wage rate. For all farm size classes,
female wages were around 58% the male level, but the child
labour rate had fallen back to around 41%. However, as a look
at Table 5.7 will demonstrate, a widened differential did
exist on the larger farms.

Possibly more significantly, the data demonstrated that there
was a fair degree of variance in wage rates across villages.
More exactly, it was found that in the Sharkiya village male
hired wage rates were over 20% higher than in the other two
cases. Conversely, child wages were the same proportion lower
than elsewhere. Female wage rates displayed little variation.

Secondly, a strong positive association was found between
farm size and the wage for hired labour and male labour, in

Table 5.7: Wage Rates by Operation and by Sex: All Villages, 1984

Operation	Code	Proportion of Labour Inputs by Operation			Wage by Operation for : (£E per day)								
		Hired Male	Hired Female	Hired Children	MALE			FEMALE			CHILD		
					Shitwi	Sifi	All	Shitwi	Sifi	All	Shitwi	Sifi	All
Manuring	401	5.9	-	23.5	4	4	-	-	-	-	1.53	1.57	1.57
Ploughing	402	4.9	-	-	4.54	4.62	4.59	-	-	-	-	-	-
Cultivation	403	5.6	12.9	4.3	4	4.12	4.06	2	2.32	2.30	1.92	1.51	1.60
Weeding	404	18.6	8.3	6.1	-	3.86	3.86	-	2.25	2.25	-	1.57	1.57
Irrigation	405	19.3	-	2.9	3.76	3.78	3.76	-	-	-	1.41	-	1.41
Chemical/ Fertilizer	406	4.2	13.3	5.8	3.65	4.12	3.81	2.10	2.10	2.10	-	1.77	1.77
Harvesting/ Picking	408	32	62	53.9	3.71	4.06	3.92	2.10	2.10	2.10	-	1.58	1.58
Threshing/ Winnowing	409	2.6	-	-	3.90	3.70	3.83	-	-	-	-	-	-
Transport- ation	410	3.6	0.5	3.1	4.20	3.80	3.86	-	2.35	2.35	1.67	-	1.67
Other	411	3.2	2.8*	-	4.35	4	4.05	-	2.26*	2.26*	-	-	-

(* = Maize Separating)

Table 5.8: Linear Regression Analysis for Hired Male Wage Rate
            (variable a25)

Dependent Variable: a25-Hired Male Wage Rate

Mean: £E3.87

C.V.: 11.29

Indep. Var.	Regr. Coefficient	Standard Error	Signif. Level
Q1-Cropped Area	0.00134	0.0004	0.0018
S1-Draught Animal Ownership Dummy	0.3518	0.0854	0.0001
S2-Tractor Ownership Dummy	-0.0302	0.2219	0.8918
S3-Irrigation Pump Ownership Dummy	0.3790	0.1355	0.0058
S4-Thresher Ownership Dummy	0.3640	0.3251	0.2645
S5-Plough Ownership Dummy	-0.2084	0.1032	0.0452
S6-Saqia Ownership Dummy	0.8441	0.0874	0.0001
S7-Tractor Use dummy	0.3806	0.0558	0.0001
S8-Irrigation Pump Use Dummy	-0.2420	0.0755	0.0001
Constant Term	3.2929	0.0805	0.0001

R^2 =.525   Observations = 170

* Two-tailed significance probability (t test)

particular.   In the case of female and child labour the
variation in wages offered across farm size was relatively
restricted, ranging from 7-12%.   However, the variation between large farm wage rates and those offered by smaller units
was quite significant.

Regressing the cropped area on the wage rate offered by household, there was a strong positive relationship which was
significant at the 1% level.   However, the male hired wage
level was negatively associated with the proportion of adult
males in total household size.   This was found to be significant at a 5% level.   In the case of female wages, the association with cropped area was altogether weaker and in the
case of child labour was absent.

From Table 5.10 it is clear that larger farms pay substantially more for hired workers than do smaller units.   Thus,
farms of over ten feddans had, on average, to pay wages 27%
higher than those paid by the smallest farms.   This points to
the fact that larger farmers were prepared to pay a wage premium not only to secure the greater number of hands required
for their cropped area, but also possibly as a means of
securing labour at the optimal time.   The 1984 survey did not
collect information on planting dates and other essential crop
tasks that would allow for a more systematic treatment of the
'timeliness' question but it should be noted that for crop
yield data (see Chapter 8) there was no consistent relationship between farm size and productivity.   This would
appear to run counter to some of the arguments, principally
presented in an Asian context, that postulate an inverse relationship between farm size and productivity.[12]   Of course,
much of this argument has hinged on the role of underemployed
family labour in crop cultivation and this approach, given
what is said here in the chapter on employment, has less relevance at present than it may have done in the relatively
recent past.   Also, the variation in farm size at the lower
end of the landholding scale is relatively limited and the
number of observations for farms in the larger size categories
was rather restricted.   Nevertheless, it is quite clear that
hired, temporary wage rates are positively associated with
farm size.   With the large farms relying almost entirely on
hired labour, it seems that the payment of wage premia is
largely a means of securing labour.

Table 5.9:   Wage Rates: By Village, By Sex, 1984

Village	Male Wage	Female Wage	Child Wage
Sharkiya	4.55	2.26	1.36
Gharbiya	3.65	2.28	1.75
Dakhaliya	3.45	2.13	1.68
All	3.85	2.22	1.57

Source: ODI/Zagazig Survey, 1984

Table 5.10:   Agricultural Wages: Egypt, 1984: All Villages -
              By Sex and Farm Size

Farm Size	Male	Female	Child	Index: (0-1=100) Male	Female	Child
0 - 1	3.75	2.15	1.60	100	100	100
1 - 3	3.88	2.24	1.62	103	104	101
3 - 5	3.97	2.29	1.56	106	106	98
5 - 10	4.15	2.25	1.51	111	104	94
>10	4.76	2.42	1.53	127	113	96

Regressing yields by crop on the wage rate for the categories of hired labour, it was found that in the case of wheat and rice output per feddan was positively associated with the male wage rate at the 1% level. No significant association was found between cotton and maize yields and the wage rate and in the case of female and child wage rates no significant association was found in any of the equations.[13]

Wage Differentials by Sector

Any discussion of the trend in agricultural wages would obviously be incomplete without dealing with the more general evolution of wages in the economy as a whole. This has been particularly important in the Egyptian context where historically there have been major variations in the wage level across sector. In addition, these sectoral wage differentials have also been associated with an urban-rural wage divide. As in the case of many ldc economies, this gap has been used principally for the construction of labour transfer models, where the critical flows have been between the rural sector and the urban areas.[14] In the context of the Delta, this distinction may not be the most apposite one. As will become clear in the chapter on employment (Chapter 7), access to non-rural employment is not a simple function of residence and distance. In the Delta, villages not only tend to be large, with population often averaging around 10,000 plus but the distances to towns and industry are not normally substantial. Given easy access to transportation and the existence of extremely competitive and relatively low-priced communications, these earlier barriers to job mobility have been superseded. Furthermore, work outside the rural sector does not necessarily have to be associated with residence outside the rural areas. With housing shortages and escalating rents in the major urban conurbations this feature may have become more pronounced in recent years.

Ideally, when comparing the sectoral distribution of income, it would be desirable to have recourse to time-series data for the development of wages and salaries by sector which could then be deflated by the labour force and consumer price index. In fact, such a series does exist and when measured in constant 1974 prices would appear to suggest that agricultural wage income remained roughly constant between 1975 and 1981/82

and, relative to other sectors may have declined. Yet this
information is unlikely to be an accurate indicator as casual
labour wages are not included, hence making the estimates for
agriculture and construction misleading. What these estimates
of per capita annual wages do suggest is that the cross-sector
differentials in nominal wages were significant even by the
start of the 1980s. Agricultural nominal wages were well below
50% of those in construction, electricity and public utilities
and the spread was even greater when compared with sectors
such as industry, petroleum or trade and finance.[15]   Table
5.11 attempts to give some indication of the level of differential that has been maintained over the last two and a
half decades. If these figures can be believed, then while
the differential between agricultural wages and other wages
has fallen over the full period, 1960-1982, the gap has not
been closed in the most recent post-1974 period. Thus, by the
early 1980s construction wages were about three times the
level of wages in agriculture and the differential was considerably wider in services and industry. This, of course has
been one significant factor in explaining the undeniable and
widespread desire of younger workers who might have been
expected to seek work in agriculture, to look for employment
in other spheres.

Although the wage pull effect has been strong and can explain
a certain part of the movement of labour away from the agricultural sector, this is not the only, or even necessarily the
principal factor explaining the transfer of labour.

Yet the trajectory of wages in other sectors of the economy
has considerable relevance for agricultural wage rates. In
the last ten years, it has been frequently argued that agricultural wage rates have tended to mimic, albeit with a lag,
the wage level generated in construction work. While the wage
level tends always to be a good barometer of the business
cycle as a whole, the interchangeable nature of labour between
agriculture and construction has made them particularly apt
for comparison. This mobility between sectors extends not
only to the usual rural-urban divide, but, perhaps as crucially, to the range of jobs on offer within the village and
local economies of the Delta. While this has always been the
case, the last ten years have seen an especially sharp
increase in the demand for construction. Indicative of the
impact of the flow of remittances on disposable income in the

rural sector is the fact that in the three sampled villages in
the 1984 survey, around 5-8% of houses in the villages had
either been newly constructed or else had major new extensions
added.   Many of the traditional houses have been replaced by
standard red-brick constructions.   The general importance
given to house construction was made clear in several recent
surveys dealing with expenditure patterns in households with
remittances. Between 28-40% of the funds transferred into the
household were spent on house construction and allied work.[16]

The importance of construction work as an alternative to agricultural labouring stems from two associated developments over
the last decade.   In the first case, there has been the
substantial outflow of migrant labour to other Arab states.[17]
Initially much of this demand for labour took the form of
construction work. In the last five years, however, as disposable revenues in the Gulf states have declined and Egyptian
construction labour has come also to be replaced by cheaper
South and South East Asian labour, the importance of this type
of work overseas has declined.[18] Secondly, in the wake of the
general upturn in the rate of domestic economic growth and
investment after 1973, the indigenous construction sector, of
which Osman Ahmed Osman's Arab Contractors is the most well
known example, underwent a very significant acceleration in
its domestic activity.   In the four years immediately
following 'Infitah' construction sector wages increased more
rapidly than for other sectors.   One estimate has, for
example, placed the annual rate of increase for construction
wages at 28% for the period from 1973 to 1977.[19] One result
was that although agricultural wages also increased at a
significant pace the differential widened between the wage
rates in these sectors in the last decade, undermining, in
part, the long term trend towards the diminution of this
differential.[20]

Yet, if most attention has been paid to the construction -
agriculture wage and labour transfer relationship, this is
only one feature of the contemporary labour market. Indeed,
it appears that the demand for construction work has fallen
off in the last two to three years and this has had obvious
employment implications.   The 1984 survey demonstrated (as
will be treated in more detail Chapter 7) that although
construction work in the village or locality is often seen as
a substitute for hired agricultural labour, the scope of work

Table 5.11: Wage Levels, By Sector per annum, 1960-1978 (LE)

Year	Construction	Agriculture	Services	Industry
1960/3	158.8	31.2	168.8	155
1964/8	169.1	47.7	206	181
1969/73	195.1	55.6	244	220.8
1974/78	334.2	101.0	326.1	310.0
1979/81/2	491.0	167.0	770.0	769.0

Source: Mohie-Eldin, 1975 : World Bank, 1983 (b).

Table 5.12: Male Wages for Types of Work, 1984

Type of Work	Wage per diem
Brick Factory-Labouring:	£E4 - 7.5 (Males) : £E2 - 4 (Females)
Construction Work-Labourer:	£E5 - 8 (Male) : £E2 - 3 (Female/Child)
Head Labourer:	£E7 - 15
Iron Worker:	£E8 - 10
Carpenter(Self-employed):	£E300 - 450 per month
Muqawwil (Contractor):	£E350 - 700 per month

now open to rural households has considerably broadened.
Indeed, a very small proportion of the sample was found to be
working in the construction sector.[21] Although construction
labour was not considered as inferior labour in quite the same
way as work in the local brick factories, there was no doubt
that strong preference was given to the securing of government
work, or at least, clerical type work, as against manual
labour.

Table 5.12 gives some indication of the degree of wage
variation by the type of work commonly considered as being a
substitute for agricultural labouring.

While it is clear that daily wages for non-agricultural work
are generally higher, it should be remembered that brick factory work is considered to be particularly strenuous, with
relatively long working days (commonly eight hours) and poor
working conditions. Thus, although the average weekly wage
can reach around £E30 for a six day week, a wage that exceeds
by far the salaries offered in the public sector or in government jobs, brick work is normally considered as employment of
the last resort. Most brick workers tend to be landless or
from the smallest farm households. As mud brick production is
now being swiftly phased out on government directive, this
employment option is likely to disappear in the relatively
near future.[22]

If brick factory work and construction are the most common
local sources of non-agricultural labour demand, in the 1984
survey it was found that the great majority of respondents
whose principal occupation lay outside agriculture held jobs
in the government or public sector. Yet, this can hardly be
explained in terms of relative wage rates, even if, as will
be seen in Chapter 7, there is a significant differential in
average non-agricultural income as against agricultural wage
income.

Government sector wages - and, to a decreasing extent, public
sector wage rates - are subject to centralised
determinations.[23] Wage controls have operated much more
comprehensively in this sector than elsewhere, although nomi-

nal wage levels often obscure the range of incentive payments
and additional rewards that have been granted in recent years.
An indication of the effect of wage controls was the fact that
while government sector wages rose by some 70% between
1966-1979, agricultural wage levels quadrupled in the same
period. However, it is important to note that an increasingly
large proportion of public sector workers now hold additional
employment, thereby making sectoral comparisons more problematic.

At present, the likely annual income from a government sector
job and from agricultural labouring appears to be roughly
equated, although the effort demanded in both sectors is by no
means comparable. Both types of employment would appear to
offer a wage rate below that for permanent agricultural work.
In the 1984 survey it was found that in the Sharkiya village,
70-75 permanent workers were employed. Most were hired by
larger farmers for livestock work. The bulk of such attached
workers were from landless or marginal farm households, with a
going wage for adult males of between £E50-80 per month and
£E30-45 for boys. Additionally, many were provided with food
by their employers, but not housing. At the highest level,
this would mean a monthly wage at least double that from
casual labouring or government sector work. However, given
the relatively restricted number of large farms in Egyptian
agriculture, the demand for such labour is insignificant.

A rational demand for labour is also characteristic of the
other major employment option, the manufacturing sector,
whether private or public. In the organised sector, wages in
public enterprises have not been of the usual low variety.
Indeed, public sector wages have consistently (at least until
very recently) run ahead of wage levels in the organised private sector.[24] For example, it was found in the case of the
Gharbiya village, that unskilled work in the publicly owned
cotton textile mills in Mohalla-El-Qobra would bring in a wage
considerably higher than for other unskilled work. Average
wages were between £E50-60 per month, rising to c.£E100-120
p.m. with overtime. As travel costs only amounted to between
£E15-20 per annum, this was obviously considered attractive
employment.

Wages in the private manufacturing sector tend to be very

strongly and positively associated with plant and firm size. However, the great majority of enterprises are small-scale, rarely employing two or more hired hands. Wage rates in these units have tended to be on par with, or slightly above, the current wage level in agriculture. A recent study of small enterprises in Qalyubia and Fayoum concluded that about one in fifteen of the population in those governorates was engaged by small scale units.[25] The focus of the study was primarily on small scale firms, so that the great majority were involved in livestock product processing. However, in those cases, where manufacture was involved, textile work tended to predominate. The work force also tended to have a major female component. In the Dakhaliya village surveyed in 1984, it was found that weaving was an important secondary occupation for some house holds. Although some of this work was done on a putting-out basis, most was done either by small workshops or at home by individual weavers. The output was marketed in the neigh- bouring towns of Aga, Mit Ghamr and Mansoura. In all, nearly 6% of sampled households had one or more family members working as weavers. Almost all such households fell in the 1-3 feddan category, suggesting that such work required ade quate working capital, possibly beyond the reach of the smallest farm households. Income from textile work was rela tively high, though seasonally fluctuating. In general, monthly earnings in the winter months were between £E50-60 but this declined quite sharply in the summer period. This was hardly surprising, given the local specialisation in pullovers and scarves.

The disparity in average monthly income for those working pri- marily as agricultural labourers and for those working outside agriculture was reasonably high. Table 5.13 suggests that non-agricultural wage income was between 30-70% higher on average than the monthly income from agricultural labouring. Given the fact that relatively few of the sample had secured work in the more lucrative sections of the private sector or that construction and brick factory labouring was relatively unimportant, this disparity may seem surprising. Government wages for unskilled and semi-skilled work varied between £E30-45 per month in this period, while wages in the informal tertiary sector may have been a little lower. The disparity can probably be best explained by the fact that income from agricultural labouring continues to have a very strong seaso

Table 5.13: Monthly Wage Earnings - Agricultural Labouring and
             Non-Agricultural Wage Work, 1984 (£E)

Village	Agric. Wage Income	Non-Agric. Wage Income
Sharkiya	42.88 (37)	73.45 (19)
Gharbiya	12.08 (3)	41.04 (59)
Dakhaliya	42.38 (17)	57.46 (56)
All	41.11 (57)	52.50 (134)
( ) = No of observations		

Source: ODI/Zagazig Survey, 1984

nal variation. Thus, although the male agricultural wage was,
by 1984, around £E3.9 per day on average, the continuing
existence of slack periods naturally tended to dilute the
actual wage received in the year by agricultural labourers.

Conclusion

Data presented in this chapter have provided a detailed breakdown of recent trends in agricultural wages in Egypt. Using
both official time-series on wages and cross-sectional wage
data generated from household and village surveys, it is clear
that in the last decade real wages in agriculture have risen
quite significantly. However, it is important to note that
this trend has not been uniform. Both female and child wages
have either risen at a much less pronounced rate or else have
remained constant in real terms. At the same time, the wage
spread - at least for male labour - was found to be quite
wide, clearly reflecting localised supply elasticities. Wage
differentials were not only substantial across the category of
labour employed, but also were significant when decomposed by
task. This could in part be explained by the wage increments
paid for hiring in semi-skilled labour, such as tractor dri-
vers. It was also found to be related   to the size of
holding.

Although the limited sample of large farms cautions against a
generalised conclusion, it appears that the male wage rate in
agriculture - particularly for seasonally compacted tasks,
such as harvesting - is positively associated with the
employer's size of holding. Bidding up wages clearly reflects
a tightened labour market at the seasonal peaks. However,
this has long characterised Egyptian agricultural wage patterns and may not accurately reflect a general scarcity of
male labour for agriculture. Such wage premia can be
explained either in terms of securing labour for highly time
constrained tasks in a competitive spot market or else can be
viewed as a form of informal contract for the securing of such
labour at required periods. In the latter case you would
expect employers to enter into contracts before the peak
season even if this implies paying wage rates superior to the
marginal product outside of the peak season.[26] Unfortunately,
there is not enough evidence to know whether this is a relatively new expedient or an established practice.

Caution over assuming that recent trends in agricultural wages necessarily denote a major shift in the labour supply parameters is further confirmed by the analysis of the performance of agricultural wages relative to those in other sectors. Although sectoral comparisons are always difficult, given the highly seasonal and hence fluctuating nature of agricultural wage income as well as the phenomenon of multiple employment, it would appear that there is still a very significant wage differential between agriculture and other sectors. Although the differential between agriculture and construction wages may have narrowed between 1960 and 1982, it is important to note that between 1974/78 and 1979/82 there was little appre ciable change in the ratio of construction to agricultural wages. Moreover, when agricultural wages are compared with those in the service and industrial sectors, it emerges that the differential has widened significantly in the same period in favour of non-agricultural wage levels. This suggests very strongly that the increase in agricultural wages should be viewed as part of a general, economy-wide trend.

While the trend in money wages over the last decade cannot be explained as a function of the trend in food prices,[27] the upward shift in wage levels and in the labour factor share has to be related to the growth in non-domestic sources of employment - international migration - as well as the expansion of employment in the urban sector and, most particularly, in the public sector. Between 1979 and 1983/4 alone wages and salaries as a share of GDP rose from 8% to over 10%. This was mainly accounted for by public sector employment which averaged a growth rate of over 7% in the same period.[28] Clearly, as Chapter 7 demonstrates, these parallel trends have had major implications both for the determination of the urban wage level and, by the linked shifts in employment and labour distribution, for the level of wages in agriculture. To that extent, the male wage trend reflects the higher level of employment diversification that has occurred and, consequently, the higher degree of competitiveness in the spot wage labour market for agriculture. The following chapters attempt to make sense of these developments by concentrating on supply-side factors and by particularly focusing on the features of the more diverse labour market that has evolved in rural Egypt.

Footnotes

1. Hansen and Radwan, 1982, pp139-161; El Issawy, 1983a
2. Richards, 1982, pp227-231; Mead, 1967, pp91-98; Radwan, 1977; Koval and Bahgat, 1980; Fitch and Aly, 1980; Mabro, 1971, pp401-417;   Abdel Fadil, 1975, pp63-70.
3. Richards and Martin, 1983, pp21-43; El Yamany, Habashy and Reiss, 1984.
4. Fitch and Aly, 1980
5. Hansen, 1969, pp305/6; Ministry of Agriculture, Rural Wage Data (unpublished).
6. Hansen, 1966, pp367-407
7. For instance, Goueli et al., FMS, No3 June 1980; Youssef, 1983; Richards and Martin, 1982; Agricultural Mechanization Project Survey Data (unpublished, 1984); El Yamany et al., 1984.
8. Egyptian Gazette, 1984
9. Hadhoud, 1982
10. Abbas, 1944, p290
11. Hansen, 1966, pp386-389; INP, Report D, 1965; Mohieldin, 1966.
12. Bharadwaj, 1974; Sen, 1975; Bardhan, 1973; Saini, 1971; Rao, 1966
13.

Dependent Variable	Independent Variable	Reg Coeff	Stand. Error	Signif. Level
v5 (wheat yield)	Male Wage	1.9155	0.3340	0.0001
	Female Wage	-0.2258	0.5921	0.7037
	Child Wage	-1.2037	0.5465	0.0298
R^2 =.3404	Observations = 109			
v7 (rice output)	Male Wage	11.3974	1.3994	0.0001
	Female Wage	-5.6749	2.5962	0.0315
	Child Wage	2.9403	2.3560	0.2154
R^3 =.4504	Observations = 90			
* Two-tailed significance probability				

14. Mabro, 1967; Waterbury, in Adbel Khalek and Tignor, 1982
15. Hansen, 1985, pp71-75
16. Hadhoud, 1983; El Dib, Ismail and Gad, 1984; Taylor, 1983, Khafagy, 1984.
17. Choucri, 1983; Arman, 1983; Richards and Martin, 1983; Ferghany,1983; Mohie-Eldin, 1980; Birks and Sinclair, 1980; Hansen and Radwan, 1982, pp81-94; Shaw, 1985,

pp21-55.

18. Choucri, 1983; Serageldin, Socknat, Sinclair, 1983.
19. Choucri, 1978; Hansen and Radwan, 1982, pp70-77.
20. Hansen and Radwan, 1982 pp75/6.
21. It should be noted, however, that the move into construc-
    tion work was at its peak prior to 1984 and that labour
    lost by agriculture to construction in the earlier period
    may have become permanent urban residents and hence did not
    show up in the 1984 sampling. Secondly, our survey did not
    cover the landless and informal sector workers and may thus
    severely underestimate the shift of labour into construction.
    I am grateful to Bent Hansen for bringing my attention to
    these points.
22. Egyptian Gazette, Cairo, 8 and 9/10/84.
23. Starr, 1983; Handoussa, 1983.
24. ibid.
25. Davies, Mead et al., 1983.
26. For an interesting discussion of labour-tying contracts
    and their rationale, see Bardhan, 1984, pp67-85.
27. De Janvry and Subbarao, in Richards and Martin, 1983,
    pp237-247.
28. IMF figures, June 1984 (unpublished).

CHAPTER SIX

Population Trends and Developments in the
Size and Distribution of the Labour Force

Demographic Developments

Despite Egypt's fixed resource base and its limited success to
date in expanding the frontier of cultivation,[1] the country's
population has continued to grow rapidly for the past 100
years. Since 1952 alone, Egypt's population has increased
more than two and a quarter times. Current rates of growth
are estimated to be between 2.5-2.8% per annum. These are
high incremental rates by any standards and, even assuming a
reduction to a growth rate of around 2% per annum, would mean
that Egypt's population would be between 63 and 66 million by
the end of this century. Assuming a broadly constant
habitable area, the density of humans per kilometre of over
1028 in 1976[2] will reach around 1780 by the turn of the
century.

A possibly more relevant indicator of the pressure on land and
agriculture would be to compute the density of the rural
population with regard to the cropped area. Assuming a level
of growth in the available cultivable area of the order of
that holding between 1960 and 1980, it appears that while in
1947 there were 0.71 feddans cropped area per caput (using the
figures for the rural population alone),[3] by 1978/81 this had
fallen to 0.48 feddans with a likely further fall to around
0.37 feddans by the year 2000. This would hold on the
assumption of an increase in the share of the urban population
to 50% of the total population.

The sharp upward trend in population is vividly discernible in
Graph 6.1. For the twenty years from 1952 to 1973 this can
largely be attributed to a decline in the birth and death
rates, with an obviously sharper fall in the latter. Since
1973 the mortality rate has continued to decline while the
fertility rate actually increased slightly. Between 1952/55
and 1980/83 death rates declined by around 45%, while the
birth rate fell by about 12%.[4] Consequently, the rate of
natural population growth was over 11% higher in the later
period.

GRAPH 6.1

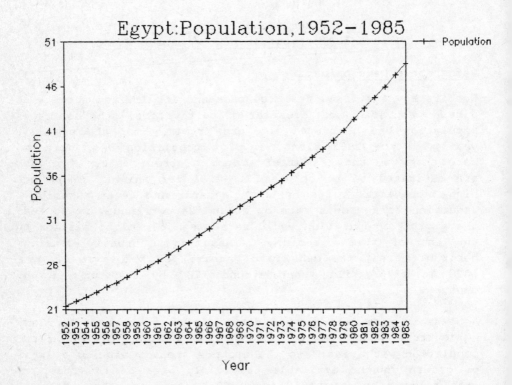

These demographic trends have been accompanied by a number of features, some representing long-run trends in the Egyptian demographic structure and, others, such as emigration, being relatively discontinuous features. In the first category, the most obvious characteristic of recent Egyptian demographic history has been continuing urbanisation of the population and economy.

The dominance of towns in Egyptian history has always been pronounced. By the time of the overthrow of the Monarchy a little under 40% of the population was living in towns.[5] Moreover, most of these were inhabitants of Greater Cairo and Alexandria. The contemporary pattern is similar, but the urban population now comprises more than 45% of the total population and Greater Cairo alone, with a current population of around twelve million, accounts for two-fifths of that number. At the time of writing, the urban population was growing at an annual rate 0.6% greater than that for the population as a whole. Although nearly 88% of the growth in the urban population between 1960 and 1976 (the two Census dates) has been attributed to natural increase and territorial redefinition, migration to the towns may have accounted for 12-13% of the overall growth. This suggests that although out-migration to the towns from the countryside is a continuing phenomenon (and a phenomenon also characterised by a flow of labour from north to south) it is no longer the principal mover of urban demographic growth.[6]

When analysing the principal determinants of fertility it appears that the decline of polygynous marriage contracts does not seem to have had any marked impact on the age at marriage for women. This remained constant between 1965 and 1975, at around 19.7 years. The level of celibacy has also remained low - 81-88% of women between the ages of 25-44 years were married.[7] The 1984 survey data broadly confirm this impression (Table 6.1).

With relatively low levels of contraception use - the most reliable figures place the proportion of women in reproductive age groups using contraception at around 26% - and early marriage, the result is a high overall fertility rate of around 5.5% (1975/6 figure). In the last decade fertility appears to have declined by around 1% p.a. but the rather weak family planning programme pursued by the state, coupled with

Table 6.1: Proportion of Females Married by Age,
            Delta, 1984 and Egypt, 1976

Age	Delta, 1984	Egypt, 1976
15-18	35%	21%
18-25	47%	59%
25-35	72%	86%
35-50	99%	82%
50-65	100%	-
Over 65	100%	-

Source: ODI/Zagazig Survey, 1984 and Population Census Report, 1976

Table 6.2: Average Household Size, 1984: By Governorate & Farm Size

Farm Size (feddans)	Sharkiya	Gharbiya	Dakhaliya	All
0-1	6.1	4.7	5.3	5.2
1-3	6.9	4.1	6.3	6.0
3-5	8.2	8.5	6.0	7.3
5-10	6.0	7.0	6.2	6.2
Over 10	5.0	-	4.0	4.7
All	6.7	4.7	5.9	5.8

the continuing high levels of desired family size, suggest
that fertility levels will not be strongly depressed in the
near future.

The 1984 survey found that average family size was still high,
although smaller than in the relatively recent past. As Table
6.2 shows, actual family size had an inverted U curve, with
middle-size farm households tending to have significantly
larger families. The largest units were characterised by
their discernibly smaller average family size, testifying
undoubtedly to the expected operation of an inverse income -
family size association. Larger households, with diversified
economic interests stretching beyond the agricultural sector,
seem to follow a demographic strategy more akin to the
Egyptian urban pattern than to the customarily higher levels
of small farm, predominantly agricultural, households.

While family size is inversely related to land ownership,
there has been a significant change in the predominant type of
family. Forty years ago, joint families accounted for a
substantial share of all households.[8] Now, the institution of
the joint family has apparently declined significantly.
Moreover, co-existence of generations under the same roof - in
extended families - tends still to be fairly common among
farms of between 1-5 feddans but not for the smallest units
and the larger farm households. Between 40-45% of these
households are organised on an extended basis.

If family size still tends to be large, testifying to the
widespread insurance effect of larger family units, the
combined impact of rates of natural increase and, possibly,
the out-migration of working age-adult males, is that the
young constitute a very high proportion of the population. The
1976 Census data revealed that almost 40% of the population
was aged below 15 years and that fully 60% of the population
was under 25 years of age. The youthful structure of the
Egyptian population could also be seen in the breakdown by age
group of the 1984 sample. 55% of the population were under 25
years of age and nearly 30% were below fifteen years. These
are rather below the national figures, but still show that the
rate of new entries into the educational process and the
labour force will be considerable in the coming decades.
Extrapolating from this data, by the year 2000 the potential
male labour force for the three sampled villages (15-64 years)

could be 8-10% larger than at present; assuming no changes in
the participation rate.

Labour Force

The persistently sharp rate of increase in Egypt's population
has had obvious implications for the size of the labour force,
and is crucial for the potential longer-term effects of labour
displacement in agriculture. Computing the trend in the size
of the labour force in the recent period is made more
complicated by the non-correspondence of the two basic sources
of data: the Population Censuses, on the one hand and the
Labour Force Sample Surveys on the other.[9] For the period of
common coverage, 1960-1976, the Population Censuses give a
growth rate of around 2.2% p.a. for the labour force as a
whole, while the latter place the figure at 3.2% p.a.
Following Hansen, the Census data will be used for
interpreting long term trends in the size of the labour force,
while the Sample Surveys can be best utilised for
understanding relatively more recent changes.[10]

After 1947 the labour force expanded initially at a fairly
gentle rate; the acceleration came after the early 1970s. By
1981/2 the labour force was at least 65% larger than in 1947
and the trend rate was consistently upwards.[11] Moreover, this
was at a time when there were substantial outflows of labour
from the Egyptian economy towards the labour scarce, oil rich
Arab states. Estimates of the size of this outflow vary
widely. Nevertheless, Birks & Sinclair have argued that this
figure had risen from a level of around 370,000 migrant
Egyptians in other Arab countries in 1975 to over 803,000 by
1980.[12] Since then, estimates - rarely compiled with any
adequate empirical justification - have commonly placed the
number of migrants abroad at between two and three million.[13]
While in the earlier period nearly a third of these went to
Libya, by the early 1980s it was thought that Iraq and Jordan
were the principal destinations. The expulsion of Egyptian
workers from Libya in August/September 1985 was supposed to
have affected at least 100,000 Egyptian migrant workers. This
would suggest that by then the stock of migrants was at less
than half its peak figure in the early 1970s.

Information gathered by the 1984 survey showed that just under
12% of all sampled households had one or more members living

away from the village at the time of the survey (two-thirds of whom were males). This amounted to 3.8% of the total sampled population. However, the majority of males in this group were serving in the army as conscripts. Roughly a quarter were, respectively, living in urban areas of Egypt or abroad. This was a rather low number, six adult males out of a total adult male sample population of 325 (Age Bracket 18-65 years). In other words, less than 3% of households had a member of their family working abroad. This meant that remittances were a rather minor component of household income. Nevertheless, the rash of new house construction and building of extensions in all three villages was indicative of a rather wider exposure to emigration over the last decade than these figures would suggest. Working in the Gulf was generally seen as an attractive and relatively speedy way of accumulation irrespective of social status. Accordingly, there was a broad spread among those who had sought work abroad, ranging from land-poor agricultural labourers through to trained accountants from the more prosperous village elite. Most emigrants were in their late 20s or early 30s and were unmarried.

In the absence of comprehensive figures on the number of emigrants for the economy as a whole in the recent period, it seems reasonable to assume that in the mid-1970s the number stood at between 400,000 and 500,000, rising to over a million by the early 1980s. By 1985 the level may have exceeded two and a half million, given the strong and continuing demand for Egyptian labour in Iraq[14] caused by the alternative demand for Iraqi manpower as a result of the war with Iran. A continuing feature of the migration process has been the drain out of Egypt of skilled and semi-skilled labour, a feature that has been pronounced in the case of emigration to Iraq. Taking account of such migration, it can be crudely calculated, that the 1975 labour force would have been around 5% larger than the total given in Table 6.3 and that by 1981/2 the total, hypothetical size of the labour force, assuming the return of all migrant workers, would have been at least 9-10% greater than in the table.

Table 6.3 collates the two available, but not strictly comparable, sources of labour force information. From this, it appears that the labour force as a whole grew by 2.2% per annum between 1971 and 1981. With a youthful population and

Table 6.3:   Trends in the Labour Force: Rural and Urban, 1960-1981

Year	-(000s)- Urban	%	Rural	%	Total
Labour Force Sample Survey [1]					
1968	3065.7	38.6	4878.8	61.4	7944.5
1971	3360.0	40.0	5045.6	60.0	8405.6
1972	3495.2	39.6	5321.4	60.4	8816.6
1973	3856.5	41.2	5125.9	58.8	8982.4
1974	3804.0	41.9	5271.9	58.1	9075.9
1975	3962.0	42.8	5302.1	57.2	9264.1
1977	4244.3	44.7	5250.0	55.3	9494.3
1978	4484.7	45.8	5317.8	54.2	9802.5
1981	4957.4	47.1	5560.5	52.8	10517.9
Population Census [2]					
1960	2737.7	35.0	5081.2	65.0	7818.9
1966	3266.4	38.5	5224.6	61.5	8491.0
1976	4770.2	43.4	6211.3	56.6	10981.5

1=12-65 years
2= 6-65 years

Source: Ibrahim El-Issawy, Labour Force, Employment and Unemployment
          Geneva, 1983, p60: CAPMAS, Labour Force Sample Survey, 1981,
          Cairo, 1982

over 40% of the labour force (excluding those under 12 years) under the age of thirty, current projections for the period through to the end of the century suggest that the labour force will continue to grow at between 2.2-2.4% per annum.[15] Naturally, this rate of increase would be higher if there are substantial re-transfers of Egyptian labour back into the domestic labour market from the Gulf. By the end of 1986, it appeared that a return flow of migrant labour had indeed been initiated and was directly reflected in the reduced volume of remittances.

Apart from the fact that, as Table 6.4 clearly demonstrates, there has been a consistent relocation of the labour force, with a significantly declining share in the rural sector, there has been at the same time a sharp, long-term fall in the proportion of the labour force employed in agriculture. Indeed, from a position where 58.4% of the workforce was in agriculture less than thirty years ago, it is now the case that less than 37% is retained in the primary sector. Furthermore, there has been a general, though less dramatic, fall in the share of employment for the commodity sector as a whole. Services, in particular, have experienced a major increase in their share of employment.

Yet, if it is generally agreed that the share of the agricultural workforce in the labour force as a whole has undoubtedly slipped, it is less easy to estimate the exact size of the agricultural labour force. In the first place, estimates put labour force participation rates - most especially for women - at a very low level. In the case of women, this is undoubtedly inaccurate, given the significant levels of crop work that are done by women. Secondly, computing the size of the agricultural labour force is always made more complex by the existence of substantial seasonal variations in labour demand. This is especially important in terms of child labour use in crop work.

The under-enumeration of the non-male labour force can be seen in the fact that barely 2% of the total recorded agricultural labour force in the 1981 Labour Force Sample Survey were women.[16] As the 1984 survey shows that women and children contribute at least 41% of total <u>hired</u> labour hours in crop production this level of labour force participation is far too low. Thus, when looking at Table 6.5 which gives the

Table 6.4: Employment: Shares by Economic Sector, 1947-1982

Sector	1947	1960	1966	1974	1978	1981/2
Agriculture	58.4	57.0	53.4	46.6	40.0	36.9
Industry, Petroleum & Mining	8.2	9.5	13.1	12.7	12.6	12.9
Construction	1.6	2.0	2.5	3.5	5.2	6.1
Electricity, Gas & Water	0.3	0.5	0.6	0.4	1.1	1.1
Commodity Sectors	68.5	69.0	69.6	63.2	58.9	57.0
Commerce & Finance	8.4	8.3	7.2	9.8	10.6	11.0
Transportation, Comm. & Storage	2.9	3.4	4.1	4.4	4.3	4.2
Distribution Sectors	11.3	11.7	11.3	14.2	14.9	15.2
Service Sectors	20.0	19.3	19.1	22.5	26.2	27.8

Table 6.5: Labour Force Participation Rates, Egypt, 1937-1976

Year	Females(%)	Males(%)	Total(%)
1937	7.9	65.1	37
1947	7.8	62.8	37
1960	4.8	55.2	30
1966	4.2	50.8	28
1970	3.5	49.5	26
1972	4.0	50.7	27
1976	9.2	52.9	31

Source: Population Censuses, 1937, 1947, 1960, 1966 and 1976

evolution of the agricultural labour force over the last
thirty-five years, it should be borne in mind that the figures
are principally referents for the trend in male labour force
size in agriculture.

However, it can be seen that the continuing movement of labour
away from agriculture towards the towns and, more recently,
abroad, has had a very noticeable effect on the size of the
labour force. Between 1947 and 1976, there may have been a
small overall increase of around 3%. More significantly, in
this context, is the fact that between 1970/75 and 1981, the
agricultural labour force declined by between 7-10%.
However, this should not necessarily be construed as a
long-term trend.

While the share of agricultural employment in total employment
has continued to fall, the actual size of the labour force in
agriculture may have risen very slightly between 1979 and
1981. Given the fact that there has not been a substantial
shift into more labour-intensive cropping patterns or that
the cultivated area has expanded significantly, the scale of
decrease in the size of the (male) labour force has not been
dramatic. When the role of female and child labour in
agriculture is taken into account, it seems unlikely that a
realistic set of labour force figures would demonstrate any
highly significant fall in the size of the agricultural labour
force.

The conclusions reached from this analysis have obvious and
important implications for longer-term manpower planning. In
particular, they have considerable relevance for agricultural
sector policies that assume, firstly, that labour shortages
exist and that, secondly, these will persist in the forseeable
future. As will become clearer later in this chapter, the
first assumption holds only in a very limited form and the
second, given the data on which these assumptions are based,
is likely to be unwarranted.

A simple exercise in projecting the size of the agricultural
labour force in the year 2000 suggests that, assuming the
present rate of drift towards other sectors, and the same
level of under-enumeration of female labour force
participation, the labour force will be about 20% larger at

Table 6.6: Female Labour Force Participation

Year	Women as % of Labour Force
1947	14.0%
1960	6.2%
1970	3.6%
1981	10.3%

Source: Mohie-Eldin, 1975: CAPMAS, Labour Force Survey, 1981,
Cairo, 1982, p9

Table 6.7: Agricultural Labour Force According to Different Sources
1947-1976 (000s)

Year	Census Labour Force+	Index	Sample Survey** Labour Force	Index
		(1960=100)		(1970=100)
1947	4267	97	-	-
1960	4407	100	-	-
1966	4462	101	-	-
1970	-	-	4298	100
1971	-	-	4469	104
1973	-	-	4222	98
1975	-	-	4425	103
1976	4422	100	-	-
1979	-	-	4002	93
1981	-	-	4006	93

+ = Census Data include ages 6-65 years
**= Labour Force Sample Survey Data include ages 12-65 years

the start of the next century. In the case of the national
labour force, assuming a rate of increase of around 2.2% p.a.,
the overall increment would exceed 50% and this figure would
rise to 60% if a rate of 2.6% p.a. were assumed. In any
event, the point that comes across most sharply, is that, with
the present population structure, the labour force both inside
and outside agriculture can be expected to grow substantially
in the medium term. The rate of increment is, moreover,
likely to rise still further if female educational standards
improve and attitudes to female work relax.

Unemployment in the Egyptian Economy

There are significant problems in estimating the number of
unemployed and the rate of unemployment. Rather than enter
into a more detailed discussion of the methodological issues,
the available and acceptable data will be marshalled below.[17]

Taking 1960 as the benchmark, two estimates of unemployment
are available. The first, from the Census, placed the level
of open unemployment at 2.2% of the labour force. The Labour
Force Sample Survey (LFS) for that year gave a higher figure
of 4.8%. Part of the difference can be accounted for by the
time of year in which the two enquiries were made. In
general, the LFS data is unsuitable for analysing longer term
trends, given changes in the sampling technique. Thus, using
the 1976 Census data for comparison, it appears that
unemployment had risen to 4.1%, adjusting for seasonality.
The LFS for 1975 and 1977 report an unemployment level of
5.3%. The latest LFS - 1981 - purports to show that
unemployment is at around 5%. More recent estimates suggest
that with a reduced level of economic activity, unemployment
levels have continued to rise through to the mid-1980s. Thus,
by whatever data source is employed, it is clear that the rate
of unemployment has increased and that, in fact, most of this
increase has come post-1973.

The increase in the level of unemployment has largely occurred
within the urban areas. Rural unemployment was thought to
account for around 46% of total unemployment in 1976 but more
recent LFS data suggests that the share is lower, somewhere in
the region of 28-35%. A sizeable village survey done in 1977
found that under 2% of the labour force was classified as
'looking for work'.[18] At the last count (1981) the

unemployment rate in rural areas was put at 3.2% as against over 7% for urban areas.[19]   Although growth in the rate of unemployment has cut across most sections of the Egyptian economy, agriculture has been the least affected.   Open unemployment rates, as would be expected, are low and have been consistently decreasing for the last twenty-five years. In 1960, it was estimated that the rate for agriculture was 2.5%; by 1978, this had fallen to 0.02%.

Common to the majority of those without work, is the fact that they are young and have mostly not held any previous jobs. Between 90-94% of those unemployed had not worked before and many of them, it can safely be hypothesised, have been waiting for government work to become available.[20]   Moreover, unlike in the previous decade, by 1976, the bulk of unemployed (52.5%) had acquired some level of education.   Over a third had intermediate, but not university education, and nearly 10% had been to university. This contrasts very markedly with the earlier situation.   In 1960, for instance, over three-quarters of the unemployed population were illiterate or could only read and write. [21]

If, as it appears, there exist shortages of labour alongside increasing unemployment, this should be interpreted, in Hansen's words, 'not as an increasingly slack labour market in general but rather as indicating increasing mal-adjustment in the labour market with the emergence of a growing fringe of unemployed, educated youngsters'.[22]   In turn, this level of mismatching is closely associated with the impact of state interventions in the labour market and in particular, by the massive expansion in government and public sector employment. At the same time - and this is of particular relevance in the context of agriculture - the growth in the numbers and proportions availing themselves of education has had a very significant impact on young people's expectations and employment aspirations.

The scale of employment offered by the government in the last decade has had a major impact not only in terms of lowering the rate of unemployment in the economy, but also on the type of work that has become available and, as significantly, in the development of a more general attitude to work that now permeates much of the society.   Quantitatively , the importance of government and public sector employment can be seen

Table 6.8: Employment by Sector 1981 Labour Force Survey Data
            (12-65 years)

Sector	Urban	Rural	All
Government	27.3	11.5	19.0
Public Sector	19.7	6.6	12.8
Private Sector	43.8	76.5	61.1
Other	9.2	5.4	7.1

Source: CAPMAS, Labour Force Sample Survey, 1981, Cairo, 1982, p.84

Table 6.9: Employment Structure of Rural Households, 1977

Occupation	Number of Persons	Percentage
Farmer	647	43.7
Agricultural Labourer	236	15.9
Craftsman or Industrial Worker	120	8.1
Construction or Service Worker	116	7.8
Government Employee	148	10.0
Military	113	7.6
Others	70	4.7
Looking for Work	30	2.0
Total	1480	100.0

Source: Hansen and Radwan, 1982, Table 43, p.101

in the fact that by 1981, just under a third of total
employment fell outside the private sector (see Table 6.8).
In urban areas, nearly half of the workforce is employed by
the government in one capacity or another. Although the
spread of government work has been less rapid in the rural
areas, it is important to note that by 1981, over 18% of the
labour force worked in the state sector. The figure would, of
course, be higher if military employment was also taken into
account. Table 6.9, which is based on a detailed household
survey done by ILO in 1977, further shows that nearly 10% of
the sample worked in a civilian capacity in government jobs
with a further 7% in the army.[23]   Since then, as the 1984
Survey results demonstrate, the importance of government and
public sector work in the employment profiles of rural farm
households has grown still further.

The emergence of the state as a major employer can be dated to
the Nasser period and the political economy of state capitalism that was its principal characteristic. Nevertheless -
perhaps paradoxically - the turning towards private and
foreign capital associated with the Infitah-el-Iqtissad of
1973 and after cannot obscure the fact that in many respects
the state's involvement in the economic life of the majority
of the country's citizens has grown rather than receded.
Indeed, when compared with the highly resource-constrained
years between 1967 and 1973, the rate of growth in state sector employment has accelerated, averaging about 7% p.a. in the
decade following 1973 (see Table 6.10).

This trend has come about largely for non-economic reasons. In
the first instance, an employment guarantee scheme for military conscripts was set up following the war with Israel in
1973. Although this scheme was abolished three years later, a
longer-running, companion employment guarantee programme for
graduates has survived. Despite the fact that few recently
graduated job seekers prefer the government work that is
guaranteed to them, (principally because of the low pay) it is
universally seen as a fall-back option. While the government
would undoubtedly prefer to abolish the guarantee, the
possibly high political cost that this might entail has
disallowed this more radical option.

Instead, discouragements are strewn in the path of any potential government job seeker in the hope that he or she will

Table 6.10: State Sector Employment 1956-1984: Growth Rates

Period	Growth Rate (%)
1956-61	10.7
1961-65/66	34.1
1965/66-67/68	8.7
1967/68-70/71	3.1
1970/71-73	4.7
1973-78	7.0
1980/81-83/84	6.9

Source: El Issawi, 1983, p.25: IMF, 1984

find alternative employment.   At present, the gap between
applying for and securing a post may be up to three years and
certainly not less than two.   Nevertheless, with government
employees commonly holding down one or more private sector
additional jobs because of their better levels of remunera-
tion, the market for graduates is relatively tight, and has
been for the last few years.   The material consequence of this
is that the government sector has become chronically over-
staffed, while the nature of the work and the pay scales mean
that productivity levels are extremely low.   At the same time,
the employment guarantee programmes - though now more akin to
grandiose social security schemes - have been important in
transmitting a new culture of employment.   Over 70% of government jobs are of an administrative nature.[24]

It need hardly be emphasised that this is unlikely to be a
productive use of human capital.   Moreover, although wages as
a share of the government budget have not risen since 1977,
they still account for about 12% of government expenditure.
The annual wage and salary bill of government has increased by
around 16.2% p.a. between 1980/81 and 1983/84.   In the case of
public sector industrial concerns, wage increments have outrun
productivity.   In the first half of 1983/84, for example,
average compensation per worker rose by 12.8% while the nominal value of output per worker rose by 10.6% in the same
period.   Wage increments in the larger government sector have
commonly been held below the rate of inflation but this has
only further aggravated the problem of over-manning amidst
low morale, motivation and inadequate material rewards.   Not
surprisingly, the effect has been deleterious for the overall
efficiency and accountability of government employees.

The growth in state sector employment has undoubtedly reduced
the level of open unemployment in the economy.   It has been
estimated that for the period 1960-1976 in the absence of
emigration and excessive government job creation, unemployment
would have risen by 1976 to nearly 26% of the labour force.[25]
Since 1976 growth in the number of emigrants has been considerable, while state employment has increased by around 8%
per annum.   Assuming that open unemployment in 1984/5 was at
the 5% level registered in 1980 and estimating the excessive
quantum of government employment in terms of the gap between
the rate of population growth and the rate of growth in
government employment, nearly 1.1 million government jobs -

mostly in administration - were created in the period
1979-1984/5 in excess of a 'normal' rate of expansion (here
assumed to be equal to the rate of growth in population).
Taking the simple assumption of a halving of current levels of
out-migration, in addition to the numbers excessively employed
by government, an open unemployment rate of around 25-28% of
the 1984/5 labour force would be generated. If a complete
absence of emigration were assumed, the unemployment rate
would have exceeded 37%. Even without such drastic assumptions, it is very clear that the most striking development in
the Egyptian labour market in recent decades has been the
sustained growth in state employment. As will become clear
from the following chapter, this growth has not been limited
to urban areas but has increasingly impinged on the employment
profiles of rural, farm households.

Footnotes

1. Gotsch and Dyer, 1982, pp129-148.
2. Population Census, 1976.
3. Waterbury, 1983, p42.
4. Nassef, 1983, pp2-13; Kelley et al, 1982, pp83-114.
5. El Kammash, 1968, pp99-105.
6. Ibrahim in Abdel Khalek and Tignor, 1983, pp375-433;
    Nassef, 1983, pp18-31.
7. IBRD, 1981, pp23ff; Kelley et al., 1982, pp152ff; Sayed
    and El Khorazaty, 1980, pp11-38.
8. Ammar, 1944; Berque, 1957.
9. For a discussion of these issues, see Nassef, 1983 and El
    Issawy, 1983b.
10. Hansen and Radwan, 1982, pp38ff.
11. El Issawy, 1983b, p38; El Kammash, 1968, pp127ff; CAPMAS,
    LFS, 1981.
12. Birks and Sinclair, 1980 and in Richards and Martin, 1983,
    pp117-133.
13. See, for example, Amin & Away, 1985 for a most useful sur-
    vey of the available evidence; also Lesch, 1985, provides
    some further information.
14. Until the recent (1986) imposition of restrictions on the
    permissible level of remittances imposed by the Iraqi
    government.

15. Arman, 1982; IBRD, 1981, pp145-183.
16. CAPMAS, LFS, 1981; see also Chaudhury, 1981; Mohie-eldin, 1975.
17. For readers interested in the analysis of the reliability and comparability of the relevant sources, see Hansen and Radwan, 1982 and El-Issawy, 1983b for a more adequate treatment of the issues.
18. Radwan and Lee, 1986, p185.
19. CAPMAS, LFS, 1981.
20. El-Issawy, 1983a, pp23-27; IBRD, 1981, pp168-171.
21. Mohie-eldin, 1975; El-Issawy, 1983a; El Kammash, 1968, pp116ff.
22. Hansen and Radwan, 1982 p41.
23. Radwan and Lee, 1986, p135.
24. El-Issawy, 1983b, p68; IMF, 1984.
25. Hansen and Radwan, 1982, pp46/7.

CHAPTER SEVEN

Employment, Underemployment and the Market for Labour
in Rural Egypt: Evidence from the 1984 Survey

The Current Structure of Employment: A Summary of the Survey Results

The 1984 survey collected information on the employment status
of all members of each surveyed household who could be considered to be in the workforce. In general, this information
was sought from all family members above ten years of age and
below sixty-five. Respondents were asked not only about their
principal occupation but also about such secondary and tertiary work that they might hold. They were also asked about
the proportion of the year that they worked in each type of
employment. In addition, a monthly breakdown was made for all
members of the labour force of the number of days worked each
month in agriculture and outside of agriculture. In all, the
employment section of the questionnaire covered the occupa-
tional involvement of 793 respondents, of whom over 20%
reported a secondary occupation. Only two respondents cited a
third occupation.

Although attempts were made to interview as many family members as possible, enumerators had, in many cases, to rely on
the household head for the information. This - amidst the
general feeling that in status terms a woman's place was far
more in or near the home than working elsewhere - led to a
significant under-enumeration of the off-farm work of the
household women. Given that hired female labour accounted for
a little under a quarter of total crop labour inputs, the
scale of female involvement in the labour market from amongst
the sampled households was extremely low.

Indicative of the imbalanced result was the fact that 75% of
female respondents cited housewife as their primary occupation. A further 18% were principally classified as students.
Less than 3% of female respondents worked principally in agriculture, either on their household land or as agricultural
labourers. Of those that did, all were young, unmarried girls
from small farm households. Six out of the 334 held primary
employment in the government or public sector. Of these women

with state sector work, it is interesting to note that while farm holding size was evenly spread, all had either passed out of secondary school, or above. However, these were among the rare cases where female education had been maintained beyond the primary level.

While the great majority of female household members cited housework as their principal occupation, it is worth noting that nearly 16% of respondents cited on-farm agricultural work as their secondary occupation. The average period in the year devoted to agricultural work (which should be construed as crop labour) was around a month and a half, with, however, the majority of observations indicating a working period of under a month. As would be expected, most of this crop labour was associated with rice transplanting and cotton picking. About seven-eighths of this peak season labour supply was provided by women whose primary occupation was noted as housework.

The data collected regarding the employment profile of the male labour force were undoubtedly more reliable, although it should be pointed out that interpreting housework in the broadest sense (ie. as including livestock work, some birseem cutting and so on) may well give a moderately accurate picture of the relatively low levels of wage employment among farm household women, save for particular crop tasks at relatively compacted periods in the year. In the case of the male labour force, two features in particular stand out. Firstly, there was the high level of retention of young males in education. Over a third of males aged above 10 years were still at school or University. As around 37% of the male sample fell in the 12-25 years age bracket, this points to a very high par- ticipation among male youth in education.

Secondly, while farming as the principal occupation accounted for a quarter of the sample, with a further 10% working pri- marily as agricultural labourers, over 14% were employed by the state and this proportion rose to 21% if army and police work was included. Thus, extracting students from the effec- tive primary labour force (as well as those unable to work), slightly under 40% of the sample were farmers, a further 15% were agricultural labourers, nearly a third were employed in one way or another by the state (including those doing mili- tary service) with barely 10% being employed in the non- agricultural private sector. Contrary to popular view, it was

Table 7.1: Males: Primary Occupation: Distribution of Employment by
            Farm Size, 1984

Primary Occupation	FARM SIZE (feddans)					All	
	0-1	1-3	3-5	5-10	>10		
Government	11.9%	8.7%	9.2%	10.3%	-	10%	(47)
Public Sector	3.4	3.8	3.1	-	20	3.4	(16)
Cooperative	-	0.5	1.5	-	-	0.4	(2)
Police/Army	6.8	7.6	3.1	5.1	20	6.6	(31)
Farmer	24.3	24.4	29.2	20.5	40	24.9	(117)
Agric. Labourer	11.9	12	4.6	-	-	9.8	(46)
Construction	0.6	1.1	-	-	-	0.6	(3)
Services	1.7	2.2	7.7	5.1	-	3	(14)
Working Abroad	1.7	0.5	-	2.5	-	1.1	(5)
Student	31.1	33.7	41.5	-	20	34.7	(163)
Weaver	1.1	2.2	-	-	-	1.3	(6)
Trader	-	0.5	-	2.5	-	0.4	(2)
Unemployed	0.6	0.5	-	-	-	0.4	(2)
Other	1.7	-	-	5.1	-	1.1	(5)
Outside Work Force (e.g. Disabled)	3.4	2.2	-	2.5	-	2.3	(11)
Number of Observations	177	184	65	39	5	470	

(   ) = No. of Observations

Source: ODI/Zagazig Survey, 1984

found that under 1% of the labour force (whether measured in potential or effective terms) was involved in construction work as a principal source of employment. However, this very limited involvement in construction work may partly be a function of sample bias, as no landless workers were included.

The importance attached to education was common to all farm-size classes and, indeed, the striking feature of Table 7.1 is that there is remarkably little variation in the distribution of education across farm size. The small-farm households maintain an equal share of their potential labour force in full time education. However, agricultural labouring, as expected, is a more common primary occupation amongst the smallest landholding households. Nevertheless, while several decades back one could have expected agricultural labouring to be the most important source of off-farm employment, by 1984 the proportion was similar to that directly employed by the state, excluding public sector enterprises and military service.

It should also be pointed out that the level of open unemployment apparently remained low. Only 0.4% of the male sample reported being out of work or waiting for work; the latter being invariably for a government position. Of course, the question of disguised unemployment and under-employment (to which we shall return in more detail later) cannot be fully addressed with this data, but it is nevertheless interesting to note that there was little variation across farm size class for employed males in the proportion of the year that they were 'in work'. On average between 88-90% of the working year was reported as being in primary employment. This would appear - at least superficially - to be close to a full employment level.

The nature of the changes in the structure of the rural labour market can clearly be seen when dealing with the question of secondary employment. A relatively recent survey dealing precisely with this issue estimated that while household heads and land holders had a low probability of entering this market, there was a high probability of housewives and students participating in the hired agricultural labour market in a secondary capacity.[1] The data for 1984 confirm that housewives and students do indeed participate in agricultural work in a significant way, but that this participation is not

Table 7.2: Proportion of Labour Force with Secondary Work

Occupation	5	6	7	8	11	15	18	19	20
Govt. Work	38.5(20)								
Public Sector	47.1(8)								
Police/Army	25 (8)								
Farmer		2.5(3)	0.8(2)	0.8(1)	1.7(1)		5.9(7)	1.7(2)	0.8(1)
Agricultural Labourer	9.4(5)		1.9(1)	1.9(1)			1.9(1)		
Construction	100 (3)								
Service Sector	27.3(3)								
Retired	53.8(7)								
Housewife	17.5(44)	1.2(3)							
Student	30.7(66)			0.5(1)					
Driver	33.3(1)								
Waiting for Work	100 (1)								
Weaver	16.7(1)								
Other	40 (2)								
Total Observations =	169	6	3	3	1	1	8	2	1

Code: 5 = Own-farm Agriculture   11 = Housewife
       6 = Agricultural Labouring   15 = Carpenter
       7 = Construction   18 = Weaver
       8 = Service Sector   19 = Trader
                                     20 = Other

       ( ) = Number of Observations

No of Households with One or More Members with a Secondary Occupation = 107
(62.6% of all households in survey)

No of Household Members with Secondary Occupation = 194
(25% of those in workforce)

in the hired labour market but occurs on their own farms. Around 3% of respondents with secondary employment found work in the agricultural hired labour market. By contrast, nearly 87% cited on-farm agricultural work as their secondary source. While over 30% of students worked for some time in this capacity, it is important to note that over two-fifths of those with government or public sector work also worked in a secondary capacity on their household land. A very small number of people worked outside agriculture in their secondary occupation.

Table 7.3 further shows that the proportion of the labour-force with own-farm work as secondary employment was strongly inversely related to farm size. This can be interpreted in various ways. It would confirm the very limited labour absorption capacity of the small farms, albeit with marked differences on a seasonal basis. Secondly, it could be interpreted to mean that with the growth of non-farm employment options, male members of the household labour force have in many cases secured work in other sectors and participate in farm labour on a purely part-time basis. Given the diminutive size of most plots, this would be a perfectly feasible option.

This securing of non-agricultural work as the principal employment, with farm work taking a subsidiary form was found to be most advanced in the Gharbiya village (see Table 7.4). Here, the average size of holding was very low and a high proportion of the work-force had secured jobs outside the village. The proximity of the large towns, Tanta, Mohalla-el-Qobra and, to a lesser extent, Santa naturally facilitated this process. Consequently, small-farm household labour was only very marginally involved in the hired agricultural labour market. Between a half and a third (for the two smallest farm-size classes) had a secondary occupation. In nine out of ten cases this secondary work took the form of own-farm labour. With particularly high numbers retained in education and with a very marked share of employment accounted for by the state, it would not be inapt to describe crop farming as a part-time activity for the bulk of land operators. Given the conditions of employment in most government offices with relative flexibility in hours and attendance this combination proves eminently feasible.

A range of hypotheses were tested with a view to isolating the

Table 7.3: Proportion of Labour Force with Secondary Employment and With
            Secondary Employment in the Agricultural Sector, 1984

	------Farm Size (feddans)------------------------				
	0-1	1-3	3-5	5-10	>10
With Secondary Employment	31.9	32.3	15.1	15.2	12.5
Secondary Employment = Own-Farm Work	28.1	20	13	13.5	-
Secondary Employment = Agricultural Labouring	1.0	1.0	-	-	-

Table 7.4: Principal and Secondary Occupations for Small Farm Households
            Gharbiya, 1984 (0-3 feddans), (both sexes)

	-------Proportion of Sample-----------	
Occupation	Principal	Secondary
Government/Public Sector	14.6%	
Army/Police	5.6	
Own-Farm Work	13.6	90%
Agricultural Labourer	0.5	3.8
Construction	0.5	5.0
Working Abroad	1.4	
Services	0.5	1.2
Student	28.6	
Housewife	30.5	
Other	4.2	
Number of Observations	213	80

determinants of household workforce members' primary occupation.   Initially, the factors behind agricultural sector work
as the principal employment were explored.   The number of
household members working either on their own farms or else as
agricultural labourers was regressed on a number of variables
denoting farm size.   In the case of the cropped area there was
found to be a relatively weak negative association which,
however, was not statistically significant.   Household size
was also found to be negatively associated with the number of
family members working primarily in agriculture.   Again, the
statistical significance was weak.   Rather, the internal composition of the household provided greater explanatory power.
The number of agricultural-sector workers was strongly associated with the number of adult males in the household and
with the number of non-resident males.   As expected, there was
a strong negative association with the proportion of educated
adult males in the household; an association that was significant at the 1% level.

The predominance of adult male household heads, and hence of
the more elderly members of the household, amongst those who
cited agricultural work as their primary occupation was pronounced.   When tested statistically by regressing own-farm
agricultural work on heads of household, a positive association was established that was again significant at a 1%
level.[2]

The possible link between the structure of technology
available to farm households and the proportion of household
members working primarily in agriculture was found to be a
rather weak one.   Although the number of full-time farm
workers was positively associated with ownership of draught
animal power (this was significant at the 5% level), no
meaningful association existed with the ownership of a variety
of machines, including tractors and irrigation pumps.
However, when using a cost proxy - the share of machine energy
costs in total costs - a fairly strong, statistically significant, negative relationship emerged.

The emergence of government and public sector employment as an
important choice in employment has also been associated with
the spread of education.   This approach would be in line with
an argument, now familiar in the Egyptian context, that education has restrained the supply of labour to agriculture.

Table 7.5: Educational Levels, 1984 : By Sex

Age Range (years)	Illiterate	Read & Write	Primary School	Secondary School	Above Secondary School	Observations
			M A L E S			
6-12	10	2.5	87.5	-	-	80
12-18	17.6	3.9	45.1	32.3	1.1	102
18-25	24.3	15.9	2.8	28	29	107
25-35	14.9	29.7	8.1	28.4	18.9	74
35-50	47.6	41.5	-	3.7	7.3	82
50-65	50	44.8	3.4	1.8	-	58
>65	62.5	37.5	-	-	-	8
All	26.6	21.1	24.9	17.2	10.2	511
			F E M A L E S			
6-12	31.7	3.3	65	-	-	60
12-18	51.9	5.5	33.3	5.6	3.7	54
18-25	65	5	1.7	5	23.3	60
25-35	78.6	16.1	-	3.6	1.7	56
35-50	93.5	4.3	1.1	-	1.1	92
50-65	87.9	12.1	-	-	-	33
>65	100	-	-	-	-	9
All	69.8	6.9	16.2	2.2	4.9	364

Source: ODI/Zagazig Survey, 1984

Richards and Martin, for example, found that in the late
1970's education had constrained the supply of full-time agricultural workers, but that this was in significant measure
compensated for by secondary agricultural work.[3] Those
entering the labour market in a secondary capacity, for the
most part at harvest periods, were largely students and
housewives. This seasonal disposition of labour has also been
confirmed by the 1984 data, but with the important proviso
that few are entering the agricultural labour market in a
secondary capacity, but work instead on their own household's
farm at restricted periods in the year. On average, males –
mostly students – worked about eight-nine weeks in the year in
secondary agricultural work, with women working for between
six-seven weeks.

Yet it would be false to suppose that this constrained labour
supply to the market for hired labour in agriculture is a
simple consequence of wider educational possibilities.
Firstly, it should be pointed out that female children continue to be excluded from school in a substantial way,
although the scale of withdrawal from education appears to be
falling.[4] The figures presented below prove this beyond
doubt, as would any cursory visit to the school classes held
in or near the sampled villages. In the Sharkiya village primary school, for instance, the ratio of boys to girls was between 3 and 4 to 1. In addition, girls' attendance was much
more sporadic and depended on other demands on their time in
the household and fields. In general throughout Egypt (and
this is even more pronounced outside the Delta) education,
even at a primary level, is the preserve of male children.

Apart from the fact that education remains strongly biased
against females, it should also be noted that there is a
notable difference in the educational levels attained by those
below 25-30 years and those in the age brackets above. The
growth of state education from the mid-1950s onwards, now
offered free to citizens, has undoubtedly had a major impact.
Secondly, despite the fact that education does not incur
significant direct costs by way of fees, the wider costs of
supporting children in education are reflected in the distinction in educational levels when looked at by farm-size class.
While in the case of the two largest farm-size categories
nearly 90% of males between the ages of 18-25 years had gone
through secondary education or beyond (to university or

training college), in the case of the small-farm households
(those below three feddans) a little over half this age group
had attained a comparable level.

But if this gap, which in large measure is an income-derived
difference, still persists despite the free availability of
state education, any comparison of current levels of education
with those holding of the previous generation is very
striking. In the case of those above 35 years of age, only a
third had gone up to or beyond secondary school in the larger-
farm category (farms of over 5 feddans) and under 5% had
achieved this level in the small-farm households. In the case
of women, educational attainment was strongly correlated with
farm size, suggesting that only the more prosperous, asset-
endowed households would invest in female education to any
significant extent. However, in general, there can be little
doubt that there has been a profound change in the availability and use of educational resources.[5]

One obvious connection between the spread of male education
and the labour market has been in the type of work taken up by
those who have progressed beyond illiteracy or a basic reading
and writing capacity. As has already been mentioned, state
sector jobs have become an important source of employment. It
can be surmised that a number of these posts have been
obtained under the graduate employment guarantee scheme and
the military guarantee scheme that operated between 1973 and
1976.[6] In addition, the general expansion of government
employment has clearly reached down as far as the village
level. The easy availability of transportation has facilitated this process for most government jobs are outside the
village.

In the case of those whose primary employment was listed as
government or public sector work, such employment was found to
be positively associated with an educational status beyond
primary school level and with proximity to major towns (a
dummy variable). The statistically significant negative association with the age bracket 10-25 years suggests that state
sector work is screened in terms of minimum educational qualifications. Indeed, the average age of those with state-
provided jobs was around 33 years, while nearly three-quarters
had been educated to secondary school level. But although
access to secondary education has increased, the quality of

Table 7.6: Educational Levels, 1984 (Both Sexes)

| Educational Level | Farm Size (feddans) | | | | | |
	0-1	1-3	3-5	5-10	>10	All
Below 6 years	10.4	11.7	6.5	4.7	20	10.4
Illiterate	43.5	43.2	33.3	18.8	10	39.9
Read & Write	14.3	12.9	11.4	15.6	20	13.5
Primary School	16.0	19.3	23.6	28.1	10	19.1
Secondary School	11.5	6.7	12.2	21.9	10	10.2
Above Secondary School	4.2	6.2	13.0	10.9	30	6.9

Table 7.7: Determinants of Primary Employment
in Government or Public Sector

Dependent Variable: Primary Employment in Government or Public Sector

Independent Variables	Coefficient	Standard Error	Significance Level
Household Head	.0552	.0249	0.0267
Male	.0569	.0183	0.0020
10-25 years Age Bracket	-.1322	.0186	0.0001
Education Beyond Primary School	.1482	.0191	0.0001
Proximity to Major Towns (Dummy)	.0538	.0179	0.0028

R^2 = .31   Number of Observations = 67

Source: ODI/Zagazig Survey, 1984

education is frequently low and possibly declining.[7] Males
from small-farm households have increasingly been drawing the
benefits of remaining at school. Indeed, when seeking to
explain the number and proportion of students by household,
neither farm size nor household income proved to be useful
explanatory devices. The only variable with statistically
significant association was that of household size where the
relationship was, as expected, positive.

Attainment of at least a minimum level of schooling appears to
be a necessary prerequisite for securing government or public
sector employment. To this extent, the combination of state
employment expansion, employment guarantee schemes and a more
general aspiration for work outside agriculture should be considered as the major features of the male labour market in the
Delta.

Demand for education in rural Egypt has undoubtedly grown
significantly over the last couple of decades. Clearly, this
has been strongly conditioned by the increased supply of
schooling facilities as well as the costing of such facilities. While direct charges for education are very small,
retention of children in education clearly entails a substantial, short-to-medium term opportunity cost. This is particularly true at the present time given current conditions in
the labour market. Households' preferences with regard to the
retention of household members in education are obviously
complex.[8]

In the first place, one would expect such preferences to be
structured by expectations of the present value of the future
financial benefits to be received, less the costs of education. Secondly, the ability of the household to sustain the
direct costs of education would be a critical factor.
Thirdly, the 'fungibility' of education time would appear to
be an important factor in arranging human capital investment
preferences. Thus, given the small average size of holding
and the fluctuating level of labour commitment to agricultural
production, retention of household members in education need
not necessarily be to the exclusion of their involvement in
agriculture. The 1984 survey results appear to point to this
conclusion. Fourthly, the non-pecuniary benefits of education, as offset by the non-pecuniary costs, if any, would
govern household decision-making on this issue. Fifthly, in

the Egyptian context the unequal attitude to male and female children has an important bearing on the demand for education.

Evidence regarding the net present value of future financial benefits from education is by no means conclusive. Although estimates of the returns to education range between 8% and 30%, depending on the educational level attained, this may not be accurate. In the first case, it is important to note that education - and with it access to 'skilled' work - does not necessarily denote withdrawal from agricultural work, even if it does tend to denote withdrawal from the hired agricultural labour market. This is directly related to the third factor - 'fungibility' cited above. Thus, education tends to be associated with a higher probability of, firstly, work diversification and secondly, a higher intensity of remunerated labour time. For small farm households education of male children is rightly viewed as a means of securing a higher, aggregate level of employment for family labour stock. This is of particular relevance given the fact that seasonal 'lay-offs' and involuntary unemployment are still prevalent in the agricultural labour market.

The structure of the labour market over the last decade, with the range of employment guarantee schemes, has further ensured that retention of male children up to and including university education has become widespread. This is governed by an expectation of increased probability of securing 'skilled' work (ie. a government job). By this means, the current amalgam of male retention in education and the prevalence of secondary agricultural work by those retained household members provides a rational and efficient solution to current employment and income signals from the labour market.

Underemployment in Egyptian Agriculture

Historically, it has always been considered that Egyptian agriculture has been marked by high levels of underemployment with relatively low open unemployment.[9] This has been a consequence of the nature of the production system and the very sharp variation by season and month in the average quantum of labour time devoted to crop activity.

By implication, the predominantly household farm system has

been seen to organise its labour disposition around the critical compacted requirements of the harvest period. With small
farm households functioning almost entirely as hirers-out of
labour, such seasonal variations were not overcome through
transactions in the labour market. Indeed, large farms hired
in labour through the year, but with seasonal peaks, while
small farm households attempted to sell their available labour
power on the agricultural labour market, at the same time as
working their own minute holdings. To this extent, previous
research has largely been concerned with the manner and degree
to which the demand for labour - largely viewed as a function
of the large-farm production framework - and the supply of
labour from the small farms was in disequilibrium. While the
continuing growth of urban centres (in particular Alexandria
and Cairo) in the pre-1952 period, suggested that out-
migration was one possible option for a largely under-employed
peasantry, in general it has been safe to assume that agricultural wage labouring was the only remunerative employment
in rural areas.[10]

The agricultural labour force was drawn not only from small-
farm households but also from the substantial numbers of
landless families. In Sharkiya, for example, it was found
that in 1937 of the total rural population over 55% were
tenants, agricultural labourers or dependents. Consequently,
Ammar found that, '......the competition between the landless
elements has inevitably raised the rental value of the land
and at the same time lowered the wages of labourers....The
living conditions of the people are still more difficult
because the land that may be rented cannot meet the great
demand of the landless class. It is not only that the arable
area is limited but many big estates are exploited by the
landlords themselves by means of hired labourers.....Most of
the labourers are not employed all the time and their already
marginal income has been greatly affected'.[11]

The situation in the Depression years described by Ammar was
modified in many crucial respects by the set of agrarian
reform measures introduced after the fall of the Monarchy.
Large estates were broken up, land ceilings were imposed and
land titles redistributed. The result was, of course, a proliferation of small farms and a substantial culling of larger
units. Although this may not have been as radical a process
as originally intended there can be little doubt that a major

series of changes in the production framework was achieved. This had obvious implications for the distribution of the demand for labour.

These land reform measures appear to have had two major con-sequences for employment. Firstly, the size of the landless population was diminished by redistribution (and continuing out-migration). Secondly, by breaking up the large estates - the traditional source of the demand for <u>hired</u> labour - and by increasing the weight of small farms with their predominantly household labour use structure, agrarian reform was thought to have depressed the capacity of the agricultural system to absorb an increasing labour force. Mohie-Eldin, for example, argued that labour surpluses were <u>highest</u> in governorates where small farms predominated.[12] Apart from the traditional seasonal variation in labour use, there was also the fact that in the 1960s small farms rarely hired in labour on a cash basis. When outside help was required, this was provided on a mutual aid or <u>mazamlah</u> basis by relatives or neighbours.

The labour surplus estimated to ensue from the prevailing agrarian structure in the early 1960s was consequently very substantial. Accounting for peak season requirements, it was thought that the quantum of surplus labour time was equal to over 65% of the potential supply of <u>male</u> labour to agriculture for farms of below 5 feddans. Actual male employed labour time was estimated to account for around 64 days per annum out of a maximum of 300. Yet, in an argument strikingly resembling that advanced at the present time, Mohie-Eldin argued that this labour surplus existed alongside seasonal shortages, caused by the extreme variance between harvest and slack season requirements.[13] Such shortages resulted either in non-optimal harvesting times, or in the release of female and child labour for such work.

Other estimates of employment in plant production suggested that average requirements were higher than the figures used by Mohie-Eldin. Hansen & El Tomy's figures estimated a labour requirement almost three times higher for males and nearly double that for females.[14] Neither estimate took account of livestock work or time allocated to capital formation, main-tenance and so on. This may have led to overestimation of the scale of underemployment and levels of seasonal variance.

GRAPH 7.1

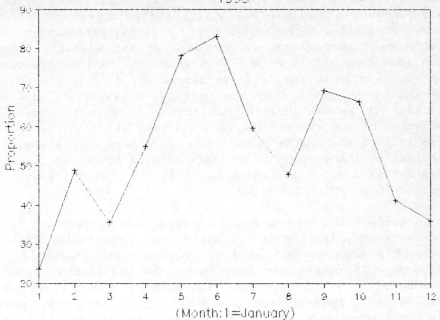

Proportion of Month Worked by Adult Males
1955

These earlier attempts to estimate the level of surplus labour, its seasonal distribution and the corresponding wage structure largely assumed that remunerated employment in the rural sector was only a function of agriculture. Indeed, by 1960 it was thought that the non-agricultural labour force constituted only around 20% of the rural labour force.[15] Wage labouring in agriculture was split into permanent and casual work. The latter category was overwhelmingly predominant. In turn, the labour force was composed of two elements, those with some land and those who were landless. Although estimates of the size of the landless labour force exist, it should be pointed out that they are residual calculations and are unlikely to be particularly accurate.[16] Table 7.8 contains estimates of the size of the landless population in the period from 1929 to 1975. The calculations have been made assuming a constant 8% share of rural non-agricultural households between 1929 and 1961 and a 20% share for 1975; an order of magnitude derived from labour force data.

It is evident that the number and proportion of landless families working primarily in the agricultural sector has fallen, even if a constant share of non-agricultural households is assumed. Of course, in many cases the distinction between someone with very little land and someone without land is a fragile one. Nevertheless, the share of landless families in the rural population appears to have fallen very significantly and possibly at a very rapid rate in the last twenty years. Given the method of calculation - by residuals - it is feasible that an increasing proportion of non-agricultural households are previously landless agricultural households. Even so, the point is clear; the number of households without land contributing labour to the agricultural, hired labour market has fallen. In the three villages surveyed in 1984 landless households constituted between 8-12% of the total number of households. It was generally held that the share of landless labour had fallen quite substantially in the last quarter century, even if the transition had only been towards ownership of minute land titles.

The growth in the absolute number and weight of minute farm holdings in the overall structure of ownership has also been closely linked to prevailing inheritance practices. Using the size class 0-1 feddan as a proxy for farms where the arable area is insufficient to provide anything near 'full-family

Table 7.8: Landless Families as Proportion of Total Rural Families,
            1929-1975 (000s)

Year	1 Rural Families	2 Agric. Land- holding	3 Non-Agric. Families	4 Landless Families	5 Proportion 4/1
1929	2116	1207	169	740	35%
1939	2333	993	187	1153	49.4%
1950	2740	997	219	1524	55.6%
1961	3224	1641	258	1325	41.1%
1975	4094	2642	819	633	15.5%

Table 7.9: Unemployment of Hired Agricultural Workers By Month, 1977

Month	1*	2**
January	33%	53%
February	35	57
March	25	42
April	16	39
May	10	25
June	0	18
July	15	36
August	30	57
September	26	46
October	0	10
November	12	35
December	37	57

1* = days worked/days available :

2** = days worked/25 days

Source: Richards & Martin, 1983, Table 29.

employment' over the year, the number of such holdings apparently increased by nearly seven times between 1950 and 1977/78. Possibly a third, at most, of this increase could be accounted for by land redistribution; the remainder has to be explained largely in terms of inheritance norms. This has ensured that the supply of off-farm labour has continued to rise, especially given probable increases in female labour force participation. However - and this is the nub of the matter - the growth in the labour force and the very substantial decline in both the number of agricultural landless households and 'self-sufficient' labour farms - has not been translated into an increased supply of hired labour to agriculture.

The emergence of non-agricultural work opportunities, has transformed the labour market. The 1981 National Labour Force Sample Survey estimated that the proportion of the rural labour force now working in agriculture had fallen to around 64%.[17] This development has been crucial in weakening the impact of farm sub-divisioning and labour force growth on the level of underemployment in the primary sector.

The 1984 survey attempted to elicit information on all household members aged between 10 and 65 years about their time allocation to agriculture and the number of days, disaggregated by month, worked in agriculture. Graphs 7.2 & 7.3 express its findings in terms of farm-size groups and as a proportion of the total male labour time potentially available in each month. The graphs demonstrate not only the very marked seasonal distribution of labour inputs, with the period from April/May through to September/October being the period of maximum labour allocation to agriculture, but also the sharply decreasing share of labour time allocated to agriculture by farm-size class. Thus, male household members from farms of between 5 and 10 feddans worked in agriculture on average around 19% of the total time available. Household members from the smallest farm units, by contrast, spent around 39% of their time working in agriculture. There was, moreover, considerable variation across village. Male labour force members in the Gharbiya village allocated less than half the share to agriculture that was found to hold in the Sharkiya case-study.

Additionally, all household members in the labour force were asked whether they had been available for hired agricultural

Employment in Agriculture,1984

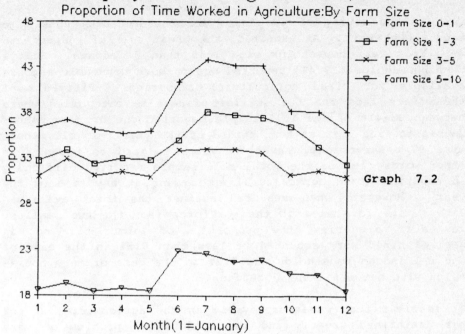

Graph 7.2

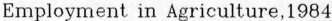

Employment in Agriculture,1984

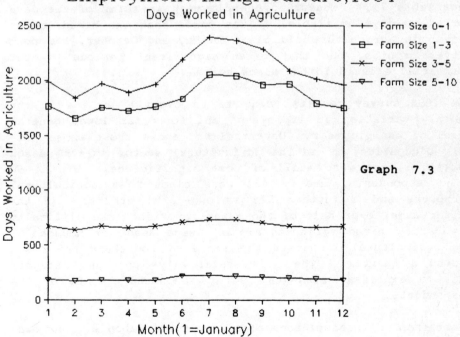

Graph 7.3

work in the course of the last year and had been unable to
secure such work. As expected, the great bulk of respondents
were from farm households with less than 3 feddans. Sixty-
four households (37.4%) reported one or more household members
available for hired agricultural labouring. Fifty-six of
these were from the two smallest farm-size categories where
between 38-41% of the full sample reported one or more member
unable to find work at some period of the year. In all, there
were 97 observations, seven of which related to women. In
other words, 19% of the total male sample reported difficulty
in securing hired agricultural employment at any time of the
year. However, when measured against the total available
labour time for males in the workforce from the two smallest
farm-size categories, the proportion of labour time not in
desired hired work amounted to less than 9.5% in the case of
the 0-1 feddan households and 6.2% in the case of farm households with between 1 and 3 feddans.

It is clear that under-employment in the agricultural sector
has diminished greatly and the traditional problem of very
slack season labour surpluses has been much weakened, even
when the 1984 data is compared with 1977/78 Sharkiya data.
(See Table 7.9) Measuring unemployment in terms of the days
worked to days available, it was found that the hired labour
market in agriculture did clear in May and October, the peak
harvest months, but that often significant periods without
work still existed in the slack season.[18]

The 1984 survey results point to an overall decline in the
monthly variation in employment and to a far lower general
level of unemployment. Nevertheless, among those whose primary occupation was in the agricultural sector, slack season
work shortages were still of some significance. Of the 90
male respondents, nearly 47% were classed as agricultural
labourers and a further 37% as own-farm workers. In the
latter case, over half of those who reporting some difficulty
in finding hired agricultural work were heads of household;
for agricultural labourers the share of household heads was
around a quarter. The other relatively important category
was, as expected, students. They accounted for 8% of the
respondents.

Apart from the predominance of agricultural labourers and own-
farm workers, principally heads of household, among those with

seasonal work shortages, another striking characteristic was
the age distribution of respondents. Nearly a third were aged
between 10 and 19 years with over 22% falling in the age category 50 years and above. This confirms the general pattern,
in which unemployment levels are higher among young entrants
into the labour force, and the elderly. 'Peak' age workers
tend to be less affected.

At the same time, it must be carefully noted that work scarcity continues to exist for those working primarily in agriculture, including those who were principally agricultural
labourers. This further reinforces doubts about the degree or
the novelty of the supposed agricultural labour shortage.
Although all the evidence points to a tightening of the labour
market in agriculture, in addition to the customary harvest
season demand for labour, the labour market does not clear
throughout the year, even at the peak seasons. This fact may
seem paradoxical. However, when controlling for students
coming on to the labour market at peak periods – in the summer
months at school and university vacation time – the proportion
of labour time without work fell in the May-September period,
in the case of the two smallest farm-size classes, to the
average levels of March, April, October and November. As
expected, December, January and February remain the relatively
slack crop months and the share of unemployed time correspondingly rose, albeit at a rather gentle rate. This implied
that household members from the smallest farms (0-1 feddans),
were without work for around 40% of their potentially
available labour time while for households with landholdings
of between 1 and 3 feddans, this share was around 26%.

It was also found that the proportion of time unemployed was
consistently higher for agricultural labourers than for own-
farm workers seeking hired work. As nine-tenths of those
whose primary occupation was registered as agricultural
labouring experienced a lack of work at some period of the
year this suggests, yet again, that 'full employment' in agriculture is still far from being a reality for those who have
not managed to secure primary employment outside the sector.
To this extent, it would be premature to suppose that the
problems of under-employment and sharp seasonal variations in
work availability have entirely disappeared. The agricultural
labour market does not clear, even when there has been a
highly significant employment shift away from the agricultural

sector.

However, where there has been a particularly strong movement of male adult labour out of agriculture, as in the Gharbiya village, both the numbers of people in the agricultural labour force and the proportion of the labour time without work was very substantially lower. In the Gharbiya case study, agricultural labouring was almost non-existant as a primary occupation and only 12% of the sample gave own-farm agricultural work as their primary employment. Of the latter, only four (13%) reported any difficulty in finding hired work. The great bulk of those who did experience problems were from the Sharkiya village where non-agricultural employment was least advanced.

Non-Farm Employment and the Supply of Labour to Agriculture

It is clear that although the Egyptian labour force as a whole has been growing at a steady rate and that medium-term projections predict a growth rate of as much as 2.6% per annum, the labour force available to agricultural producers has not increased at a corresponding rate. Indeed, such statistics as are available suggest a decline in the agricultural labour force of the order of 7% between 1970-1981.19 Yet these figures are open to strong criticism, largely because of the assumptions that underpin them.

In the first place, as has been demonstrated in the previous chapters, the participation rate for women, though increasing, remains artificially low, in official statistics. Female members of the labour force are consistently underenumerated, as are the important child labour inputs used in crop production. Secondly, the problem of calculating the size of the male agricultural labour force has become even more complex with the prevalence of multiple employment and part-time or secondary involvement in the agricultural process. It is unlikely that the sample surveys on which most of the labour force data are based were sufficiently well designed to pick up these features.

Therefore the picture of a declining agricultural labour force in the last decade may not be a true representation of the course of events. There can be little denying that the market

for agricultural labour has grown tighter, but the 1984 survey
has shown fairly conclusively that tasks in agriculture
historically the preserve of male labour are now, in part,
done by hired and family woman labour as well as child labour.
In short, there has been some substitution of adult male
workers, principally for harvesting. At the same time (see
Chapter 4) there is little evidence to suggest that average
male inputs in crop production have declined to any major
extent or that the quantum of labour inputs commonly committed
to crop tasks has been deflated.

Nevertheless, even if the scale of the implied permanent
withdrawal of labour from the agricultural sector has been
considerably over-stated, it is undoubtedly true that the
principal components of this growth path have lain outside the
agricultural sector despite high rates of domestic economic
growth post-1973. Indeed, agriculture's rate of growth, for
reasons dealt with elsewhere, was significantly and consistently lower than that of other major sectors. Growth in
the domestic economy has tended to be accompanied by a shift
of resources away from agriculture, particularly in the case
of human capital. Seeking work abroad in the urban informal
sector,20 in construction and in government and public sector
enterprises, a significant proportion of the potential agricultural labour force has found employment outside the sector.
Although this shift has not always been permanent - and this
has been the case for migrants overseas, for example - one
consequence has been that agriculture now accounts for around
37% of total employment. Twenty five years earlier agriculture's share was over 57%.21

An indication of a very widespread perception of labour shortage in agriculture can be gained by looking at Graphs 7.4 and
7.5. Both were constructed from data collected in 1984 in
which farm households hiring labour were asked, on a monthly
basis, whether they found difficulty in securing it. Graph
7.4, which includes all farm size classes, demonstrates, as
expected, that the perception of labour shortage is strongest
in the sifi harvest season (September to November) and, but to
a lesser extent, in the shitwi harvest period (April/May).
While in the winter period, from December through to February,
over 70% of households considered labour to be readily
available, this proportion fell to a little over 20% in
October and around 40% in April. As the shitwi harvest period

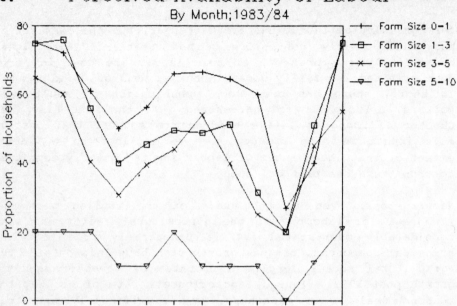

Perceived Availability of Labour
By Month;1983/84

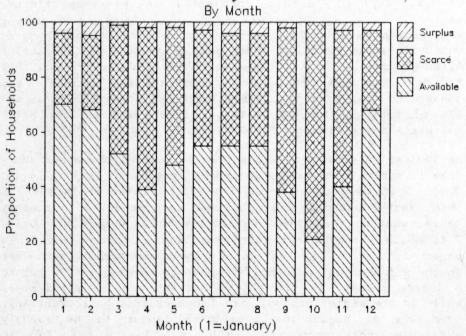

Perceived Availability of Labour:1983/84
By Month

has always been considered the main <u>male</u> labour bottleneck, this difference is interesting. Amongst other things, it suggests that the <u>sifi</u> harvest has become - with the coincidence of cotton picking and cutting, maize harvesting and separating, rice cutting and the subsequent preparation of the fields for the <u>shitwi</u> crops - the principal period of tightness in the labour market.

Graph 7.5 further elaborates these findings while decomposing household response by farm size class. As might be expected, the perception of labour shortage is universal amongst the largest farms (over 10 feddans) and very widespread among farms with between 5 -10 feddans. Perceptions of shortage are strongly and positively correlated with farm size. Nevertheless, in all farm-size categories labour availability was considered to fall sharply in the usual peak periods. There was a strong equalising trend particularly with regard to the <u>sifi</u> harvest period. In over 70% of the smallest farm units it was considered that labour was scarce in October.

Although the widespread belief in labour shortages - amply demonstrated in a range of enquiries and surveys22 - undoubtedly primarily reflects changes in the supply of labour to agriculture, there are few reasons for supposing that such 'shortages' are chronic or necessarily structural. Indeed, labour force projections do not support the view that this is necessarily a long-run feature of the Egyptian economy. To the extent that this might be the case, it would presuppose the continuance of exceedingly high rates of domestic economic growth and the continuing provision of employment by the state delinked from productive requirements. At the same time, despite the widespread view that it is socially degrading for women to work in hired agricultural employment, all currently available evidence points to a <u>growing</u> involvement of women and children in the crop production process.

The coexistence of severely tightened labour markets at peak seasons with considerable under-employment and slackness in the market at other periods of the year has long been a feature of Egyptian agriculture. What is more novel is the relative decline in the variance of employment over the course of the year. This has been strongly linked to the emergence of employment options outside agriculture, though not necessarily in urban areas. Indeed, the entire urban/rural distinction has if anything, been weakened in recent years.

Conclusion

The constrained supply of labour to agriculture has been linked to a number of inter-related factors, associated with a series of state interventions, not only in the labour market, but also in to the basic distribution of assets.

Firstly there has been the provision of free education, extended in 1962 to intermediate and university levels. Although the quality of instruction has tended to fall in recent years and attendance is likely to suffer if child labour inputs in agriculture continue to grow in importance, the easier availability of education has had a major impact on the labour force. For the most part, women remain uneducated, except for a few from asset-endowed households employed at a relatively skilled level in the labour market. Secondly, job guarantee programmes have both encouraged male children to remain in education up to university level, despite high short-term opportunity costs, and swelled the overall share of the state in total employment.

The rate of increase in government and public sector employment throughout the last decade has been more rapid than at any time since the heyday of Nasserism.23 Much of this employment generation has to be viewed as a largely unproductive and increasingly burdensome intervention in the labour market.

At the same time, profound changes have occurred in the aspirations of those entering the labour force, both through education and widened employment openings. When linked to the emergence, in the last decade, of emigration as a short to medium-term source of accumulation, the economy-wide effects of these changes have been highly significant.

These changes have manifested themselves in a variety of ways. Firstly, out-migration to the towns by household members is a continuing feature. Secondly, there has been a growth in non-agricultural work in the smaller urban centres, like Santa, Mit Ghamr, Minyet-el-Qam and the major Governorate towns, Mansoura, Tanta and Zagazig (Dakhalia, Gharbiya and Sharkiya respectively). Employment in these Delta urban areas no longer requires transposition from the village as communications networks have opened up and heavily subsidised transportation has become widely available. Most government and public sector jobs are still urban-located but the arc of recruitment has undoubtedly spread beyond the urban areas. The 1984 survey shows beyond doubt how important such employment opportunities have become to male members of the labour force. These opportunities have been particularly pronounced for the younger members of the labour force, even if private sector work - either combined with a government post or else held as the principal employment - is preferred because of superior private-sector wage levels. However, job creation in the private sector, or at least in the more organised sections, has been relatively weak. This has meant that state-provided employment has generally been more readily available and, in the case of those with sufficient educational qualifications, has been provided, albeit with a lag, as a right.

The emergence of non-farm employment opportunities has had an obvious impact on the supply of labour to agriculture and on the supply price of such labour. The effect on farm profitability of such factor cost increments is explored in <u>Chapter 8.</u> When dealing with the quantitative aspect - the volume of labour inputs available to agricultural producers - a number of aspects have to be separated out.

In the first place, institutional intervention in the distribution of land titles and assets - the period of the Land Reform measures - has resulted in a fall in the number of landless households. Some of these formerly landless units were granted land while others hired-in land on a seasonal or crop-specific basis. In the 1984 survey, tenancy was certainly present both for those without any owned land as well as for those with small own-farm holdings. However, there was a very considerable across-village variation both in the number of tenancies and in the number of tenancies where no land was also owned by the leasing-in household. The great bulk of leased-in land was tenanted by farms of up to 3 feddans and the rented area as a proportion of the total village area ranged from around 2.1% in the case of the Gharbiya village to 13.4% for Dakhaliya and over 26% in the Sharkiya case-study. A similar range of variation existed when computing the share of units where the operated area was entirely rented.   These ranged from 1.8%, 9.3%, to 27.7% of all farm units (Gharbiya, Dakhaliya and Sharkiya respectively).

In all cases, the factor most satisfactorily explaining the proportion and area under tenancy was the number of landless households in the village.   Where smallholdings predominated almost entirely - as in Gharbiya - tenancy was almost non-existent.   This suggests that the proportion of larger farms in the village is strongly associated with the level of tenancy.   Although between a half and a third of all units renting-in land were also landholders in their own right, the majority of renters were households without any owned land.24

Thus, the post-1952 redistribution of land not only led to a direct decrease in the number of landless households dependent on agriculture, but also stimulated a market in tenancies at the base of the land operating structure.   This has naturally tended to constrain the supply of hired labour to agriculture. In other words, the consequences of both the redistributive and employment-generating interventions of the state over the last three decades have been to whittle down the reservoir of available labour in the agricultural sector.

In the case of adult male labour, two features stand out most strikingly: firstly, the growth of non-agricultural work opportunities, including education, and secondly, when looked at in terms of the household male labour supply function, (with nearly 80% of farm units falling below 3 feddans in size) farming has increasingly become a part-time occupation. However, it is important to know whether the ownership or renting of land has actually been a major constraint in itself on the release of labour.   This point was strongly emphasised by Hansen & Radwan who argued that small farms 'locked-in' labour,   thereby   reducing   the   level   of   labour   market participation.25   It has been further argued that this has been particularly prominent in the case of the poorer house-holds, where non-agricultural work had rarely been secured. Using the Farm Management Survey Data for 1976/77, Goueli further argued that heads of household for small farms worked, on average, for around ninety days in a year.26   In other words, heads of household were normally employed for a third of their available time. With much importance still accorded to the ownership of land, both as security and status, the prevailing system of land distribution tended to trap labour resources in a situation of quasi-structural under-employment.

The 1984 evidence does not fully substantiate this line of reasoning. As this chapter has shown, very significant num-bers of male household members, irrespective of farm size, work off the farm for their principal employment. However, many with non-agricultural primary employment work on their own farms in a secondary capacity. One consequence of this has been a significant growth in the hiring-in of labour by small farms.

In the case of male heads of household for farms of below 3 feddans, it was found that just over half worked on their own farms as primary employment. A further 13% worked as agri-cultural labourers. For the former, nearly two-thirds worked on-farm for the entire year, with a further 25% working on-farm for 7-9 months in each year. For the full sample of male household heads, over 40% reported having secondary work. Of those with secondary work, on-farm work accounted for between 10-11 weeks in each year on average. Of the total sample of those reporting an inability to secure hired agricultural work at some point in the year, household heads with farming as their primary employment comprised some 35% of respondents.

Roughly 17% of the available labour time for those who reported such difficulties could be classed as 'without work'. When this was computed in terms of total available labour time for for household heads with farming as their primary occupa-tion, the share fell to below 4%. This suggests very strongly that the 'locking-in' of family, particularly household head, labour on small farms is no longer a major feature of the rural employment structure. Seasonal scarcity of work appears to be far more acute among male workers principally employed in agricultural labouring. To that extent, households with limited endowments of land and assets which have not diver-sified the employment 'portfolios' of their labour force have continued to fare more poorly than others.

This chapter has demonstrated that the widespread perception of labour scarcity in the agricultural sector can best be understood in terms of the growth in non-farm employment and, in particular, growth in state sector employment. This has had major implications both for the distribution of household

male labour time and for household income levels. In addition, the growth in current demand for non-agricultural
employment has been dynamically associated with a deepened
demand for education. This has not had drastic implications
for own-farm labour requirements, given the small size of most
farms, but it has resulted in two associated trends. Male
household members with non-farm employment as their primary
occupation have a high probability of working on-farm in a
secondary capacity. Secondly, employment diversification has
deepened the demand for hired labour, even among these
smallest farm units. Thus, the apparent tightness in the
labour market, itself largely a tightening in the male agricultural labour market, can be explained in terms of the
substitution effect generated at farm level by the allocation
of family male labour time outside agriculture.

However, it appears that the commonly postulated labour supply
lag has been rather less general than imagined. Rather,
labour scarcity remains a significant issue for the limited
number of larger farm households. Most small farm units have
undergone a complex process of adaptation, involving both the
introduction of mechanical energy and the substitution of
female and child labour for male labour as a result of recent
shifts in the framework of the labour market. Before exa-
mining how far machine energy has replaced human and animal
energy, Chapter 8 analyses the implications of recent shifts
in employment and wages for farm profitability and aggregate
household income.

Footnotes

1.   Richards and Martin, 1983.
2(a) Determinants of Number of Agricultural Sector Workers
      per Household, 1984

      Dependent Variable: K40 = Number of Workers whose
      Primary Employment is in Agricultural Sector.

      Mean: 1.05
      C.V.: 75.68

Explanatory Variable	Regression Coefficient	Standard Error	Significance Level (PRT)
K2	0.3033	0.0614	0.0001
K4	0.1169	0.1741	0.0855
K9	1.0125	0.1713	0.0001
K14	1.3828	0.6794	0.0436
Constant	0.6022	0.1751	0.0008

R^2 = 0.3099 F Value = 13.47 No. of Observations = 156

Variables Dictionary:
K2 = Number Adult Males : K4 = Number Adult Females
K9 = Proportion Educated Males : K14 = Number
Non-Resident Males

2(b) Dependent Variable: Own Farm Work as Primary Employment

Independent Variable	Estimate	Standard Error	Significance Level
Head of Household	0.4412	0.0240	.0001
Constant	0.0467	0.0098	.0001

R^2 = 0.26

3.   Richards and Martin, 1983, pp22/23; El Issawy, 1983(b), pp44-47.

4.   Cochrane and Oubouzar, in IBRD, 1981, pp106-109.

5.   It should be noted that, while in the recent past Egypt has devoted over 5% of its GDP to education, both capital and recurrent expenditures have been biased towards secondary and higher education. In the mid-1970s expenditures were allocated as follows; 30% to primary education, 14% to preparatory, 18% to secondary and 24% to universities.

6.   For details of those schemes, see Hansen and Radwan, 1982, pp43-45.

7.   Shortage of teachers, linked to large classes and low investment in infrastructure have commonly resulted in inadequate standards of instruction. The shortage of teaching staff is closely associated with the demand for such skilled labour in the Gulf states. See, Abdel Fadil, in Abdel Khalek and Tignor, 1983, pp351-374.

8.   Fields, 1974, pp906-925; Blaug, 1973.

9.   Mohie-eldin, 1966; Mead, 1967.

10. Abdel Fadil, 1975; Radwan, 1977, pp22; Hansen and Marzouk, 1966, pp37-39.

11. Ammar, 1944, pp289-290.

12. Mohie-eldin, 1975.

13. ibid., See also, Hansen, 1969, pp304-306.

14. Hansen and El Tomy, 1965, p408.

15. Mohie-eldin, 1966.

16. See, Abdel Fadil, 1975, pp42/3; Radwan, 1977, pp34-36.

17. CAPMAS, LFS, 1981.

18. Richards and Martin, 1983, p42.

19. CAPMAS, Labour Force Sample Surveys, 1971, 1974, 1976, 1981.

20. Abdel Fadil, 1983.

21. Hansen and Marzouk, 1965, p35.

22. For instance, Reiss, Lutfi et al., 1982, p41; Hopkins et al., 1982.

23. Abdel-Fadil,1980,pp5-26.

24. Most rented areas fell below 2 feddans and were cash rented. Sharecropping was virtually non-existent.

25. Hansen and Radwan, 1982, pp144-153.

26. Goueli, 1980.

CHAPTER EIGHT

Output, Costs and Income

Introduction

This chapter seeks to examine the production framework of the
Egyptian farm household, concentrating on the output households generate by employment of a combination of productive
factors, the costs engendered in so doing and the overall
income configuration of the sampled households. The
discussion will be broken down into a number of sections. In
the first place, the focus will be on the relative productive
efficiency of farm households in Egyptian agriculture.
Although, given the impact of land reform, differences in land
endowments are far less substantial than in most ldc economies
and variations in the quality of land and availability of
inputs have a relatively limited role in generating a wide
spread of productivity levels, the relationship between farm
size and productivity is explored in some detail. Secondly,
analysis is made of the evolution of returns to particular
crops and rotations in the recent period. Thirdly, the nature
of market engagement and sales is dealt with on a crop basis.
A number of hypotheses are tested with regard both to the
determinants of food - as proxied by cereals - production and
marketing. Apart from deriving the co-ordinates of household
crop income, this exercise was undertaken as a means for
establishing whether small farm crop production follows a
strategy of minimising market purchases. This traditional
characterisation of basic self-sufficiency as the goal of that
portion of output not subject to forced delivery is examined.
Lastly, the source and volume of crop revenues and values are
combined with information concerning non-crop income.
Aggregate household income, as also adjusted per capita incomes, have been estimated and some tentative conclusions
regarding the incidence of poverty among rural land holding
households have been reached.

Productivity: Evidence from the 1984 Survey

Discussions about productive efficiency of agriculture in economies with broadly comparable production frameworks, cropping

Table 8.1: Crop Yields per Feddan, 1984 by Farm Size

Farm Size Feddans	Wheat (Ardab)	Cotton (Qantar)	Rice (Ardab)	Maize (Ardab)
0-1	8.97 (1.98)	7.83 (1.71)	18.86 (5.21)	13.37 (2.87)
1-3	7.97 (2.58)	8.27 (1.31)	21.87 (3.60)	12.83 (2.53)
3-5	7.95 (1.56)	8.90 (1.04)	21.07 (3.27)	12.54 (1.52)
5-10	8.20 (1.68)	8.80 (1.07)	22.67 (2.98)	12.81 (2.25)
>10	6.05 (3.42)	9.50 -	28.33 (2.36)	13.88 (1.31)
All	8.25	8.21	20.87	12.99

(Standard deviation in brackets)

Table 8.2: Proportion of Households Growing Major Crops

Farm Size	Wheat %	Cotton %	Rice %	Maize %
0-1	57.1	84.3	54.2	77.1
1-3	84.3	85.7	61.4	94.3
3-5	83.3	94.4	66.6	100.0
5-10	100.0	70.0	90.0	100.0
>10	66.6	33.3	66.6	100.0

patterns and input utilisation have commonly concluded that
productivity per acre tends to be inversely related to the
size of operated holding. This argument has been advanced at
most length and with considerable debate in the Indian context.[1] Even so there is little general consensus and a wide
range of empirical findings has been unable to produce conclusive evidence one way or other. The debate has had virtually
no resonance in the Egyptian context as, firstly, land reform
measures have already been implemented and in a comparatively
thorough-going manner. Secondly, the variance in productive
conditions - at least within the core area of Egyptian agriculture, the Delta - has been slight. The fact that all
cultivation is irrigated, that fertiliser has been heavily
subsidised and that distribution has been a quasi-monopoly of
the state has had obvious implications for the level of
variance in productivity.

Amongst other results, this has meant a relative homogeneity
in the cropping pattern and in the volume of output per unit
of land across farm size class. Table 8.1 presents data concerning the variation in crop yield by farm size class. The
four principal crops grown in the sampled villages are listed.
However, given the nature of birseem's end product, it was
impossible to estimate differences in productivity across farm
size. Yields for cotton and rice were between 15%-20% higher
than the national average, while maize output was around the
national mean. Wheat yields were around 18% lower. However,
this was caused largely by the very low level of productivity
in the Dakhaliya village. In the other two villages wheat
output per feddan was comparable to or in excess of the
national average.

The evidence presented here displays no one uniform trend for
crop production. While wheat yields tend to fit an inverse
pattern, this is not the case for cotton and rice. In the
case of maize, it is interesting to note that yields for the
smallest farms tend to be higher than for intermediate categories. However, large farms (over 10 feddans) have comparable or higher levels of land productivity.

The relationship between land productivity - measured both in
value terms for output as a whole and in physical terms for
the major individual crops - and farm size was tested statistically. However, it would be as well to remember that

where, in the Indian context, an inverse relationship has been
satisfactorily estimated the principal explanatory variables
have been the higher intensity of cultivation and the cropping
pattern.[2]   In the equations specified here, the latter was
implicitly accounted for in terms of the variable, total value
of crop production.   The former factor was not explicitly
included.   This was because there was little variation in the
cropping intensity across farm size.   Secondly, fallow land
was almost non-existent and the reference period for the survey comprises a two-crop cycle.   In other words, the total
land cultivated in any one season measured the land used by
the household in the agricultural year.   Lastly, no attempt
was made to grade the quality of land. This would in any event
have provided a measure of productivity, precisely the phenomenon that one is attempting to measure.   Information was
however collected on the value of owned land and the level of
variation in average land values can be seen in   Table 8.3
below.   There is a clear positive association with farm size
which suggests that the larger units either control better
quality land, or, more likely, have higher land values on
account of investment (drains, irrigation and so on).   Land
values are around a third higher for larger farms than for the
smallest category.   However, all farms have access to irrigation and the degree of variance in land quality in the Delta
remains relatively slight.   For these reasons, variation in
land quality was not included in the equations. Nevertheless,
it should be remembered that the levels of variance in yield
across farm size class are consistently lower than the imputed
variation in land quality, using land values as the proxy.   If
land values were a true reflection of a difference in the productive endowment, this would suggest that, controlling for
this feature, small farm yields were generally superior or at
least equal to those registered by the larger enterprises.

Data for the four major crops where information concerning
physical yields was available (wheat, rice, maize and cotton)
were included.   With birseem these crops accounted for over
96% of the cropped area in the sampled villages.

Regressing physical yield per feddan for individual crops on
operated area yielded the expected positive association between operated area and land productivity from the cotton and
rice equations, but for the other crops no coherent pattern
emerged that was statistically significant.   However, when the

Table 8.3:   Average Value of Land per Feddan, 1984:By Farm Size

Farm Size (feddans)	Value (£E per Feddan)
0-1	9740
1-3	10800
3-5	11150
5-10	13090
>10	12700

Table 8.4:   Average Labour Productivity: By Farm Size and Crop, 1984; Output per Labour Hour (Physical Units - Kgs)

Crop	0-1	1-3	3-5	5-10	>10
Wheat	8.4	8.1	9.4	10.8	7.5
Cotton	2.1	2.1	2.7	2.3	1.5
Rice	5.7	5.3	6.0	7.7	8.3
Maize	5.0	6.0	6.4	6.3	6.9

total value of crop production per feddan was regressed on the
operated area (or gross cropped area) in linear form, a coefficient of £4.46 per qirat, or £107.04 per feddan, was yielded
with a constant term of 1796 and a mean value of £2002 per
feddan. The positive sign for the constant indicated that the
crop value per operated area tended to decline with area
operated. This was confirmed when the regression was run in
log-linear form where the coefficient was significantly below
one.[3] The regression results are further confirmed by Table
8D (Appendix) where it emerges that crop values per feddan do
indeed rise for farms of up to ten feddans but fall off for
the larger units. Nevertheless, the value differential between the smallest farms and those with the highest per unit
values - the 5-10 feddan holdings - exceeded 50%. This may
partly be due to soil quality differences. In particular, it
is likely to reflect the level of investment in drainage on
farm, as well as the relative accessibility of irrigation.
With cropping intensities varying to a very small extent
across farm size this latter factor has limited implications
for intra-farm size productivity variation. What proved more
significant were differences in the cropping pattern.
Although virtually all farms had sown the standard crops, the
rotational combination was an important factor in determining
the overall value of crop output when measured over the full
agricultural year.

The information presented above demonstrated that, in the
first place, productivity of land varies within a relatively
narrow band. Secondly, there was no clear trend when
disaggregating by farm size. In the case of two of the major
crops - rice and cotton - there appears to have been a positive association between output per feddan and farm size.
This is interesting, if only because both crops are the most
labour intensive of the core crops sown in the sample catchment area. At the same time - as will become clear in Chapter
9 - such yield differences cannot be explained by differences
in the availability and utilisation of machinery. The labour
intensive tasks - cotton picking and harvesting, rice
transplanting and cutting - have not been subject to any
degree of mechanisation. With relatively homogenous production functions, the idea that small farms devote labour time
to crop production without regard for conventional marginal
product-wage valuation does not hold. In any event, it is
clear that land productivity exhibits no real bias towards

small farms whose labour endowments and scarcity of land assets might, in other circumstances, have been conducive to higher levels of average land productivity.

The small farm labour surplus model, with its possible implications for output levels, would appear to lose further credibility if labour use patterns are taken into account. As Chapter 4 demonstrates, there was relatively limited variance in labour inputs committed to crop production across farm size. Moreover, small farms did not, when estimating labour use over a two-season period, have higher labour commitments to arable farming, even though, as expected, the hired component of that labour time was lower than for the larger farms.

When yields were regressed on, firstly, the number of household members with primary employment in the agricultural sector and, secondly, the number of standardised household members, no meaningful association was found to exist. This suggests that productivity cannot be linked to small farm labour retention, given that the smaller units tend still to have a higher proportion of household male members primarily working in agriculture. Furthermore, the hypothesis that productivity might be a function of the relative effort devoted to cultivation, where that effort was itself a function of endogenous (ie household) demand was not sustainable. Household demand - with the implicit assumption that on-farm consumption was the primary rationale for the enterprise outside of the forced deliveries system - proved to have little explanatory power in relation to the level of productivity. However, when individual wheat crop yields were regressed on the proportion of hired to total labour time used in crop production, a negative association was found to be significant at the 1% level.[4] This suggests that family labour may put in greater effort or sustain a higher quality of work. This result did not hold for the remaining crops and the overall significance of the effect cannot have been substantial on average yields by farm size class. With family labour predominating only on the smallest farms, this would have implied a productivity advantage at that level which, it would appear, does not in fact exist.

Leaving aside mechanical and draught animal inputs to crop production, a further set of regressions were run which aimed

to estimate the level of association between labour and
material inputs and yields. Material inputs included seed,
organic and inorganic fertiliser as well as pesticide applica-
tions.   When the gross value of annual crop output was
regressed on the value of the material inputs in linear form,
the coefficient was 1.84 and was significant at the 1% level.
In a hypothetically 'pure' competititive environment the coefficient would have been 1.   However, the regression result
suggests that the value marginal product of material inputs is
not far short of double its price.[5] When analysis was made of
the variation in the use - as represented by the value terms -
of material inputs by crop, although the per feddan values
displayed relatively limited variance across farm size class,
there was overall a definite, though not very   pronounced,
positive relationship between the value of material inputs and
farm size.   The relatively limited variation in inputs use can
largely be attributed to the role of public institutions -
particularly the gamiya - in the distribution of seed and fertiliser.   In addition, in one of the surveyed villages cotton
pesticide spraying was done aerially with a standard charge
being levied in terms of area.

While it is widely believed that larger farmers purchase additional inputs on the open market, despite its formal interdic-
tion, open market prices were generally double those for state
distributed inputs.   Since 1973 input subsidies by the state
have grown very substantially, at a rate roughly commensurate
with the growth in expenditure on food subsidies.[6] Domestic,
state distributed, nitrogen prices have been held down at a
level barely two-fifths of the international equivalent price
in recent years.   One consequence has been that input subsidies (deflated) increased by around six times between
1972/73 and 1980.[7] Another consequence - at the farm level -
has been to restrict the scale of open market purchases of
fertilizer.   Open market purchases - given the price wedge -
tend to occur only when supply is heavily constrained.
However, on the basis of extra-economic considerations large
farms may receive inputs before other farm households, given
the fact that the timely supply of inputs remains both a
bottleneck and a condition for higher productivity.

The relative homogeneity of both material inputs and labour in
crop production across farm size class clearly shows that no
inverse relationship between productivity and labour use and

farm size is observable in Egypt. This may, of course, be
partly a function of the relatively limited spread of holdings
due to land reform, but it would also appear to be closely
related to the changing employment and household labour use
patterns. Thus, even though small farm households continue to
have a higher level of earners or potential earners per feddan
and a higher proportion of the labour force primarily working
in agriculture, this is no longer reflected in higher overall
labour intensities, even if the proportion of family to hired
labour remains inversely associated with farm size. This is
the case despite the continuance of seasonal underemployment
among small farm male household members. This suggests that
levels of labour utilisation in particular tend to be equated,
despite high variation in initial factor endowments. The competitive structure of the agricultural labour market and the
link to farm level labour use would appear to mark a relatively recent departure from earlier practices, although there
has been considerable debate about the relevance of labour
surplus paradigms even for the earlier period.[8]

The balance between family and hired labour and the nature of
the tasks, together with the effort associated with such
tasks, has obvious implications for labour productivity
levels. When average productivity per labour hour was
measured by crop and by farm size, it was found that although
there was a positive association between farm size and labour
productivity, the trend was not discernible for all crops,
nor, as with rice and maize, where productivity increased with
farm size, was the differential between large and small farms
that substantial. Only in the case of rice, where output per
labour hour was over 45% higher on the largest farms than on
the smallest, was the differential substantial.

These results further confirm that small farm production does
not rely on relatively high (and by implication, inferior productivity) inputs of labour, drawing on a readily available
stock of family labour. Physical output per labour unit
showed relatively limited variation across farm size class.
This may best be construed as a reflection of the changing
conditions in the labour market, where standard assumptions
that market prices reflect the opportunity cost of resources
have greater relevance than in the past, at least in terms of
male household labour allocation.

Market Releases

In addition to their traditional typification as labour-rich but asset-poor enterprises, Egyptian small farms have commonly been characterised as largely gearing production towards the satisfaction of their own farm consumption needs. Indeed, it had been the quasi-autarkic nature of the production strategy that had emerged as a hallmark of peasant agriculture in underdeveloped economies. And it has been the shortfall in actual consumption satisfaction and the required level of self-provisioning that has attracted a great deal of practical, let alone scholarly, attention.

In Egypt, while few have historically doubted that self-provisioning was the principal rationale of small farm production, the matter has been further complicated by the long-standing requirement to provide cotton as forced deliveries within the three year rotational system. This has been augmented by the requirement to transfer, at prices generally below the domestic market, let alone border price, rate shares of output of a range of other crops (see Table 8.5). In the survey area, the only other crop that was directly affected in 1984 was rice where a minimum 40% share was compulsorily acquired by the state through the gamiya. In fact, as Table 8.6 demonstrates, somewhat higher proportions were sold to the state, even though the administered farm-gate price was at least 25% lower than the open market price in the immediate post-harvest period.

Although, with the exception of birseem and cotton, all the other major crops that predominated in the survey area were food crops, wheat and maize have always been, and still are, the principal farm food items. In recent years, this picture has become more complicated with the spiralling value of fodder and of wheat straw in particular. This also applies in the case of maize which has emerged as a major summer fodder source. Given the considerable importance of small farm livestock husbandry, the very substantial areas under birseem and maize can be largely understood in this light. Thus, wheat cropping, though still providing a proportion of small farm households' consumption needs (all surveyed villages had at least one miller in the village) also provides livestock feed. While this aspect was not explicitly explored in the 1984 survey, Alderman and von Braun reported that between

Table 8.5: Egypt: Crop Procurement by the Government, 1985

	Output to be sold to Government[a]	Average yield	Proportion of output procured by Government
	Units per Feddan		%[b]
Cotton (metric qantars)	All output	6.8	100
Wheat (ardeb)	1-2-5	10.5	17
Rice (ton)	1-1.5	2.5	50
Sugarcane (ton)	All output	37.6	100
Onions (ton)	6-8	8.7	80
Lentils (ardeb)	1-2.5	3.5	50
Sesame (ardeb)	1-2.5	3.5	50
Groundnuts (ardeb)	2-8	10.9	46
Horsebeans (ardeb)	2-3.5	6.8	40

[a] The upper and lower limits of the range depend on the estimated productivity of the land.

[b] Estimated on the assumption that the average quantity delivered to the Government falls at the midpoint of the range of procurement.

Source: Ministry of Agriculture

Table 8.6: Share of Cereals for Human Consumption and
            Animal Feed, 1981/82

Commodity/ Use	----------Farm Size (feddans)----------				
	0-1	1-3	3-5	5-10	Total
Wheat					
HC	79.5	65.4	62.3	39.6	59.7
AF	0.9	1.6	3.2	3.1	2.3
Maize					
HC	68.5	62.9	63.9	49.1	62.4
AF	19.7	21.1	15.4	12.6	18.5
Sorghum					
HC	38.3	41.7	33.4	49.6	41.1
AF	49.1	47.6	36.1	13.4	39.7
Rice					
HC	29.2	21.9	26.2	22.8	24.1

HC: Human Consumption   AF: Animal Feed

Table relates to farm households' own production.
Shares not consumed by people or fed to animals were sold.

Source: Alderman and Von Braun, 1984 p54

63-79% of wheat and maize output was consumed on farm by humans on units of below three feddans, a further 1%-1.5% of wheat output was used as animal feed with around 20% in the case of maize[9] (see Table 8.6). Where sorghum was grown the latter share rose to nearly half total output. Even for farms of above five feddans it was found that on-farm human and animal consumption accounted for over 42% of total output in the case of wheat, 62%-63% for maize and sorghum and 23% for rice. As expected, the proportion of output retained on-farm declined substantially with an increase in farm size. Although relatively little difference existed between farms of up to five feddans, units with more than this area at their disposal had market release levels at least 50% higher.

The data collected in 1984 show rather high levels of on-farm retention of commodities. As would be expected, the share of farm consumption is inversely related to farm size, with the exception of birseem (see Table 8.7). The association between operated area and marketed releases for cereals was further tested when regressing total crop cash income on operated area. The equation proved to be significant at a 1% level and the shift coefficient indicates that crop cash income increased appreciably with operated area.

The information regarding rice and maize marketing should be seen as rather less reliable than for the other crops. These figures were based on intentions, rather than actual practice, as the data was collected shortly after the sifi harvest. However, the distribution of output according to end-use that is displayed in Table 8.7 gives a slightly misleading picture. While small farm production appears to be largely organised around the human and animal consumption needs of the household, representing the distribution of output income in terms of monetary income flows as a proportion of total crop value gives a somewhat different view of the matter (see Table 8.9). Although a substantial proportion of cash income accrued from forced deliveries of cotton and rice, with the sifi harvest realising over 85% of cash inflow, the variance across farm size is relatively slight. This is partly because birseem output, which is commonly a tradeable for small farm households within the village, tends to be used almost entirely on-farm by the larger units whose livestock holdings are commonly quite substantial. Secondly, the production strategy of most small farms results in cash income being largely the product

Table 8.7: Utilisation of Output by Farm Size and Crop, 1984

Farm Size		Wheat	Beans	Long Birseem	Cotton	Rice	Maize	Short Birseem
0-1	A/C	93.0	87.5	79.5	--	36.7	85.3	75.7
	FMS	7.0	12.5	20.5	--	16.0	14.7	24.3
	GQ	--	--	--	100.0	47.3	--	--
1-3	A/X	80.0	0.2	79.8	--	31.5	70.3	57.9
	FMS	20.0	99.8	20.2	--	20.8	29.7	42.1
	GQ	--	--	--	100.0	47.7	--	--
3-5	A/C	57.5	60.0	70.3	--	35.1	55.5	71.4
	FMS	42.5	40.0	29.7	--	11.5	44.5	28.6
	GQ	--	--	--	100.0	53.4	--	--
5-10	A/C	55.6	--	61.0	--	30.8	48.2	54.3
	FMS	44.4	100.0	39.0	--	16.8	51.8	45.7
	GQ	--	--	--	100.0	52.4	--	--
>10	A/C	21.0	--	91.4	--	18.8	51.3	100.0
	FMS	79.0	100.0	8.6	--	40.0	48.7	--
	GQ	--	--	--	100.0	41.2	--	--

A/C = On-Farm Consumption
FMS = Open Market Sale
GQ = Government Forced Delivery

Table 8.8: Regression Analysis: Total Crop Cash Income on Operated Area

$$\log\ X2 = 0.891 + 1.183\ (\log x\ 12)*$$
$$(0.065)\ (0.04) \qquad R^2 = 0.82$$

where X2 = Crop Cash Income and X12 = Operated Area

*Significance at 1% level - two tailed 't' test
 Standard errors in brackets

of the _sifi_ crop, hence available in November. With even small farms selling around a fifth of their birseem output, this leaves wheat as the only major crop where on-farm consumption is overwhelmingly dominant.

These utilisation patterns have been confirmed by other survey data. An EMCEP survey in Gharbiya, dealing only with farms of below three feddans, estimated that although the proportion of households selling a significant share of total maize output was not much over 10%, off-farm sales for both rice and birseem were substantial.[10] Wheat, as in the 1984 survey, was also marked by its low level of market release, with human, rather than animal, consumption being its most important enduse.

The information presented above strongly suggests that the idea of the small farm as the conjoined site of production and consumption has fairly little relevance in Egypt. This is not only because of the diminutive size of holdings, but also because of marketing strategies and the role of forced deliveries. The IFPRI study referred to earlier estimated that farms of below one feddan had less than 30% self-sufficiency in cereals, but that this rose sharply to over 81% for farms of between one and three feddans.[11] Moreover, the existence of state run distribution systems for subsidised commodities had a crucial role in farm consumption levels and decisions regarding the utilisation of output. Amongst other things, this meant that own-produced commodities were effectively competing not only with open market products, but also with the heavily subsidised commodities distributed through the _gamiya_. In two of the three surveyed villages, consumer co-operatives had been established and these provided a range of products from bread through to frozen fish, meat, soap and jam. It was not possible to test with any precision the effect of subsidised outlets on marketed output in the 1984 survey, but the more extensive IFPRI survey demonstrated that the availability of subsidised cereals did not significantly affect grain sales but was associated with higher levels of per capita consumption.[12] Moreover, for farms of below three feddans, consumption of subsidised cereals exceeded, quite substantially, the share of total cereal production sold to the government at relatively deflated farm-gate prices.

In the 1984 survey, where output was released onto the open

market, the price level variance across farm size was
insubstantial, although there was considerable variance between villages. In the case of rice, open market prices in
November 1984 varied by around 25% across village and in the
case of maize the discrepancy was much higher, approaching
80%.However, monthly variation in open market prices for
cereals was quite pronounced. The price of maize was at least
25%-30% higher three months after the harvest than in the
immediate post-harvest period, while eight months later the
price was over 50% higher. The post harvest price of rice of
14.3 piastres had risen to around 20 piastres by
December/March, 25-29 piastres for April/July and 29-36
piastres for September/October. However, with a ration price
of 14 piastres available to card holders through the consumer
gamiya, the wedge between the open market price and the subsidised rate widened dramatically through the year.
Nevertheless, it is important to note that availability of
ration rice and subsidised commodities has tended to fluctuate
widely while in general lagging substantially below current
demand. In Sharkiya, for example, it was found that allocations of subsidised rice through the gamiya were consistently
constrained because of supply shortfalls. Generally, rice
stocks delivered at the start of each month were exhausted
within two days of arrival. In the case of subsidised flour
and bread, quantity constraints have been far less binding.
In addition, most bread is available through private bakers
rather than through state controlled outlets.

The relationship between food production - as represented by
the output of cereals - and farm consumption and market sales
was explored further by regression analysis. In the first
instance cereal production was regressed on a variety of
variables representing, or proxying, either crop substitutions
or the availability of non-farm derived food sources. In the
latter case, this was taken to mean the presence of state-run
distribution outlets in the village - a consumer co-operative
- or else the presence of private market channels - for
example, bakeries - for the provision of basic consumption
needs. In both the marketing and production equations, cereal
production was the summation of the normalised products from
the three principal cereals: rice, maize and wheat. Neither
sorghum nor barley were grown in any of the villages but, with
the exception of the variable for the price of wheat straw, no
attempt was made to incorporate subsidiary products.

Table 8.9: Cash Income as Proportion of Total Crop Value (primary output): Major Field Crops, 1984

Farm Size (feddans)	Proportion %	Sifi Season Cash Income as % of Total Cash Income
0-1	51.5	91.6
1-3	61.7	87.2
3-5	60.4	87.3
5-10	64.9	67.6
>10	48.0	82.2
All	57.8	83.5

Table 8.10: Determinants of Cereal Production, 1984

Dependent Variable: Cereal Output per household (normalized kg) [v10]
Mean: 3470.71
C.V.:   49.41

Independent Variable	Coefficient	Standard error	Significance level
x12	59.651	3.491	.0001
k1	- 31.102	63.830	.6267
x300	-6239.088	1339.911	.0001
x19	0.598	0.031	.0001
x400	7170.398	1367.344	.0001
x500	-1512.587	372.499	.0001
x600	524.817	90.631	.0001
Constant Term	-3765.614	971.863	.0002

R^2 = 0.93;   F value = 314.97;   No of Observations = 171

Variables Dictionary:

x12 = Operated Area	X300 = Bakery (dummy)
x19 = Livestock Value	X400 = Consumer Cooperative (dummy)
k1 = Household Size (equalised)	X500 = Cotton cultivating household
	x600 = wheat straw price by village

In equation 1, a static investigation of the determinants of cereal production in the sampled villages is attempted. Cereal output (v10) is assumed to be a function of both area and labour endowments, with a range of other market and price features included in the equations. The household's consumption level is proxied by the adjusted number of household members (k1), while x300 and x400 - the presence of a bakery and consumer co-operative - represent non-production associated cereal distribution outlets. The livestock feed/cereal relationship is implicitly tested through the variable (x600), the price of wheat straw in each village. As expected, given the strong positive ratio of secondary output prices to the cereal price, the association between cereal output and the price of wheat straw was positive and statistically highly significant.

The results of the regression are contained in Table 8.10. With the exception of k1 - household size, all variables are significant at a 1% level. Cereal output was found to be positively associated with operated area (with increasing returns). Both livestock variables (x19 and x600) were likewise strongly positive, suggesting that the function of both wheat and maize as livestock feed was a critical factor in the decision to sow cereal crops. The lack of association with adjusted family size further suggests that cereal production was not regulated by endogenous consumption requirements. While the presence of a bakery in the village was, as hypothesised, negatively linked to cereal production, the reverse effect exists for x400 - the presence of a consumer co-operative. The latter's presence might have been assumed to affect rice production levels, but this was not supported by the model's outcome.

A second linear functional form was fitted with the aim of explaining the determinants of marketed cereal output. A number of additional variables were used: y60, the area under birseem; y70, the share of cereal output sold as forced delivery (rice) to the state; and an additional dummy variable for rice cultivation, (y4). As with the production equation, the overall explanatory power of the model was high and the majority of variables were statistically significant. Again, household size (k1) was not a factor explaining the volume of open market cereal releases. Although the sign was negative, the estimate was not statistically significant. The birseem

area variable (y60) displayed a negative association with
market releases which was statistically significant. This
obviously derives from the fact that, for the <u>shitwi</u> season,
wheat and birseem are competing crops. It would appear that
cultivation of birseem as livestock feed does not result in a
higher level of cereals market release and hence should not be
viewed as a complementary output. With regard to farm size
(x12), the relationship is positive and highly significant.

It emerges from the preceding analysis that small farms' production and marketing strategies are not strictly determined
by the aim of maximising food consumption requirements. This
is not only a result of the system of forced deliveries that
operates in Egyptian agriculture. Crop selection has become
increasingly biased towards livestock feed production.
Moreover, small farms market a significant quantum of birseem
output, the principal livestock feed. In addition, marketing
of traditional food crops occurs even for the smallest units.
This cannot, in general, be explained in terms of 'distress
sales'. Rather, this reflects both the shift in the production and marketing strategies of farm households as well as
the growth in the availability of subsidised food distributed
through the consumer co-operatives and ration shops.

Production Costs and the Structure of Returns

The previous sections have concentrated on the relative productive efficiency of Egyptian farms as well as the utilisation of the outputs created by that production process. Both
the utilisation of labour on-farm and the disposal of non-
forced delivery output suggest strongly that the small farm
enterprise can no longer be adequately theorised within a
simple, quasi-autarkic, labour abundance framework.
Production and marketing decisions are strongly coloured by
the growth of non-farm male employment and by the availability
of subsidised food commodities. Production for home consumption can better be understood in terms of the provision of
domestically produced livestock feed, rather than provision of
sufficient cereal output. To that extent, the cropping pattern and broader allocation of resources in the sample area
closely replicate the trend that has emerged at a national
level. Accordingly, this section examines the role of prices
in the allocation of land and resources to particular crops.

Table 8.11: <u>Determinants of Open Market Cereals Releases</u>

<u>Dependent Variable:</u> Cereal Free Market Sales (normalized kg) [v51]
<u>Mean:</u> 1208.9kgs
<u>C.V.:</u> 87.00

Independent Variable	Coefficient	Standard error	Significance level
Y4	- 217.812	253.401	0.3913
Y3	- 231.151	239.479	0.3359
K1	- 69.876	40.439	0.0860
Y60	- 34.251	6.602	0.0001
X600	64.835	59.191	0.2750
Y70	456.666	820.238	0.5785
X300	- 220.824	223.542	0.3247
X12	47.559	3.253	0.0001
X19	0.343	0.023	0.0001
Constant Term	- 547.689	624.648	0.0038

R^2 = 0.89;   F value = 150.8;   No of Observations = 168

<u>Variables Dictionary:</u>

     Y4   = Rice Cultivation (dummy)
     Y60 = Area under Birseem
     Y70 = Proportion of total cereal output as forced deliveries
     Y3   = Cotton cultivation (dummy)
     X600 = Wheat Straw Price
     X300 = Bakery (dummy)
     X12 = Operated Area
     X19 = Livestock Value
     k1   = Household size (equalised)

Emphasis is placed on analysis of farm production costs and the structure of comparative returns within the range of available crops. At the same time the cross-sectional data from the 1984 survey is complemented by recent time-series data.

An examination of the distribution of the cropped area over the recent past shows that while birseem, wheat, cotton, maize and rice are the staples of lower Egypt agriculture, their relative shares and the importance of horticultural crops have varied considerably. Furthermore, evidence suggests that, with suitable lagging, area-price and area-revenue response models account very well for such variations.[13]

At a simple descriptive level, it appears that since the early 1970s the area allocated to fruit production and to vegetables has risen particularly sharply. In a rather longer-term frame-work, it is also possible to see that the area allocations to birseem have continued to rise, while crops that to varying degrees have been controlled - cotton, rice and beans - have all experienced downward area/allocations. In the early 1950s cotton accounted for around 19% of the cropped area, beans 3.5% and wheat 16.7%, but by the early 1980s their respective shares had fallen to around 11%, 2.2% and 12.4%.

Trends in the respective area allocations, in gross output and in yields are shown in Graphs 8.1 and 8.2 which cover the last decade. From these, it can be seen that both wheat and rice output have either fallen or stagnated. Despite higher variability in output the same trend has also held for beans. Only maize and cotton have shown a reasonably consistent upward trend.

The physical measure of land productivity over the last three decades is given in Table 8.12, where it can be seen that for the major Delta crops productivity growth in the full period has been quite impressive. However, in the last ten years only cotton and, to a lesser extent, maize have experienced a continuing rapid rate of increase. Thus, even though Egyptian crop yields are undoubtedly high when compared with world averages, recent performance has been rather disappointing with yields tending to decline in the 1970s. This might be construed as a classic Ricardian condition, but it is also

Graph 8.1

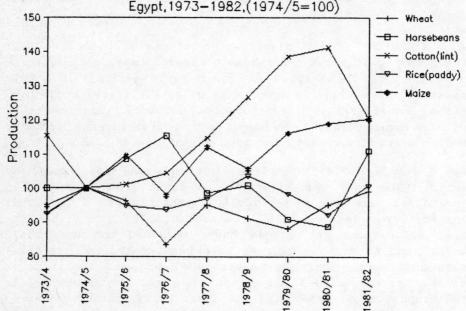

Indices of Agricultural Production and Yield
Egypt,1973−1982,(1974/5=100)

Graph 8.2

Indices of Agricultural Production and Yield

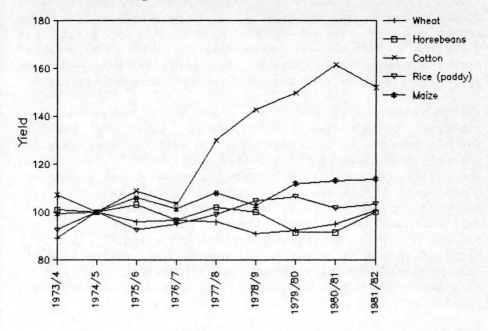

true to say that productivity has continued to be constrained
because of poor drainage and sub-optimal cropping practices.
Recent estimates have suggested that actual yields are around
60% of their potential level in the case of food crops and
around a third that level in the case of vegetables.[14]
However, any analysis concerned with developments over the
recent past has to acknowledge that land productivity has
risen at a very gradual pace for the main farm outputs.
Recent attempts at introducing new packages - as with the
Tobruk 4 rice package - have had a very chequered history.

The relationship between areas planted and prices has been
explored in a standard regression model by Cuddihy.
Significant correlation was found to exist between relative
prices, yields and cropping patterns, with both planted area
and yield varying with changes in relative prices of
outputs.[15] At the same time, there is a fair amount of evidence to suggest that area controls have themselves been subject to 'market pressure' through non-compliance and the
payment of fines rather than forced cultivation.[16] Until the
start of this decade, the actual cotton area was consistently
below the planned area. Recent price increments have reduced
this gap. In the case of rice, actual allocations have fallen
consistently below planned levels.

There is no doubt that the state can control area allocations
if it desired but in recent years there have been signs that
enforcement has been relaxed and fines less rigorously levied.
In 1984 it was found that in Sharkiya fines for non-growing of
cotton were c. £E100 per feddan. However, actual levying of
these fines was less consistent and, as evasion of planned
allocations was very strongly correlated with farm size, the
question of local power and extra-economic considerations
become factors of significance. With lower allocations to
cotton, large farms had, as expected, higher proportions of
the cropped area under long birseem and maize than was the
case for the bulk of agricultural producers. Possibly the
most direct way of understanding the shifts in cropping over
the recent period is by looking at the structure of returns to
particular crops. Graph 8.3 presents this information for the
period 1965-1980, where net returns are calculated as primary
and secondary output by price minus the cost of production,
where the latter figure includes wages and rent. From this
graph it is obvious that over the period 1973-1980 returns to

Table 8.12:   Yields for Major Field Crops 1950-1982 (1950/4 = 100)

Year	Wheat	Cotton (lint)	Rice	Maize	Sugarcane	Sorghum
1955/59	116	104	133	98	109	107
1960/64	129	120	140	118	112	121
1965/69	128	134	132	167	113	142
1970/74	157	151	140	172	107	145
1975/79	164	163	141	177	99	133
1980/82	167	208	150	191	99	133

Sources: El Tobgy, 1976 pp91ff: ARE, Ministry of Agriculture

Table 8.13:   Returns per Feddan, 1980

Crop	Net Return (£E)	Rank	Crop Duration (months)	Return per Month (£E)	Standardised Man-Days	Return per Man-Day (£E)	Rank
Wheat	28.2	6	7	4.03	28.1	1.0	4
Maize	83.0	4	5	16.60	64.3	1.3	3
Rice	46.6	5	5	9.32	79.1	0.6	6
Cotton	107.8	2	8	13.48	124.2	0.9	5
Long Birseem	190.0	1	7	27.14	38.5	4.9	2
Short Birseem	94.6	3	4	23.65	17.7	5.3	1

Source: Ministry of Agriculture, A.R.E.

Graph 8.3

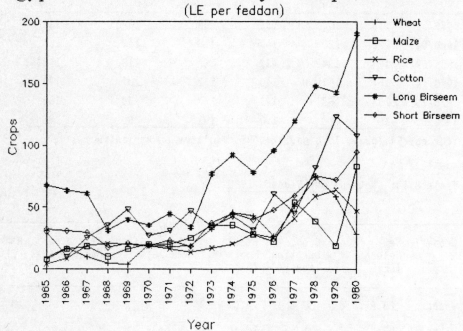

Egypt:Net Returns for Major Crops,1965-1980
(LE per feddan)

birseem cultivation (particularly long birseem) have been
significantly above other crops, even though net returns to
cotton cultivation rose quite sharply after 1977. In terms of
the principal rotations it emerges that for the three-year
period 1978-1980 the most attractive rotations all involved
cultivation of long birseem in the <u>shitwi</u> season, with rice or
maize as the <u>sifi</u> crop returning roughly comparable rates.

However, a somewhat modified picture emerges when account is
taken of both the volume of standardised man-days' input by
crop, and the period over which the specific crop remains on
the ground.   Table 8.13 presents this information for 1980
where it can be seen that, controlling for labour time and the
period of maturation, both varieties of birseem offer private
rates of return considerably in excess of those realised
through the choice of other crops. Returns per labour day
were, on average, around five times the returns from other
crops. This structure of profitability, even allowing for
full use of shadow wage rates for family labour, naturally
explains the growing land allocations to birseem in the winter
season and maize in the summer. It should be emphasised that
in the 1984 survey 30% of the cropped area was under long and
short birseem with a further 24% accounted for by maize. Even
if soil conditions in the sampled villages were unfavourable
for the cultivation of vegetables or fruits, these two crops
accounted for over half the crop allocation.   Official
Ministry of Agriculture data on alternative crop profitability
for 1984 and 1985 also indicate that, with the exception of
onions, the returns for long birseem cultivation were significantly higher than for other field crops. One need look no
further than the comparative distribution of returns to fathom
the reasons for this set of preferences.

Earlier analysis of the area response to revenues yielded particularly high levels of association. However, given the nature of farm production in Egypt, actual calculation of
comparative net returns raises a number of methodological
issues. In the following analysis, a range of cost and returns
estimates will be listed, where the principal differences will
be in the attribution of shadow wages to family labour and the
inclusion of imputed rental charges. While, at this stage,
attention will be paid principally to calculation of gross
margins, some attempt will be made to compute the changing
distribution of factor shares in the production cost structure.

This is of particular significance given the apparent increases in real wage levels in Egyptian agriculture.

Graphs 8.4 to 8.7 represent, in index form with 1970-72 as the base year, the relationship between four variables. In addition to the official figures relating to costs of production the trend in such costs, exclusive of wages, is given alongside the direction of producer prices for the individual crops and the rural cost of living index. From these it can be seen that with the possible exception of maize at the end of the reference period, costs of production have significantly run ahead of both farm-gate prices and the general rural rate of inflation. In other words, if labour was consistently valued at its opportunity cost, farm producers have been progressively squeezed by the inflation in costs over the last decade. However, if the cost of production minus wages index is compared with the trend in producer prices and the rural cost of living, the disparity still holds, except in the case of cotton (where labour is, of course, a particularly prominent input but at a lower differential). For both wheat and rice, irrespective of which production cost measure is used, farm-gate prices have consistently lagged behind the rate of increment in incurred costs. However, returns to wheat are probably understated in so far as the value of secondary output has increased at a rapid rate in time with the expansion of the domestic meat market. As regards the internalised structure of comparative crop costs, it appears that the ratio of cotton (the crop with the highest absolute production cost) to maize, rice and beans, costs of production have remained broadly constant but have widened significantly with regard to wheat. While the wheat:cotton cost ratio was around 1:1.8 in the early 1970s,[17] a decade later this had shifted to 1:2.6.

If production costs have tended to run ahead of the rate of increase in farm-gate prices for the major field crops, it is clearly of interest to disaggreate these trends and isolate those factor costs that have been primarily responsible, mostly post-1979, for this disequilibrium. Given the widespread belief that labour costs have spiralled in this period, the share of wages in total costs requires detailed analysis. Close scrutiny of the evolution of the shares of total costs over the last ten years reveals that the proportion of total costs accounted for by material inputs (seeds,

Graph 8.4

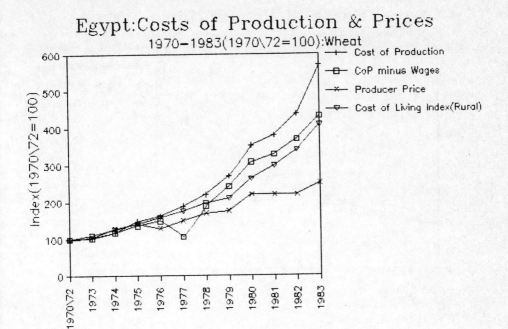

Egypt:Costs of Production & Prices
1970–1983(1970\72=100):Wheat

- —+— Cost of Production
- —□— CoP minus Wages
- —×— Producer Price
- —▽— Cost of Living Index(Rural)

Graph 8.5

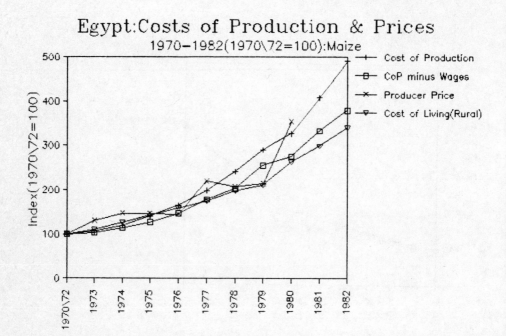

Egypt:Costs of Production & Prices
1970–1982(1970\72=100):Maize

Cost of Production
CoP minus Wages
Producer Price
Cost of Living(Rural)

Graph 8.6

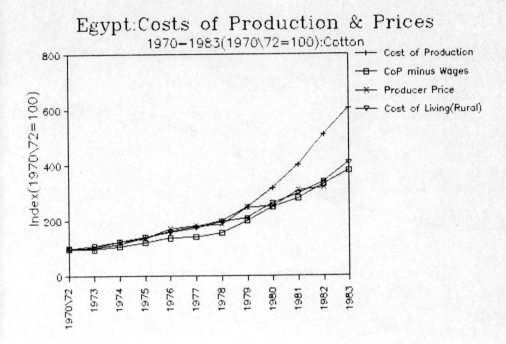

Egypt:Costs of Production & Prices
1970—1983(1970\72=100):Cotton

Graph 8.7

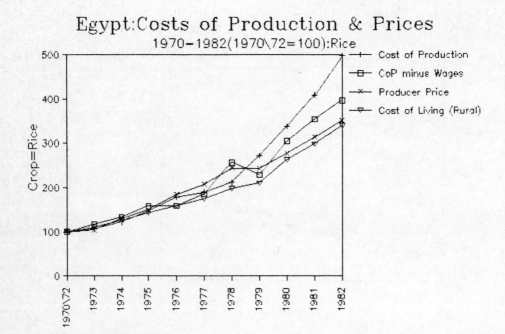

Egypt:Costs of Production & Prices
1970−1982(1970\72=100):Rice

fertiliser and pesticides) has declined, as has the share of
rent. In general, the proportion appropriated by draught animal charges declined and, as expected, this was accompanied by
an increasing share of machinery charges in total costs. Even
so, mechanical energy costs were as low as 7%-8% for cotton.
It is only in the case of wheat (15%-16%) and rice (13%-14%)
that machine charges have exceeded a tenth of total costs.
Moreover, in the case of rice, mechanical energy costs were
broadly the same share as in the early 1970s. This confirms,
once again, the fact that wheat is the only major field crop
that has seen a relatively wide spread of mechanisation.

What is striking in the analysis of official cost of production data is the degree to which costs have been ratcheted
upwards through increased labour factor shares. This is
revealed in Table 8.14 which demonstrates that labour cost as
a proportion of total cost rose for all field crops between
1970 and 1984. These calculations are, it should be remembered, based on shadow rates for family workers. To that
extent they clearly overstate _actual_ money costs as a proportion of total costs.

The data collected in the 1984 survey regarding costs of production, proportions of output marketed, prices received and
net returns have the advantage of being decomposed by farm
size category. Unlike the information presented by official
data, this allows for analysis of the variations in cost
structure and cost shares across farm size. Two sets of
results were tabulated. In the first place, nominal costs of
production were estimated. Here, no shadow rate was imputed
to family labour or to owned machinery or livestock. However,
in the case of machinery, basic running costs, but not depreciation, were included. The second calculation involved
imputing opportunity costs to owned inputs and family labour.
However, the cost of material inputs (seed, pesticide, fertiliser) remained unchanged. In both estimates no attempt was
made to impute a shadow water cost, irrigation being a free
good in Egypt, nor, when it came to calculating net returns,
was any allowance made for asset deterioration or interest
payments. This can be excused as the aim was to chart the
input:output relationship. The returns were generated by a
given use of assets.

Given the prominence of labour charges in production costs,

Table 8.14: <u>Labour costs as a proportion of Total Costs of</u>
<u>Egypt: Production 1970-1984</u>

Years	Cotton	Maize	Wheat	Rice	Beans	Birseem
1970-72	30.9	23.3	16	26.5	19.8	27.4
1973-75	35.7	27.7	19.2	28.8	25.9	25.6
1976-78	36.5	33.3	34.5	35.1	30.8	28.8
1979-81	47.3	35.6	26.5	34.5	31.8	25.8
1982-85	58.6	45.1	38.7	46.8	42.7	30.2**

** 1982/83

Source: Ministry of Agriculture, A.R.E.

Table 8.15: <u>Determinants of Production Costs: Labour</u>
(log-linear)

Rice-log m68 $= 1.6390 + 0.3368Y*$ $\quad R^2 = 0.51$
$\quad\quad\quad\quad\quad (0.0728)\ (0.0326)$

Maize-log n68 $= 1.3031 + 0.4812Y*$ $\quad R^2 = 0.68$
$\quad\quad\quad\quad\quad (0.0607)\ (0.0280)$

Long Birseem $= 1.4743 + 0.3290 *$ $\quad R^2 = 0.42$
-log p68 $\quad (0.1067)\ (0.0529)$

Short Birseem $= 0.9684 + 0.0802 *$ $\quad R^2 = 0.70$
-log o68 $\quad (0.0802)\ (0.0479)$

Cotton-log r68 $= 1.1461 + 0.5233 *$ $\quad R^2 = 0.56$
$\quad\quad\quad\quad\quad (0.1004)\ (0.0387)$

Wheat-log t68 $= 1.6132 + 0.3066 *$ $\quad R^2 = 0.38$
$\quad\quad\quad\quad\quad (0.0644)\ (0.0362)$

All Crops $= 1.4480 + 0.5284 *$ $\quad R^2 = 0.66$
-log q68 $\quad (0.0834)\ (0.0294)$

* significant at 1% level

the structure of nominal costs shows the cost of production rising, almost uniformly, by farm size class. In general for the major field crops, the cost differential between the smallest and largest units averaged over 60%, falling to around 25% in one of the villages where average production costs were almost half those of the other two sampled villages.

When shadow rates were imputed for family labour and owned animal or mechanical energy inputs, the picture changed considerably with production costs per feddan tending to be inversely related to farm size. With the possible exception of wheat, costs on the largest farms were around two-thirds the levels registered by the smallest enterprises.

In disaggregating total costs, it was found that (exclusive of rent) labour charges exhibited a relatively limited band of variation. In the case of nominal costs the smallest farms had a labour share in costs of around 43%, rising, for the largest enterprises, to 61%. In the shadow cost calculation wages accounted for between 54.4% to 54.8% of total charges. As expected, the labour share was significantly lower for birseem (particularly short birseem) and for wheat, where the share of mechanical energy costs was noticeably higher than for other crops. With the exception of wheat, shadow labour charges tended to rise, as a proportion of total costs, in proportion to farm size. This points, yet again, to the fairly limited impact of labour-substituting technology, even on the larger units.

When comparing the 1984 data with the most recent Ministry of Agriculture figures for the labour share (and eliminating the rent element in costs) it seems that over the period 1982/3-1984/85 the share of wages rose slightly for wheat, more strongly for rice and maize but remained roughly constant in the case of cotton. This is also confirmed when using survey-generated figures collected for the 1980/81 season by the EWUP project as the benchmark.[18] The labour share appears to have risen by about 10% for wheat, around 15% for maize but remained constant in the case of cotton.

The relationship between costs of production and share of labour was further estimated by fitting the following functional form: $logX = loga + blogY$, where X = nominal cost of

production per feddan (by crop) and Y = hired labour hours.
In all cases the equations proved significant at a 1(*)%
level. Standard errors are given in brackets.

The variable q68 - all crops - effectively represents the
basket of crops and inputs in the agricultural year 1983/84.
With the exception of birseem, a crop which uses substantially
less hired labour time than the other major field crops, the
results listed above suggest that for a 1% increase in hired
labour hours, nominal production costs experience an increase
of between 0.3% and 0.5%

As for the distribution of costs it is interesting to note
that, other than those appropriated by labour, the share of
machinery charges has increased, but largely at the expense of
draught animal costs. Although this point will be explored in
more detail in the chapter on mechanisation (Chapter 9), it
seems apt to point out here that in a weighted two-season cost
framework, machine costs comprised nearly 13% of total shadow
costs (20% of nominal costs). This calculation excluded rent,
with machine costs also comprising technology such as the
saqia. In the case of most hired equipment there was also a
hidden labour component. This is because tractor and thresher
hire, for example, comprised not only the hire cost of the
machine, but also its operative. To this extent, the share of
machinery will tend to be overstated. However, it does
suggest that if cost proportions are indicative of the scale
and depth of machine usage in Egyptian agriculture, then the
level of mechanisation has remained relatively constant over
the last eight years. Although machinery costs have probably
declined in real terms, the types of machinery currently
available have changed to a very limited extent in this
period.

Two methods for the calculation of the structure of returns
for crop production were employed, one using nominal costings
and the other where shadow rates were included for draught
power, mechanical energy inputs and family labour. In neither
calculation was rent included, at least initially. Table 8.16
lists returns to the cultivation of the major field crops.
When actual costings were employed it is readily apparent that
long birseem and cotton returned the highest rates.
Particularly substantial margins existed for birseem on the
larger farms and this was a function of the intensity of the

Table 8.16:

i) <u>Returns per Feddan (Nominal Costs), 1984</u>

Farm Size (feddans)	Cotton	Wheat	Rice	Maize	Long Birseem	Short Birseem	Beans
0-1	305	193	182	170	280	79	31
1-3	241	137	178	130	301	50	90
3-5	249	146	158	96	172	41	9
5-10	247	125	140	110	327	120	77
>10	233	41	258	84	571	136	48

ii) <u>Returns per Feddan (Shadow Costs), 1984</u>

Farm Size (feddans)	Cotton	Wheat	Rice	Maize	Long Birseem	Short Birseem	Beans
0-1	-30	92	-120	-98	118	-17	-256
1-3	47	59	-121	-38	145	-11	37
3-5	171	99	10	12	70	-36	-70
5-10	196	103	72	54	285	101	77
>10	233	33	239	67	551	121	28

crop's cultivation. On the largest farms, especially in the
Sharkiya village, between 4-5 cuts of birseem were taken. In
general, margins per feddan rose in time with farm size, but
this was by no means a universal trend. For both wheat and
cotton, the smallest units earned the highest return. This
is of particular significance in the case of cotton.
Likewise, returns to rice cultivation, where over 63% of output was marketed on the smallest units, most of it as forced
deliveries, were relatively high for the smallest farms.

When shadow wage rates were imputed and own technology costed,
as expected, the result for most crops was that on the small
farms returns were negative. On the larger units, shadow and
nominal rates show predictably little divergence.

Two sets of estimates on margins were calculated with their
corresponding rankings (see Tables 8.17 and 8.18). In the
first case, returns were deflated by the period of average
land occupancy per crop. The return per standardised man-day
(the aggregate of hired and family labour inputs) was then
calculated using coefficients by farm size, for labour use.
The rankings changed quite noticeably as a result. While birseem offered the consistently highest rate of return, wheat
appeared to offer relatively high margins for farms under five
feddans. Cotton, if labour time was the deflator, offered
relatively low returns, as did rice and maize. Given the fact
that nearly 24% of the cropped area was allocated to maize
production, this would suggest that its cultivation is
sustained at a high area level, firstly because of its traditional role as the major food item, and secondly on account of
its enormously expanded function as the provider of summer
fodder.

The table on returns per standardised man-day - a crude index
of the average productivity of labour in agriculture - shows
that the return per man-day for birseem, and wheat on the
smallest farms, was over double that for the other crops.
This gap got wider as farm size increased.

Income

The strong variation in crop-derived income levels across farm
size naturally reflects the prevailing inequality in the basic

Table 8.17: Returns per Month (£E) and Ranking (by Crop), 1984

Crop	Duration (months)	0-1	Rank	1-3	Rank	3-5	Rank	5-10	Rank	>10	Rank
Cotton	8	38	(2)	30	(3)	31	(2)	31	(2)	29	(4)
Wheat	7	28	(5)	20	(5)	21	(4)	18	(6)	6	(6)
Rice	5	36	(3)	36	(2)	32	(1)	28	(4)	52	(2)
Maize	5	34	(4)	26	(4)	19	(5)	22	(5)	17	(5)
Long Birseem	7	40	(1)	43	(1)	25	(3)	47	(1)	82	(1)
Short Birseem	4	20	(6)	13	(6)	10	(6)	30	(3)	34	(3)

Farm Size (feddans)

Table 8.18: Returns per man-day (£E) and Ranking (by Crop), 1984

Crop	Duration	0-1	1-3	3-5	5-10	>10
Cotton	8	2.6(5)	1.8(6)	2.2(5)	1.9 (5)	1.2(4)
Wheat	7	6.6(2)	4.7(2)	5.8(1)	5.4 (3)	0.9(6)
Rice	5	2.3(6)	2.1(4)	2.3(4)	2.3 (4)	3.9(3)
Maize	5	2.5(4)	2.2(5)	1.5(6)	1.8 (6)	1.1(5)
Long Birseem	7	7.0(1)	7.9(1)	3.9(2)	11.3 (1)	24.2(1)
Short Birseem	4	4.5(3)	2.7(3)	2.3(3)	6.8 (2)	9.3(2)

distribution of land. For most households, however, income is
not simply derived from asset ownership. While it is clear
that the latter is strongly associated with household income
levels and is also highly unequally distributed, it is important to note that off-farm remunerated employment increasingly
offers not only a wider range of income source but also has a
very significant equalising impact on farm income. In other
words, wage income tends to compensate for low, initial asset
endowments. This is indicated, with the use of a simple index
measure, when comparing aggregate household income disparities
in terms of crop-derived income and total income, including
non-farm earnings.

The importance of income generated from work outside the farm,
or as a return on non-land household assets, has been a relatively recent phenomenon. A glance through the range of
earlier studies of the pre-1970 agrarian system shows that
virtually all of them view income and its distribution in
rural areas as a function both of crop and livestock returns
and also of income from agricultural wage labouring. Abdel
Fadil further noted the possibility of cash remittances from
workers who had migrated to the towns.[19]

The first systematic analysis of the changing configuration of
income can be found in the ILO survey of 1977/78.[20]
Emphasising the effective collapse in the difference between
town and country, when viewed in employment terms, this study
found that nearly a quarter of total income for the surveyed
respondents was derived from non-farm wage work outside of the
village of domicile, a further 9.3% was drawn from village
non-farm work and about 5% from remittances.[21] When aggre-
gated with income from non-agricultural productive assets, the
share of total income gained outside of the agricultural sector approached 49%. As expected, this income profile was
reflected in the employment pattern, where about 40% of the
labour force was employed on non-agricultural work.

The importance of non-farm employment has continued to grow in
the period since 1977 and, while the employment aspect is
dealt with more explicitly in Chapter 7, the income consequences of this employment diversification are treated in this
section. The survey classified income in terms of crop

Table 8.19: Income Differentials by Farm Size: 1984
             (0-1 Feddan Class = 100)

Farm Size	Crop Income	Total Income
0-1	100	100
1-3	234	135
3-5	387	228
5-10	1104	516
>10	2995	1162

(Crop Income = Crop Value - Nominal Cost of Production-Rent)
(Total Income = Crop Income + Non-Crop Income)

Table 8.20: Structure of Non-Crop Farm Income, 1984
             by Farm Size

Source	-------------Farm Size (feddans)-------				
	0-1	1-3	3-5	5-10	>10
Rent	6.2	6.3	20.6	44.7	13
Dairy	20.3	12.6	12.4	15.3	44.6
Agricultural wages	18.9	23.1	5.6	--	--
Non-Agricultural wages	41.6	45.7	48.2	24.2	29.9
Remittances	2.9	2.6	--	--	--
Trade	3.0	1.5	2.5	10.1	--
Other Income	1.5	3.2	8.4	2.0	--
Sale of Livestock	5.6	5.0	2.3	3.7	12.5
Average Income (£E)	918	994	1583	2977	5344
(Index)	(100)	(108)	(172)	(324)	(582)

income, and non-crop income, the latter being decomposed in terms of income from livestock (principally dairy), rents for land, buildings, machines and animals, agricultural wages, non-agricultural wages, remittances, sale of livestock, trade and other sources. The results for non-crop income are presented in Table 8.19 and are notable for the prominence of dairy and non-agricultural wage income for the smallest farm households. Income from household animal stocks, when sale of livestock was included, accounted for over a quarter of total non-crop income on small farms, and it also clear that dairy farming was a significant source of income for the largest units. Over 57% of non-crop income was derived from milk sales and sales of livestock for farms of over ten feddans; principally those households situated in the Sharkiya village who had invested in purchasing Frisians and supplied their milk to a Cairo dairy.

Non-agricultural wage income was a major component for all farm size classes, but as a share it tailed off quite sharply for farms of over five feddans. As expected, agricultural wage income was almost entirely confined to the small farms, while rental payments, largely from land and from hiring-out machinery, were more prominent for the larger units. Interestingly, remittances constituted a very low proportion of total income and were restricted to the smaller farms. For the larger enterprises, although some household members had migrated abroad for work, their earnings were generally viewed as their own and were not remitted back to the family.

If non-agricultural wage work did not tend to have any significant seasonal properties, agricultural wage work and dairy income had a strong seasonal profile. In the case of agricultural wages, income peaked in the principal harvest seasons of April-June and September-October, while for dairy income an average of over 60% was earned between December and April with a sharp decline over the remaining months. The continuance of such seasonal variations in income was obviously associated with the character of agricultural production and the presence of seasonal underemployment in agriculture. However, it should be noted that the degree of variance was relatively slight and more stable than earlier studies have suggested.

Of increasing importance in the non-crop income profile of rural households was the hiring out of machinery. This

principally took the form of tractors and irrigation pumps.
With demand strong, particularly in the harvest periods,
returns were high. Moreover, hiring-out of irrigation machinery, while concentrated in the period November/January and
May/June to August, had a relatively flat seasonal variation.
This was also the case for tractors, where, with highly subsidised fuel prices, task limitation had not occurred.
Tractors are consequently used for a wide gamut of tasks
including transportation and haulage, as well as the habitual
field tasks of ploughing, harrowing and, for wheat especially,
threshing. This is discussed in more detail in Chapter 9.

The importance and widespread prevalence of machine-hiring
amongst machine-owning households can be seen in Table 8.21.
Of the tractor owners sampled - 80% hired-out their machines.
The two households that did not hire-out were the largest
farms in the Sharkiya village and whose on-farm requirements
precluded following the general pattern. In the case of irrigation pumps around 78% of pump-owners also hired out their
equipment. Indeed, while it is clear that pumps were used for
irrigating their owner's land, a number of households continued to use the saqia for their own land, preferring to hire
out the newer technology. Although the majority of owners
were households with over three feddans of land, it is important to note that small farm units had actively invested in
machinery. One household, with less than one feddan of land,
had managed to purchase a tractor and thresher, largely
through remittances. The head of household estimated that
hire charges amounted to around £E15-20 per day, resulting in
not only a highly expanded aggregate gross income but also a
drastically modified composition of household income. Hire
income was around twelve times greater than the household's
incomings from non-agricultural wage work and livestock sales,
the only other sources of income.

The level of income increments accruing from hiring out machinery can also be seen in Table 8.21. For all farms, average
income per annum amounted to over £E1730 per annum. While it
appears from the Table that the smallest farm units had rental
incomes as high as the larger farms, this is somewhat
distorted by the case of the tractor/thresher owner.
Subtracting this household's income from the first farm size
class average, the figure falls to £E770 per annum.

Although information on the age of machinery was not collected, rough valuations of the machinery were made at the time of survey. It was found that the tractor stock had an average value of around £E6800 and irrigation pumps an average value of £E950. These figures are likely to be over-estimates, insofar as they appeared to represent farmers' perception of their undepreciated value. Nevertheless, a rough estimate suggests that the capital cost of an irrigation pump can be covered within two years, given the current state of demand in the rental market. Assuming a working life of ten years, an annual operating time of 1400 hours and the hire of a permanent driver, the financial rate of return on a standard Nasr 65hp tractor with a capital cost of around £E6000 would exceed 25%. In the case of a Romanian 76hp tractor where the initial cost rises to around £E9000, the financial rate of return would fall to between 15%-20%.

While machinery hire can clearly be seen as having a relatively high return it should be born in mind that less than 6% of the full sample owned or shared in the ownership of a tractor, while 10.5% owned an irrigation pump. Moreover, tractor ownership, in particular, tended to be concentrated among the large farm households. As an obvious consequence, hire income and rental income in general constituted a significant proportion of aggregate farm income, principally for the farm households with over three feddans. Where small farmers had purchased such machinery, rental income, in these limited number of cases, tended to provide the principal component of total farm income.

The importance of non-farm income can most readily be understood in terms of its share in total household income. In this calculation, income from the crop sector was adjusted to take account of (nominal) costs and rent. Table 8.22 shows not only the importance of non-crop income for all farm size classes, but also its particular significance for the smallest farms, where over three-quarters of total income was derived from non-crop sources.

The 1984 survey further demonstrated that the generation of non-agricultural income was a major and continuing feature of the Egyptian rural economy. In 1977 the ILO survey estimated that a little under half total income came from outside the primary sector. The 1984 results suggested that this

Table 8.21: Machinery Hire and Income, 1984

| Type | Farm Size (feddans) | | | | | |
	0-1	1-3	3-5	5-10	>10	All
Tractor	3(3)	1(1)	0	4(4)	0(2)	8(10)
Irrigation pump	2(3)	6(6)	2(3)	4(4)	0(2)	4(18)
Pick-up	1(1)			1(1)		2(2)
Average Annual Income (£E)	2054	440	2665	2587	-	1732

Proportion of tractor owners hiring-out = 80%

Proportion of irrigation pump owners hiring-out = 77.8%

(Figures in brackets = numbers owned)

Table 8.22: Non-Crop Income Share in Total Income and Non-Agricultural Income Share in Total Income, 1984

| | Farm Size | | | | | |
	0-1	1-3	3-5	5-10	>10	All
Non-Crop	76.8	60.0	60.7	50.4	40.2	60.0
Non-Agricultural	37.6	31.8	36.0	36.3	30.0	29.8

proportion was currently around 30% for all farms, with nearly
37% of total income for the smallest farms earned outside the
agricultural sector. In the case of farms of between 1-3 feddans this proportion was around 32%, rising to 36% for units
of between 3 and 10 feddans. The largest farms derived
approximately 30% of their total income from outside the agricultural sector.

Apart from signifying the increasing importance of employment
outside agriculture, one very marked result, as already
observed, has been to reduce the disparities in household
income across farm size. This obviously has the effect of
diluting the impact of initial inequalities in asset
endowment.

Determinants of Household Income

The results of the 1984 survey show very clearly that,
although access to non-farm employment and income has had an
important effect on the overall income profile of farm households, farm income - income derived from either crop or
livestock activity - still constituted the major component of
aggregate household income. The proportion of farm-generated
income to total income was, moreover, strongly positively
associated with farm size. In addition, large farms, through
their rotational selection, secured higher crop values per
feddan over the agricultural year. In general, large farms
had standardised crop values at least 50% higher than in the
case of the smallest farms.

This is not a strict function of larger farms tending always
to receive higher farmgate prices. However, the larger units
devoted a far smaller area to administered crops while
tending, through their greater storage capacity, to gain
higher prices through selling outside the post-harvest period.
Prices of the major farm productions varied substantially between the two seasons in the usual manner, yet the tendency of
small farms was still to sell early for liquidity and storage
reasons. It is important, however, to note that the earlier
system of market interlinking, associated with the pumping-out
of surplus through debt and other linkages, appears no longer
to be a feature of the rural economy. The emergence of the
gamiya as the conjoint site for credit, input provision and,

for some crops, marketing, has had a crucial impact in weakening these earlier features.

The relationship between household income and a number of key variables was tested in the income regressions. Net household income was regressed in linear and log-linear form on the operated area. The results suggest that income per land area declined with land operated; the shift coefficient, 0.71, fell below one. This was as expected given the compositional features of net income for all farm size classes. When run in linear form it was found that each additional qirat yielded an incremental net income of £E20, or roughly £E480 per feddan.[22] When productive assets and a set of variables representing the human capital endowment of the farm were entered, the results were mixed. No meaningful association was found to exist between net income and normalised household size. However, k40, the number of household members with farming or agricultural labouring as their primary occupation, displayed a positive relationship with net income, although with weak statistical significance. Of particular interest is the fact that k41 - the number of adult males with more than secondary education - did not, as hypothesized, have a positive and significant association with the aggregate level of household income. This could be explained in part by the fact that retention in education naturally depressed <u>current</u> income streams, this being a function of the fact that males of above 16 years were included. When the variable was modified so as to include only males of above 25 years (ie those that had entered the labour force and had left education) a positive association with net household income was found to be significant at the 5% level. This association was, as hypothesised, particularly strong when aggregate non-crop income (j10) was regressed on the number of adult males above 25 years of age with more than secondary education.

This was indirectly confirmed when household income was regressed on the number of household members whose primary occupation was outside agriculture (k42) (excluding housewives, unemployed, disabled and so on). The association was found to be strongly positive and statistically significant. For every additional member with primary non-agricultural work, net income rose by £E955. The primary occupation of the head of household was not, however, a significant factor in explaining the level of household income. No clear pattern

emerged in the regression. Although for the smallest farms,
mean household income was considerably higher when the head of
household worked outside agriculture, this relationship did
not hold in the case of farms of between 1-5 feddans.
Moreover, it is interesting to note that when the head of
household's primary occupation was as an agricultural
labourer, household income levels tended to be higher than
when the head of household farmed his own land as his principal occupation. This can best be understood as a function
of current wage rates in agriculture.

In terms of the overall structure of household income, the
regression analysis strongly confirmed the critical role of
asset ownership. Both livestock ownership and tractor
ownership were positively associated with income at statistically significant levels. The overall explanatory power of
the equation was also high. In addition, livestock and tractor ownership was strongly positively correlated with farm
size, a factor emphasising the income-asset linkage. This
merely reinforces the point that while the human capital
endowment of the household and the level of non-agricultural
employment are important factors explaining the level of
household income, the principal disparities are, as expected,
derivative of basic inequalities in the distribution of
assets.

The Distribution of Income

Information on the distribution of income in Egyptian agriculture has been severely hampered by the lack of systematic
data. Most attempts at computing income shares have relied
heavily on inferential use of the limited available data and,
in many cases, on spurious interpolation from fragmented sources. In particular, these shortcomings have adversely
affected calculation of the share of agricultural landless
households in total agricultural income. This is hardly
surprising, considering that the number of landless households
has been reckoned in terms of a residual. In the discussion
that follows, reference is made only to the distribution of
agricultural income across landholders. While it would be
preferable to frame some estimate of the share of the
landless, neither official statistics nor information from
recent surveys provide sufficient data to warrant such an
exercise.

There now appears to be general agreement as to the trend in
the relative share of the landholding groups for the period
from the early 1950s through to the mid-1960s.   Thereafter,
with no Agricultural Census in 1971 and the results of the
1981 Census as yet unpublished, the terrain is far less well
explored.

Between the early 1950s and mid-1960s one major consequence of
land reform was a redistribution of income away from the previously dominant large landholding classes.   However, it is
generally thought that the redistributive swing moved more
towards the middle range of landholder, this being rather
broadly defined as those holding between 5 and 50 feddans.
Nevertheless, it would seem that farm households with less
than 5 feddans improved their overall share of agricultural
income from around 19% in 1950 to 37% by 1965 (excludes
landless).[23]   The principal losers were the traditional dominant large farmers and landed estates whose assets were either
redistributed under land reform or parcelled out into a larger
number of holdings to avoid such confiscation.   El Issawi
attempts, in the absence of direct information about the
distribution of income, to use family budget survey data on
expenditure distribution as a proxy.[24]   These purport to show
that between the late 1950s and 1974/75 the distribution of
rural consumption remained broadly constant.   However, this
reference period cannot include the major effects in terms of
consumption that have resulted from the growth in the subsidy
and ration system since 1973.   As with farm income distribution, it is this very period that is of the most interest
currently.

While many commentators appear to believe, almost as an
article of faith, that _infitah_ necessarily worsened income
distribution in both rural and urban areas as also between
rural and urban areas,[25] there is as yet no satisfactory
information against which to test these assumptions.   However,
recent work by IFPRI/INP on the distributional implications of
food subsidies has demonstrated that the net effect of food
price and subsidy policy has been biassed towards the rural
sector, while subsidies transferred through _gamiya_ marketing
have a bias towards urban areas.[26]   One result of this has
been that food price policy has probably had positive implications for income distribution but the regressive impact of the
food distribution programme has had some countervailing

effects.   In this latter regard, it was estimated that a 10%
increase in income level was associated with a 0.42% increase
in income transfer.   In general, it was concluded that the
exceedingly complex and costly system of subsidies and prices
had progressive income distributional results.

Taking a rather more limited appraisal of the distribution of
agricultural income among landholding groups at this stage, it
appears that comparing the available data for 1961 with that
for net crop income derived from the 1984 survey, the share of
total agricultural crop income appropriated by farms of below
five feddans had increased substantially in the intervening
decades.   However, the differential in net crop income may
have widened to some extent since 1965, at least between the
farm size categories beneath ten feddans.

For the more recent period, estimates of income distribution
in the agricultural sector have relied on manipulating official data concerning average gross income per feddan by crop
with data concerning the cropping pattern and the distribution
of landholdings.   Zaytoun has employed this rather crude
method to compute income shares by class of holding.[27]   The
principal thrust of her article was to estimate the effect of
the cropping pattern on gross crop income.   It was argued that
this approach was taken because large farms tended to have a
higher proportion of the cropped area under higher value
crops, such as vegetables and fruits.   Accounting for this
cropping variation a Gini coefficient of 0.495 was calculated.
Table 8.24 uses the estimates which do not take account of
variations in the cropping pattern.   This is because in the
1984 data, with which this information is being compared, such
marked differentiation in cropping pattern was not present.
As can be seen from Table 8.24, the 1977/78 and 1984 figures
demonstrate fairly close approximation in terms of the distribution of shares in the gross crop income.   This does not
appear to support the contention that in recent years the
trend in income distribution in agriculture has been sharply
regressive.

While it is indeed difficult to come to any clear conclusion
regarding the overall trend in income distribution in the most
recent period, the breakdown of mean household incomes by farm

Table 8.23: Net Crop Income 1984

Farm Size (feddans)	Net Income	Mean	Index	Share of Total Agricultural Income 1984*	Share of Total Agricultural Income 1961**
0-1	18,536	265	100	13.9%	(
1-3	43,145	616	232	32.4%	(36.2%
3-5	18,455	1025	387	13.8%	(
5-10	29,257	2926	1104	22.0%	(41.7%
>10	23,811	7937	2995	17.9%	(
>50	---	--	--	--	22.1
Total	133,204	799	--	100%	100%

*Excludes landless share:
**Excludes landless and rental payments to absentees

Table 8.24: Gross Income: Crops 1977/78-1984

Farm Size	Gross Crop Value 1984	Mean	Percent Share in Total Gross Crop Income 1977/78	1984
	(£E)		%	%
0-1	38,279	547	15.0	13.8
1-3	93,859	1,341	33.0	33.8
3-5	44,815	2,490	19.1	16.1
5-10	52,394	5,239	12.9	18.8
>10	48,612	16,204	20.0	17.5
Total	277,959	1,625	100	100

Sources: Abdel Fadil, 1975 pp58/59 (1961 figures)
           Mohaya Zaytoun, 'Income Distribution in Egyptian Agriculture'
           in Abdel-Khalek and Tignor, 1982 pp292/4 (1977/78 data).

size (Table 8.24) demonstrates beyond doubt that there remain very substantial income gaps across farm size class. Although the access to non-farm employment and the increasing share of wage and non-crop income in total income for the small farm sector had tended to narrow the differential, the fact remains that initial asset endowments, principally land, obviously skew income distribution in a very marked manner. Thus, mean household income for farms of over ten feddans was over twelve times the mean income for the smallest farm households. As a consequence, 1.9% of the sample population controlled between 12½-14% of total income. By contrast, over 81% of sample households whose holdings fell below three feddans controlled between 51-56% of total income. This yields a Gini coefficient of 0.48 for this income distribution.

It should be noted that the sample distribution fairly accurately mirrors the national distribution of holdings. However, there was a fair degree of variation in farm incomes by village, and all the villages were in the Delta. Combined with the limited size of the sample, this cautions against any extrapolation to a wider plane.

The 1984 survey did not collect any information regarding expenditure and consumption patterns. However, the IFPRI/INP survey that was conducted in 1981/82 systematically collected information dealing with these aspects. As Table 8.25 shows, nearly 8% of rural households fell below the calorie and protein cutoff point. Furthermore, over 20% of rural households in the lowest expenditure quartile suffered principally from calorie deficiency. This was double the level for the equivalent urban expenditure quartile. Although it is not possible from this data to distinguish between households with and without land, these figures demonstrate that, despite high general levels of economic growth, widespread subsidised food distribution and rising real wages over the last decade, the problem of undernutrition still remains significant even if much reduced when compared to the relatively recent past.

This same database has been used to estimate the general level of rural poverty in Egypt, where the conventional poverty line has been derived from consumer expenditure behaviour, rather than from income sources. Setting this information alongside that derived from earlier budget surveys, Adams has estimated that, while the proportion of rural households below the

poverty line fell from around 27% in 1958/59 to 24% by the
mid-1960s, the economic slump between 1967 and 1973 resulted
in over 60% of rural households dropping below the poverty
line in 1973/75.[28] This dramatic shift appears exaggerated,
even allowing for constrained government investment and relatively high levels of implicit taxation of agricultural producers in this period.   However, what is of considerable
interest is the fact that by 1982 slightly under 18% of the
rural population was beneath the poverty line. Leaving aside
the rather questionable 1974/75 estimates, this suggests that
the proportion of 'poor' households fell by around 6% in the
period 1964/65-1982.   However, if measured in terms of the
distribution of expenditure, it would appear that in the same
period the share of expenditure accruing to the lowest 20%
fell from 7.4% to 6% while the share appropriated by the top
20% increased by roughly the same proportion.

Other standard measures of inequality show a general trend of
declining inequality between 1958/59 and 1964/65, sharply
rising inequality between 1964/65 and 1974/75 with a subsequent return to a near 1958/59 level by 1982.   Table 8.26
suggests that even if inequality in the distribution of expenditure has remained fairly constant since the late 1950s, the
infitah period has not witnessed, as has been commonly
hypothesised, a major regressive effect on the distribution of
income. However, the distribution of income has been shifted
regressively when comparing the most recent period with the
situation that prevailed in the mid-1960s.

Using the estimated basket of food commodities deemed to
satisfy a minimum daily calorie requirement (2510) and
controlling for the rate of food commodity price increases
since 1982,[29] it can be calculated that the cost in rural
areas of the minimum caloric intake per caput was just over
£E131 in 1984.   Assuming a similar share of food to total
expenditures since the mid-1970s - 64% - this would yield a
crude per capita poverty line of £E205 per annum.

Table 8.27 gives the per capita figures for household income,
citing two measures, one where nominal crop costs were
deducted and one where shadow cost rates were used.   In addition, two methods of normalising household consumption units
have been employed.   In the first case, the commonly used 0.83
coefficient has been applied.   In the second case, adult male

Table 8.25: Share of Households Below Calorie & Protein Cutoffs, 1981/82

Position	URBAN Expenditure Quartile				All Urban	RURAL Expenditure Quartile				All Rural
	1	2	3	4		1	2	3	4	
Below calorie and protein cutoff	10.6	4.9	1.2	0.8	4.3	20.3	6.0	3.2	2.0	7.9
Below calorie cutoff	20.8	15.5	9.8	6.2	13.1	17.4	8.9	4.3	2.9	8.4
Below protein cutoff	0.4	0.8	0.2	0.0	0.4	0.3	0.0	0.0	0.0	0.1

Source: Alderman & Von Braun, 1984, IFPRI, p34.

Table 8.26: Inequalities in the Distribution of Expenditure 1958/59-1982

Year	Proportion of Rural Population in Poverty	Average poverty gap in 1975 £E pa.	Sen's Index of Poverty	Gini coefficient	Theil's Entropy Measure
1958/9	27.4	9.94	0.079	0.343	0.161
1964/65	23.8	32.56	0.178	0.290	0.122
1974/5	65.4	30.46	0.212	0.348	0.174
1982	17.8	23.38	0.061	0.337	0.167

Source: Adams, 1985 pp709-710

household members have been assigned a weight of 1, adult
females a weight of 0.75 and children 0.5. In general, application of the second and rather more preferable set of weights
shifted mean per capita income upwards by around 15%, except
in the case of the large (over ten feddans) farm sample. What
emerges from the table is that, although mean small (0-1) farm
per caput incomes touch the poverty line when shadow costs are
used, the majority of small farm households' incomes appear
above this critical level.

In the mid-1970s it was estimated that nearly three-quarters
of rural households in the lower 50% expenditure range were
households without land. To this extent, one would expect the
1984 survey to have ignored the main reservoir of rural
poverty. However, it is important to note that between a
quarter and a third of small farm households (0-3 feddans) had
incomes on or below a household adjusted poverty line. This
was the case irrespective of the normalisation procedure used
for household consumption units. This is a high figure and
cautions against any easy acceptance of the view that rural
poverty has been significantly abated. Many small farm households, despite a growing involvement in the non-agricultural
labour market and rising real wages in agriculture, have only
made very limited material progress. Access to non-farm
income and employment and the increase in the agricultural
wages have been of undoubted benefit to small farm households,
but the limited degree of labour market participation by women
combined with the age structure of the population and the
relatively high levels of child retention in education
(particularly male children) has somewhat limited the overall
level and spread of benefits.

Conclusion

This chapter has concentrated on analysing the output
generated by Egyptian farm households from the combination of
inputs used in production. No consistent trend in terms of
productivity was found to exist across farm size class.
However, average labour productivity tended to be superior on
the larger farms. However, there was little evidence that any
inverse relationship between farm size and productivity
existed. To that extent, it is important to note that the
longer-term effect of land reform, now coupled to the changing

Table 8.27:　Income per Caput According to Different Measures: 1984

Farm Size feddans		Income (x34) (-nominal costs) £E	Income (x33) (-shadow costs) £E
0-1	(i)	271	203
	(ii)	314	234
1-3	(i)	311	226
	(ii)	366	262
3-5	(i)	460	373
	(ii)	519	420
5-10	(i)	1114	1038
	(ii)	1263	1177
>10	(i)	4801	4572
	(ii)	4830	4599

(i) = Normalizing coefficient, 0.83.
(ii) = Adult Males = 1: Adult Females = 0.75: Children = 0.5

profile of the labour market, has tended to equalise the
volume of inputs across farm size class. One significant difference did, however, emerge from the analysis. Larger farms
tended to gain higher crop values per unit of land, this being
both a result of price and storage factors, and also as a consequence of the evasion of forced deliveries through the non-
growing of cotton.

The shift in the patterns of allocation of household and hired
labour to crop production outlined in earlier chapters was
shown to be paralleled in the market and consumption structure
of farm households. Rather than being characterised as own-
producing consumption maximisers, small farm households could
be seen to gear their production to requirements other than
those of household consumption needs. Both the production of
livestock feed and the availability of subsidised or ration
food were found to be important determinants of farm production strategies.

The section on the costs of production and the structure of
relative returns to crops demonstrated that the former have,
over the last decade, tended to run ahead of both farmgate
prices and the general rate of inflation in rural areas. This
conclusion would hold even if shadow wage rates were not
imputed to family labour. Farm households have responded to
this squeeze on farm income through the growth in the labour
factor share by shifting as much as possible into crops with
relatively high returns and - particularly in the case of birseem - rather lower labour input requirements. Nevertheless,
the system of forced deliveries continues to ensure that
substantial areas are maintained under both rice and cotton
where farmgate prices are kept artificially low.

The analysis of farm incomes that concluded this chapter
demonstrated that non-farm sources of income have remained of
considerable importance. Around 30% of household income was
on average generated by work outside the agricultural sector.
Just as striking was the fact that, for all farms, some 60% of
aggregate household income derived from non-crop activity.
Access to off-farm employment and income sources has thus had
a major impact on the income profile of farm households,
while, at the same time, tending to lessen the inequality of
income levels that results from the continuing skewedness in
the distribution of assets. However, despite this equalising

effect it is important to note that between a quarter and a
third of all farm households with less than three feddan
holdings had income levels in 1984 that were on or somewhat
below the estimated poverty line. This strongly suggests that
despite the positive shifts in the labour market over the last
decade there remains a significant residue of poverty embedded
in the rural social structure. Recent recessionary trends in
the economy are likely to have exacerbated this problem still
further.

Footnotes

1. See, inter alia, Bardhan, 1973; Bharadwaj, 1974; Rudra,
    1968; Sen, 1964.
2. Bharadwaj, 1974, p18.
3. Crop Value per Feddan (y20) on Operated Area (x12) -
    Linear and Log Linear

    Linear: 1795.749   +   4.464
                 (60.821)   (0.888)* $R^2 = 0.31$
    Log-Linear   2.979   +   0.198
                 (0.042)   (0.027)* $R^2 = 0.24$
    * Significant at 1% level

4. Dependent Variable: Wheat Yield per Feddan (v15)

Independent Variable	Estimate	Standard Error	Significance Level
Proportion Hired to Total Labour Hours	-3.280	0.5737	0.0001
Constant	10.051	0.3566	0.0001
$R^2 = 0.21$ F Value = 32.7 No of Observations = 126			

5. Dependent Variable: Crop Value per Feddan (y20)

Independent Variable	Estimate	Standard Error	Significance Level
Material Inputs Value per Feddan (Q61)	1.845	0.252	0.0001
Constant	1526.763	77.397	0.0001
$R^2 = 0.24$ F Value = 53.4 No of Observations = 171			

6. von Braun and de Haen, 1983, pp25-28.
7. ibid., p28.
8. See,   Hansen,   1969;   Mead,   1967;   Hanson,   1971.
9. Alderman and von Braun, 1984, p54.
10. EMCEP Survey, 1983.
11. Alderman and von Braun, 1984, p60.
12. ibid., p67.
13. Cuddihy, 1980, pp33-42; Hansen and Nashashibi, 1975, pp317-346.
14. IBRD, 1983(a), p190.
15. Cuddihy, 1980.
16. Habashy and Fitch, 1980.
17. ibid., pp51ff.
18. Rehnberg et al., 1984; El Shinnawy et al., 1984 and Haider et al., 1984.
19. Abdel-Fadil, 1975, pp56ff.
20. Lee and Radwan, 1985; See also, Hansen and Radwan, 1982.
21. Hansen and Radwan, 1982, p100.
22 (i)Dependent Variable: Net Income (x5) (log-linear)

Mean: 3.13

C.V.: 10.99

Independent Variable	Estimate	Standard Error	Significance Level
Operated Area (x12)	0.7068	0.1252	0.0001
Constant	2.0552	0.0808	0.0001

$R^2 = 0.32$ F Value = 77.29   No of Observations = 170

(ii)Dependent Variable: Net Income (x5) (linear)

Mean: 2067.84

C.V.: 69.82

Independent Variable	Estimate	Standard Error	Significance Level
Operated Area (x12)	20.071	1.048	0.0001
Constant	371.528	141.558	0.0095

$R^2 = 0.68$ F Value = 366.54   No of Observations = 171

23. Mohie-eldin, in Abdel-Khalek and Tignor, 1982, pp236-267; Abdel-Fadil, 1975, pp56ff; Radwan, 1977.
24. El Issawi, 1983(a) and 1983(b).
25. See, for example, the volume edited by Abdel-Khalek and Tignor, 1982 and Abdel-Fadil and Salah, 1984.

26. See, Alderman and von Braun, 1984 and von Braun and de Haen, 1983.
27. Zaytoun, in Abdel-Khalek and Tignor, 1982, pp268-306.
28. Adams, 1985, pp707.
29. ibid., pp721-723.

CHAPTER NINE

Mechanisation in Egyptian Agriculture

Introduction

For the last five years agricultural mechanisation has been at the cornerstone of government policy. Most major government pronouncements have listed the establishment of mechanisation extension centres and the diffusion of new technology in the countryside as among the foremost achievements of the administration. This strategy continues to be at the heart of government policy, and it is particularly important in relation to bilateral and multilateral aid transfers and development programmes within the country. At a recent count all the major national donor bodies were involved to varying degrees in the country's mechanisation strategy. By 1985 the World Bank had already committed over $32m to the Agricultural Development Project with around £E14m going to its mechanisation project in the governorates of Minoufiya and Sohag.[1]

The World Bank has also agreed to fund a Second Agricultural Development project.[2] Originally intended to begin in late 1985 with an IBRD allocation of $139m, total finance for the project was estimated at $359m, of which nearly 50% would be foreign exchange costs. The Egyptian government was to fund only local charges, around 13% of total costs, while the remaining finance was to be mobilised from project beneficiaries and a co-financier. Yet despite the World Bank's approval of the project, disbursements had not commenced by mid-1987, because of financial and other constraints at the Egyptian end.

In addition to IBRD/IDA financing, USAID had also allotted over $45m to mechanisation or mechanisation-related projects by the end of 1985 and the Japanese Agency for International Cooperation had allocated nearly $35m to mechanisation projects with the possibility of a further $20m loan.[3] Clearly this allocation of resources to programmes designed to accelerate the diffusion of mechanical technology has fully matched the government's political priorities.

While the government has sought with some success to draw in

donors for soft financing of the mechanisation programme, it
has also set aside considerable resources itself in domestic
currency and foreign exchange. Thus, for example, it is estimated that the government/IBRD Second Agricultural Development
project will require over £E180m from local sources over five
years, these comprising both direct costs to government, or
else through the public sector PBDAC (Principal Bank for
Development & Credit) as well as project farmers.   The Five
Year Plan drawn up by the Egyptian Agricultural Mechanisation
Project for the period 1982/3-1986/7 required further allocations exceeding $678m.[4] These allocations have been made just
as much on political grounds as on the availability of
assistance, in this case from USAID. At least three different
units within the Ministry of Agriculture have been concerned
with the mechanisation programme, excluding the project-linked
staff of each national programme.

By exercising considerable leverage on major donors, particularly on the US, and playing off one donor body against
another, the Egyptian government has achieved a proliferation
of donor-agency sponsored programmes. The result of this
policy has been further diffusion of agricultural machinery in
the countryside, but progress has been relatively slow, given
the resources set aside for the purpose.   Bureaucratic
rivalries and competing interests, fuelled and fanned by often
ill-conceived and uncoordinated donor activity, have resulted
not only in duplication but also a weak developmental impact.

The circumstances surrounding the Agricultural Mechanisation
Centre programme, the continuation of which is now part of the
IBRD project, strongly suggest that the profile of the government is a major consideration in the entire programme. What
is also very evident is that the relative economic costs of
such programmes are not taken seriously into account in the
determination of their feasibility. To some extent this represents a continuation of the Nasserist preoccupation with the
state as the leading edge of developmental activity, but it
also represents an often ill-thought out response to the relatively recent transfusions of aid that have become available
to the Egyptian economy. The material consequences, at least
at the producer level, have been varied but, as will become
clear later, the direct impact of state-supported mechanisation programmes has been weak.   More indirect subsidies,
leading to a proliferation of private sector machinery holdings,   have   had   a   substantially   greater   impact.

Table 9.1: Donor Commitments to Agriculture and Irrigation Sectors
            Projects with Major Mechanisation Component, 1985

Country/ Donor	Loan	Grant
IBRD	139.0	
USAID		52.0
Japan	20.0	32.5
West Germany		0.5
Romania	37.7	
Denmark	0.5	
France	7.4	
UN (FAO/UNDP)	7.3	
Total	211.9	85.0

Table 9.2: Total On-Going Donor Aid Commitments, 1984

Sector	Loan	Grant
Agriculture	300.56	394.50(188.7)
Irrigation	285.58	226.99(213.0)
Total	586.14	621.49(401.7)

Figures in brackets are allocations by USAID
(on a grant basis)

Irrespective of the pace of implementation, the government
continues to view accelerated mechanisation as a key priority.
The Agricultural Mechanisation Five Year Plan thus established
an ambitious set of targets including the mechanisation of the
principal agricultural tasks - land clearing, seedbed preparation, planting and harvesting - except for particular crops
such as sugar-cane and potatoes. In addition, certain crop-
specific tasks were singled out for attention. These included
rice puddling and transplantation as well as cotton and potato
harvesting. It was envisaged that progress towards these
goals would be achieved by the import of new technology and
the proliferation of machine ownership among Egyptian agricultural producers. While some emphasis was placed on the
establishment of pilot machine rental service stations - an
aspect that has since been given the most prominence by the
government - initial stress was on expansion in and through
the private sector.[5]

Although replacement of the tractor stock was estimated in the
Plan, using a simple area/availability index, it was argued
that the tractor stock in 1982/3 was sufficient for agriculture's needs. The main stress was placed on increases in
the stock of pesticide sprayers, threshers and winnowers, as
well as irrigation technology. Targeted horsepower for the
mechanical lifting of water was estimated at 70% more than
existing levels, while a further range of gaps for particular
crop operations was highlighted. These included such items as
rice transplanters, where a plan requirement of nearly four
thousand was estimated, as well as increased diffusion of
American-designed disk and rotary ploughs.

In addition to increments in the stock and variety of implements, considerable emphasis was placed on improving the range
of repair and servicing facilities as well as the training of
manpower. The plan called for the establishment of over 500
field workshops, 134 central workshops and over 1000 machine-
hire stations. With an estimated budget of not far short of
$700m (1983$) this scale of activity was believed to be commensurate with an overall mechanisation level of 100% for land
clearing and seedbed preparation, 80% mechanisation of harvesting and 40% mechanisation in planting. While a major
mechanisation survey in 1982 estimated that over 90% of
ploughing work was already mechanised and over 60% of irrigation was achieved through machine use, the ambitiousness of

the plan can be understood when noting that for planting and
harvesting the level of mechanisation in 1982 was almost non-
existent.[6] The 1984 survey demonstrated that these targets
have not been met. In particular, virtually no progress had
been made in the introduction of mechanical energy for harvesting. With regard to the extension component of the
government's strategy, some twenty agricultural mechanisation
stations had been opened by the end of 1984, including one
near the surveyed Sharkiya village. A further thirty were
planned to be opened in the following eighteen months.

The entire government mechanisation strategy has been based on
the assumption of chronic labour shortages in agriculture.
Mechanisation has thus been presented as a labour-substituting
process. At the same time, machine-energy use has been advo-
cated for its cost-saving features, given the rising labour
factor share and its substitution of machine for draught-
animal energy. The latter is an ambiguous aspect of government policy given the entire structure of relative crop and
meat prices, but it has been emphasised by other proponents of
enhanced mechanisation.[7] Nevertheless, the important point
to note is that official and donor-driven policies towards the
introduction of mechanical energy have explicitly been based
on the positive labour substituting aspect of mechanisation.
The IBRD-financed Second Agricultural Development project, for
example, has been explicitly justified in terms of its potential for labour-substitution in the context of a postulated,
growing shortage of labour and a rising wage-factor share.
This is in marked contrast to policy in India, for example,
where mechanisation is argued not to have labour displacing
properties and where the supposed rationale for increments in
the machine stock of the country is completely different.[8]

The demand for agricultural machinery in Egypt currently tends
to be presented as a natural consequence of the labour
endowment in agriculture, thereby fitting a general pattern in
the history of agricultural mechanisation of machine adoption
spurred by a combination of constrained labour supply and
rising labour costs.[9] In addition, some emphasis has been
placed on the potential yield-enhancing properties of machinery.

A major report on the subject concluded, rather optimisti-
cally, that with unconstrained mechanisation yields per feddan

could rise by around 55%.[10] The principal components of this
increase - accounting for around half the potential growth in
productivity - were better seedbed preparation and timely
planting of crops. However, the scale of such increments was
undoubtedly overstated, while at the same time several
simplifying but misleading assumptions were made. Thus, it
was argued that mechanical harvesting of birseem could
suppress the 20% nutritive loss of current early cutting practices. This overlooks the fact that birseem is commonly
grazed on-field, or that when multiple cuts are taken, timing
is dictated by the fodder requirements of the household's animal stock. Longer maturation periods have little meaning when
birseem is viewed as a continuous feed input and when the
pricing structure favours the retention of significant animal
holdings. Moreover the argument that machine adoption results
in higher productivity conflicts with most available evidence
from other countries,[11] even if mechanisation appears to be
positively associated with cropping intensity and higher
levels of seed, fertiliser and pesticide application.[12]

The cost savings and the labour release effected through the
introduction of mechanical energy have obviously had potentially beneficial implications for productivity. In other
words, gains associated with mechanisation are, for the most
part, indirect features of the process. Moreover - and this
is of particular relevance in the Egyptian context - these
increments assume a societal, economic rationale, just as much
as a private rationale, for releasing or substituting labour
power by machine energy. The evidence presented in earlier
chapters strongly suggests that these assumptions cannot be
made lightly. In any case, the very premise on which the
mechanisation programme has been based and continues to be
based - the scarcity of labour - is open to considerable
doubt. Furthermore, any currently proposed set of advances in
machine introduction would obviously have very major implications for longer-term labour absorption in agriculture.

In other words, accelerated mechanisation must not be seen as
a short-term response to shifts in the labour supply curve,
but rather as a shift with permanent consequences for agricultural activity and for the agricultural labour force. The
government and donor agencies realise this very well, but have
assumed that constrained labour supplies are a long-run
feature of the economy. Many sceptics point out that it would

only require a major fall in the stock and flow of migrants to the Gulf states to disturb this new equilibrium very severely. Others, including the administration, respond that even if there is a major reflux of migrant workers, many originally from the rural sector, they would not in general be willing to re-enter the agricultural labour force. Expectations have changed and with them the willingness to work in activity now commonly considered to be inferior, or at least unremunerative. While there is an element of truth in this, it does depend on levels of labour demand outside agriculture and these levels are themselves an increasingly strict function of government spending. At the same time, the trend in the labour force remains strongly upwards and is unlikely to fall substantially in the relatively near future. This suggests that, assuming a permanent fall in agriculture's labour absorptive capacity, counter-cyclical employment creation would have to run at levels even greater than those of the last decade. Needless to say, this would present immediate budgetary problems and have inevitable inflationary implications caused by the likely acceleration in deficit financing. At the same time, the nature of employment generated by the state has led to contraction in the relative size of the 'productive' sector and a growing lack of correspondence between aggregate labour productivity and the wage path (see Chapter 2).

Recent Trends in Mechanisation

The central importance of mechanisation should now be clear, both for the agricultural sector and for the economy as a whole. This chapter examines these issues in more detail, using available national-level data and data generated by the 1984 survey. Particular emphasis will be placed on charting the degree and range of current levels of mechanisation and estimating the pace of introduction of new technology. The impact of machine-energy use on labour and draught animal inputs in the production process is examined, as well as the cost implications of such substitution. The latter aspect is shown to be the crucial feature determining the adoption of machine use. In addition, attention will be paid to analysing the market for machinery and the returns to machine ownership and use. A concluding section attempts to estimate the likely longer-term effects of government and donor sponsored mechanisation policies on employment in agriculture.

There can be little doubt that the stock and usage of agricultural machinery has increased substantially in the recent
past. While a significant proportion of that machinery has
been produced within Egypt, a considerable share has been
imported, not only from industrialised countries but also from
East Germany and Romania.

If the machinery stock has grown at a steady rate, it is
important to note that the range of machinery has remained
restricted and ownership of such machinery, as distinct from
use, tends to be strongly correlated with farm size. However,
the association with farm size and machine ownership may have
weakened over time. In 1950 farms of over fifty feddans
controlled nearly 80% of the tractor stock, by 1961 this had
fallen to 45%.[13] More recent field studies continue to
demonstrate the expected positive link between farm size and
ownership of tractors and other machines. Hopkins, for
example, has found that in one Minya village farm households
with over twenty feddans owned two-thirds of the stock of
tractors.[14] Irrigation pump ownership, by contrast, is far
more broadly distributed among farm households; it is not
uncommon to find partnerships formed for pump purchases. This
is broadly reflected in the ratio of tractor to pump
ownership. The major mechanisation survey of 1982 found that
the tractor/pump ratio was 1:5.4 in the ten surveyed
villages.[15] By contrast, however, the 1984 survey found that
the ratio had fallen to 1:8. However, when ownership by farm-
size class was taken into account, 60% of tractors were owned
by farms of over 5 feddans with the proportion falling to a
third in the case of irrigation pump ownership. In both
instances, ownership was linked to custom hiring of the
purchased machinery with only the largest farms possessing
sufficient area and range of activities to warrant full-time
use of the machinery on-farm.

Complementing the private sector stock of basic agricultural
machinery is machinery owned and operated through the gamiyas.
In the late 1970s 17% of the tractor stock was owned by the
co-operatives.[16] Many of these have been poorly maintained
and serviced. In the Dakhaliya village surveyed in 1984, for
example, although the gamiya had a rentable tractor, it was
kept in such a poor condition that farmers preferred to use

the private sector custom hire market. Similarly it was last reported that only 55% of the tractors on the state farms in reclamation areas were in working condition. This is a common enough tale, testimony to the changing set of fashionable pre-ferences for mechanical diffusion.

The volume and type of machinery are listed in Tables 9.3. and 9.4. Unfortunately, time series data are only available for the supply of tractors, where it can be seen that the func-tional stock more than quadrupled between 1953 and 1981. Since the early 1970s this stock has more than doubled, a direct reflection of the range of government policies aimed at accelerating the pace of mechanisation.

Domestic production of the larger 60-65hp tractors has shown a fluctuating trend. Until 1977 domestic production comprised between 35-40% of annual supply. This share appears to have fallen substantially since 1977 with the liberalisation of import rules and the increased inflow of agricultural machi-nery under the various donor assisted schemes. Imports of tractors and related implements increased from around 1500 units in 1973 to over 4000 in 1982. Ministry of Agriculture imports of machinery under USAID's Commodity Import Programme are estimated to have cost over $13m since 1975.

In the medium term, given the diversifying and ambitious nature of current government mechanisation plans, the share of imported machinery is likely to rise. This will mostly be accounted for by imports of non-basic machinery. Public sec-tor production of tractors (Nasr Automative Company, Helwan) and farm implements (Behera Company, Alexandria), as well as the smaller private sector companies' output, is likely to provide the bulk of these domestic requirements. Imported equipment - such as Japanese rice transplanters and combines - is likely to be concentrated in areas where mechanisation has so far been weak and where indigenous technology or licensed production fails to fill perceived needs.

Table 9A (in the Appendix) highlights one important aspect of mechanisation in contemporary Egyptian agriculture. Apart from tractors, irrigation pumps, threshers, winnowers and devices for crop transportation the stock of machines is rela-tively undiversified. As has been already mentioned, current tractor stocks are probably in excess of local requirements,

Table 9.3: Tractor Stocks, 1953-1982

Year	Stock	Imports	Domestic Production**
1953	8850	-	-
1955	10750	-	-
1960	10994	-	-
1965	14500	-	788
1970	17500	1901	1176
1971	18500	1632	950
1972	18500	1670	1227
1973	20036	1500	1143
1974	21000	1952	1259
1975	21500	2850	1435
1976	-	3398	1694
1977	-	6061	2236
1978	29784/24680*	-	-
1982	38639	-	-

Source: Richards, 1982, p.204:
   * ERA 2000, p.x3 and p.x.10
   ** Nasr Automative Company

Table 9.4: Current Stock of Principal and Agricultural Machinery 1982

	Wheel Tractor (50-65HP)	Ploughs (Chisel)	Pesticide Sprayers	Threshers/ Winnowers	Trailers	Irrigation pump (hp)
Number	388639	35997	12610	7712	17819	863572(hp)

Source: Ministry of Agriculture: Egyptian Agricultural Mechanisation Plan,
   1982/83-1986/87, pp72-74.

given the predominantly custom-hire nature of the market.
There may be a current shortfall of irrigation pumps of around
30% when measured in horsepower. However, saqia use remains
highly competitive in many areas of the Delta, and taking
water through gravity flows is also a feasible and costless
option for many cultivators at or near the canal head. These
factors suggest that irrigation pump requirements have been
over-estimated.

The variety of machines currently available is naturally
reflected in the prevailing patterns of usage. The
Agricultural Mechanisation Survey of 1982 estimated the level
of mechanisation by task and by crop with some precision.[18]
As expected, seedbed preparation and associated tasks are
almost entirely mechanised, as is threshing where tractor dri-
ven threshers have almost entirely supplanted the nourag
(save, to some extent, in Fayoum and Upper Egypt). Irrigation
was nearly two-thirds mechanised using both diesel and
electric-powered pumps. Use of sprayers and, increasingly, of
state-organised aerial spraying has likewise shown considerable progress.

However, animals were still predominantly used for transportation and manual harvesting, weeding and fertiliser application was the norm. Almost no progress had been made in
mechanising these tasks. This pattern of adoption confirms
that power-intensive operations have been the first to be
mechanised. This has undoubtedly affected demand for labour
for land preparation and ploughing, but has had virtually no
impact on labour use in the peak harvest seasons. It is for
this reason that the current focus is on reducing the labour
bottleneck at harvest through a substitution effect.

The 1982 Survey did not present its results in terms of
machine use by farm size category. Historical experience from
other countries - and from Egypt's own pre-1953 experience -
has suggested that adoption of new technology has been positively associated with farm size.[19] For current machine
ownership this is still born out, as can be seen in Table 9.5.
However, in terms of machine use, it appears that small farms
may actually use machine inputs more intensively than larger
farms and that there is very little variation by farm size in
machine application for the principal tasks of ploughing,
irrigation and threshing. That this is the case has clearly

Table 9.5: Machine Ownership: by Type & Farm Size 1982

Farm Size	New Tractor	Used Tractor	New Pump	Used Pump
Landless	4	1	4	0
0-1	3	1	2	1
1-2	4	2	9	2
2-3	6	1	20	0
3-5	6	7	17	8
> 5	37	11	42	7
Total	60	23	94	18

Source: Hopkins et al., 1982, p169

Table 9.6: Machine Use: by Operation and by Crop 1982

	Crop					
	Cotton	Maize	Rice	Wheat	Birseem	Vegetables
Ploughing	97.9	94.4	99.1	96.3	94.6	96.3
Levelling	76.1	71.1	97.0	73.0	76.0	94.9
Furrowing	71.8	64.1	-	-	-	89.3
Weeding	0.3	2.1	-	-	-	4.4
Irrigation	62.9	55.7	63.6	59.2	60.3	76.7
Pest Control	86.1	67.5	-	-	-	69.7
Harvesting	0.1	2.4	1.8	1.1	-	-
Threshing	-	-	97.5	98.2	-	-
Winnowing	-	-	97.3	64.8	-	-
Transportation	17.9	13.9	19.5	16.4	11.3	38.3
Cutting/Picking	-	-	-	-	0.4	3.0

Source: Hopkins et al., 1982, Appendix Tables B1-B7

to be attributed to the existence of a well established rental market.

Custom-hiring

The predominance of custom-hiring in the market for agricultural machinery has been evident for the last decade. Indeed, most serious studies of mechanisation have recognised that, given the fragmented small farm nature of production, a developed rental market would be the only efficient and relatively swift means for accelerating the pace of machine adoption. In turn, this approach has assumed that the returns to investment in machinery through leasing will remain as positive as they have done in the recent past. Gotsch and Dyer, for example, have estimated financial rates of return to tractor use for tillage of between 102%-377% and economic rates of return of between 37%-322%.[20] In general, there appears to be a strong positive association with the rate of return and farm size.

Apart from timely completion of on-farm work, the 1982 survey discovered that investment was a consistently important factor in explaining purchases of agricultural machinery, and tractors in particular. This reflected the strong returns flowing from custom hiring. Although farmers preferred, at least in theory, to use co-operative or agricultural mechanisation station equipment, because the hire charges were lower, such equipment was often not available at the right time, ensuring that the private rental market remained dominant. Over 70% of tractor hirers resorted to the private market. Even when the gamiya tractor was rented, over half of the respondents reported a waiting period in excess of a week and a further third had to wait on average for between 3-7 days. By contrast, in nearly 80% of cases when a private tractor was hired, the machine was either available on the day or with a one day wait. Only 20% of cases reported having to wait for longer than a week. A similar pattern existed for other private market machine-hire transactions where threshers or pumps were involved. The same survey also showed that over half the sample of tractor owners, but only a quarter of pump owners habitually rented out their plant.[21]

More recent evidence suggests that the proportion of machine owners hiring out their equipment has grown. Thus, although

the number of machine owners, whether singular or in part-
nership (this latter form frequently comprising resource
pooling by family members) has continued to expand, the supply
of custom hire services has multiplied, with obvious implications for the price of such services. This is particularly
true for tractors and threshers. Ownership of pumps - the
purchase price of which can currently vary between £E600-3000
- has also continued to rise. This is not only a function of
the smaller size of initial investment but also reflects less
bunched and restricted periods of use over the course of the
agricultural year. This also helps to explain a far lower
level of hiring out by pump owners.

Machine Finance and the Level of Subsidy

The financing of machinery investment has not been satisfactorily analysed. However, it appears that although remittances occasionally play an important role, domestically derived
savings and temporary financial transfers within families
account for about half the tractor and pump purchases. In
40%-45% of cases, purchases were financed by bank or co-
operative loans or dealer-instalment plans. Bank or co-
operative loans accounted for 27% of tractor purchases; their
share has continued to rise since 1982, reflecting the structure of incentives, mirrored in differential interest rates,
established by the government.

Clearly, the range of subsidies, explicit or implicit, is an
important factor determining the pace of mechanisation. In
Egypt, where price interventions remain at the heart of the
system, two factors in particular can be isolated; the cost of
capital and the cost of energy. Specific, preferential
interest rates for purchasing machinery are offered by co-
operatives and public sector banks, particularly PBDAC. Under
the present system interest on machine purchases has been held
down to an 8% annual rate (the standard market rate for capital has varied between 13-15%). The real cost of capital has
been significantly and consistently negative over the last
decade.

Conditions of access to such loans have been relatively
unrestrictive. Entry in the hiyaza records and a down payment
equal to around 25% of the capital cost have been necessary

conditions for benefiting from state credit schemes for tractor purchase.   In the case of irrigation pump credit no down
payment has been required.[22] The distribution of state provided credit to agriculture can be seen when analysing the
utilisation of funds released by the PBDAC. Although it was
established in 1931, only since 1976 has PBDAC has been able
to deal directly with farmers.[23] To this extent PBDAC functions have in part supplanted those previously carried out by
the co-operatives.   Thus although both gamiya and PBDAC are
credit sources, the PBDAC function has expanded at the expense
of the co-operatives, which are used as distributive points
for loans-in-kind, fertiliser and seed.   At present, PBDAC
offers a range of credit options defined in terms of duration,
activity and level of interest.   While production or seasonal
loans are given either in cash or kind with a nominal interest
charge of 3% per annum, allocations are also made under the
food security title – principally poultry and livestock activity – in addition to loans for land reclamation and mechanisation.   Loans for food security attract interest of 7%, for
mechanisation 8% and for land reclamation 4% p.a. Other activities can command credit, but at the normal commercial rate
of 13-14 %.   Thus, all major credit functions of the bank
involve the supply of capital at negative real rates.

Credit allocations to particular activities vary substantially.   By 1984 of the £E700m set aside for the four principal subsidised loan spheres, roughly 90% was allocated to
food security and production loans, a further 6% for mechanisation and 4% for land reclamation.   Table 9.7 decomposes the
distribution of credit for the three Governorates in which the
1984 survey occurred.   Apart from demonstrating regional
variations in credit offtake, with allocations to livestock
and poultry accounting for almost half total credit in
Sharkiya and Gharbiya, it can also been seen that loans for
mechanisation vary between 2.3%-5.4% of total credit.   This
excludes credit gathered from other public sector banks or
taken directly from the co-operative.

In addition to these standard sources of credit, specific projects have also been set up geared to enhancing investment in
livestock, poultry and machine ownership.   The Small Farmer
Project, which originally functioned in three Governorates,
Qalyubiya, Sharkiya and Minya, but has now been generalised,
concentrated specifically on these activities.   For the two

Table 9.7: Distribution of PBDAC Credit: by Activity & Governorate, 1982/83

Activity	Gharbiya	Dakhaliya	Sharkiya
Crop Loan	22750586 (38.3%)	37687266 (79.1%)	27810984 (49.5%)
Livestock & Poultry	28640377 (48.3%)	7250610 (15.2%)	26267016 (46.8%)
Agricultural Mechanization	3208287 (5.4%)	2303338 (4.8%)	1266352 (2.3%)
Other	4787011 (8.0%)	392963 (0.8%)	790891 (1.4%)
Total (£E)	59386261	47634177	56135243

Source: PBDAC unpublished figures

Table 9.8: Farm Equipment Loans Under Small Farmer Project to October 1984 - Qalyubiya and Sharkiya

Type	Number of Disbursements	Amount Disbursed (£E)
Tractors	110	437813 (16.6%)
Implements	180	287804 (10.9%)
Irrigation Pumps	879	920917 (35.0%)
Sprayers	276	30566 (1.2%)
Generators	218	223299 (8.5%)
Trucks	42	135700 (5.2%)
Poultry Equipment	1183	218725 (8.3%)
Other	401	378508 (14.3%)
Total	3289	2633332 (100%)

Source: Director, Small Farmer Project, Ministry of Agriculture, Cairo, October 1984.

original Delta Governorates loans for farm equipment amounted
to just under 12% of total disbursements to the end of 1984.
Credit under this scheme has been given at commercial rates
(13%-14%) and the distribution of that credit would therefore
give a clearer idea of the relative structure of preferences
and, by implication, returns to particular machines. In this
regard, it is interesting to note that investment in irrigation pumps was, in value terms, the most significant while
loans for tractors were the second most important. Table 9.7
also serves to illustrate the relatively narrow range of
investment choices for agricultural machinery. Excluding
poultry equipment, tractor and pump credit accounted for
nearly half the number of cases and over 56% of the value of
loans.

Apart from subsidisation of the cost of capital, the price of
energy also remains highly subsidised. Domestic energy prices
in 1983 for fuel oil and gas oil were, respectively, 5% and
14% of their international price equivalents. By December
1985 gasoline prices had been raised to between 49%-62% of
border prices, but diesel fuel was under 10% of the border
level. The overall weighted average for refined petroleum
products was of the order of 15%-20%, rising to nearly 40% by
June 1986, largely because of the fall in the international
price of fuel oil. The financial cost to the government of
such energy subsidies (including gas and electricity) exceeded
£500m by 1983 with the implicit economic subsidy amounting to
around $2.5bn.[24] Such significant subsidisation of running
charges has obviously enhanced the attractiveness of machinery
acquisition, hire and use.

Public Sector Mechanisation Programme

In attempting to accelerate the pace of mechanisation in agriculture, the Egyptian state has, as already mentioned, not
only entered into major loan arrangements with bilateral and
multilateral donor agencies, but has also offered hire services for farmers (partly as a consequence) at rates considerably below the private market rate. This has been a
long-standing policy - gamiyas have offered subsidised rates
for over a decade. Co-operative tractor hire rates have
generally been fixed at around 60% of the private market rate.
In the newly-established Agricultural Mechanisation Centres,

of which over twenty have now been opened, the hire charge is
simply fixed at half the market rate. This includes the services of directly competitive machine types - such as tractors
- as well as newer machine types where the extension aspect is
more prominent. The small rice combines and transplanters now
being demonstrated by these Mechanisation Centres are a case
in point.

Given the emphasis placed on these outlets by the government
and major donors, such as IBRD, it is worth dealing with this
aspect of machine subsidisation and extension in more detail.

The functions of the Mechanisation Centres include the acceleration of the pace of adoption of such machinery through the
provision of additional stocks of basic agricultural machinery
- particularly tractors. By making available such machinery
at rates that are half the current market level, the government aims to drive down the price of custom hiring operations.
Furthermore, these centres are intended to be points from
which new untried technology is disseminated, after experimentation at the large state farm in Saha, Kafr-el-Sheikh. By
demonstrating the use of new technology - such as rice combines - it is hoped to encourage private investment in such
machines. The present requirement, it is argued, is firstly
to demonstrate their efficacy, at competitive prices, prior to
providing subsidised credit support for their purchase by
individual farmers. Under the IBRD-supported Mechanisation
Programme it was originally intended that a further 50 of
these centres would be functioning by the end of 1989. In
addition, it was envisaged that around 220 mechanised farming-
co-operatives would be set up, providing mechanised farming
services for about 10% of the cultivated area, and profiting
from the proposed revamped extension service. At present, it
is not unjust to say that the extension service is virtually
non-existent. Farmers in the three villages surveyed in 1984
reported almost no contact with the appropriate extension
officer. Furthermore the currently established Mechanisation
Centres, as well as the additional ones proposed, are linked
to the entire credit strategy in which for the proposed mechanised farming co-operatives, negative real interest rates (8%)
would be maintained (with further reduction in the initial
down-payment).

The demonstration effect in terms of new technology clearly
has some rationale, particularly when initial investment costs

are lumpy and where it is unlikely that the private sector
will venture, at least in the early stages. However, this
begs the question as to whether, firstly, there are coherent
reasons for accelerating the substitution of labour by mechanical energy and secondly, whether the current practice and
stock of the Mechanisation Centres is designed to achieve
these aims. Thirdly, the entire strategy is problematic in
terms of the longer-run function of state-controlled outlets
for technology. To date, mechanised services have been provided overwhelmingly by private operators. Experience with
co-operatives as the organising point for tractor and pump
hire services has been poor and a sceptic might well wonder
what likely difference could result from the newer proposals
for establishing mechanised farming co-operatives. Fourthly,
while Mechanisation Centres are conceived largely as
demonstration centres, the practice of hiring out standard
equipment at heavily subsidised rates suggests that the function of demonstration is conceived of in a rather broad sense.
With the administration now under considerable pressure to
curtail the level of subsidies through the economy, such ambitious programmes clearly add to the overall subsidy bill, even
if soft loans and outright grants of machinery are responsible
for initial stocking of the centres. Clearly, as long as any
major uncertainty remains regarding the level of subsidy, both
through the interest rate and, most particularly, in terms of
the price of energy, investment in new, limited-purpose machinery will remain restricted. This would provide some justification for the substantial state investment in these centres
while raising the obvious question as to the suitability of
the technology being demonstrated. If the cost structure and
advantage of such technology can only be sustained in a
heavily subsidised regime, this raises doubts about its
longer-run feasibility, unless it is assumed that subsidisation will remain a constant.

To date, the stock of machinery commonly held by the
Mechanisation Centres betrays a heavy bias towards machines
already well adopted in agriculture. In 1984 over 80% of the
stock in the Sharkiya Mechanisation Centres comprised tractors, threshers and irrigation pumps. With the exception of a
number of disk ploughs, maize planters and seed drills, the
principal new items of equipment were Japanese rice transplanters and combines. However, the stock of these latter items
was relatively small, particularly given the wide area

coverage of each centre. The Mashtoul Centre, for example, had a catchment area of around 45,000 farm households with a stock of 22 tractors and some eighty (tractor-driven) threshers. At best, this satisfied no more than 8% of actual demand for machinery services. In both Mashtoul and Minyet possibly as much as 90% of utilised machine time was accounted for by the hiring out of tractors and pumps at these preferential rates. While in theory priority was given to the use of tractors for field tasks, they could also be hired for transportation purposes.

The 1984 sifi season was the first in which the rice transplanters and combines were hired out. Charges varied between £E30-50 per feddan for harvesting with the combine while the transplanting rate was £E75 per feddan, a charge which included the cost of the variety planted.[25] For the latter activity, one feddan normally required between 6-7 hours with harvesting taking between 3-4 hours. Both Centres reported very intensive use of the rice combines and transplanters with demand for the technology considerably in excess of the supply capacity. However, it was clear that, even with highly subsidised rates and substantially-accelerated work schedules, off-take of the services was strongly biased towards larger farmers. This was in part a reflection of the inevitable preference shown towards farm households with more substantial holdings where fragmentation and small field size was not a barrier to efficient use of the machinery. In the absence of consolidation, most small farmers considered that the new technology was unsuitable to their needs. At the same time they viewed with scepticism the obligation to plant a new variety of rice, if the Mechanisation Centre's transplanter was used. Most preferred to await the outcome of others' experimentation. In that sense, the machinery clearly was fulfilling a demonstration role.

A more significant problem concerned the suitability of the technology for small, non-consolidated areas, given the widespread reluctance of small farm households to contemplate voluntary consolidation of fields and machine use. This could suggest that any successful long term offtake of the technology amongst small- and medium-sized farm households would be contingent on a comprehensive consolidation programme or area consolidation for rice cultivation, in common with the enforced bloc cultivation of cotton.   This would allow for optimal utilisation of the available machinery.   However, in neither circumstance would ownership of such technology be an attractive proposition - assuming the continuing numerical dominance of small farm units and multiple cropping.   To this extent, it seems likely that rice mechanisation will depend not only on the existence of subsidised, state-provided hire services but also on the increased provision of such services by the private sector.   The restrictive nature of the technology and its lack of potential subsidiary earning capacity heavily reduces the incentive for investment.   This is further reinforced by the maintenance of forced deliveries for rice with obvious implications for the relative profitability of the crop.

While hire services from the Mechanisation Centres were charged at half the market rate, in the absence of any private ownership there was no market rate for rice machinery other than that fixed by the Centres.   In the Sharkiya village the charge for harvesting one feddan was £E30 in 1984, with a work time of 3-4 hours.   This rate was 25% higher than the going wage rate for manual labour.   Rice harvesting was still carried out almost exclusively by male labour with a wage rate determined in area terms.   For the 1984 sifi season, harvesting one qirat (24 qirat = 1 feddan) commanded a wage of £E1, with one adult male worker covering around 3-4 qirats in a day.   Thus, while manual harvesting was a cheaper option in area terms, machine use had the obvious advantage of minimising time and supervision.   For the larger farms this was clearly a major factor in the choice of technology.   In one of the large farms sampled, seven feddans of the seventeen feddan holding was put under rice in the sifi crop.   In theory, using a combine the work could have been completed within four days (c.28-30 hours operation).   In the 1984 season this farmer did commence harvesting with the combine but found that the results were poor, particularly because of spillage.   He then reverted to the traditional system of harvesting by hired male labour.   In all, the task required between 80-90 man-days of labour input (448 man-hours) with a final cost per feddan of £E48.   It is interesting to note that while in general wage rates for male labour in this village were positively associated with farm size, the wage for rice harvesting (£E6 per day) was nearly 50% higher than the standard wage rate in the village.   This undoubtedly reflected the wage premium opera-

tive at times of bunched demand for particular time-
constrained tasks.

In the case of rice transplanting, where female hired labour
is commonly employed on the larger farms, the hire charge in
1984 (inclusive of the cost of the variety planted) was £E75
per feddan. Using the example of the same farm, work that
could be accomplished with 6-7 hours of machine time required
between 20-24 man-hours (standardised) of labour input.
However, the lower wage levels commanded by female hired
labour (half the male wage rate) meant that production costs,
inclusive of other inputs, were around £E40 per feddan,
slightly over half the charge levied for the use of mechanical
technology. This measurement in nominal terms fails to cap-
ture the respective economic costs implied in both technology
choices, but it does illustrate succinctly the current
barriers to mechanisation of rice production, assuming, of
course, that the new technology can deliver comparable or
superior levels of productivity. However, it is also important to note that the assumption that small farm households
would not be responsive to machine adoption because of the
intensive use of family labour inputs in production does not
hold. It is instructive to note that in the two smallest farm
size categories (0-1 and 1-3 feddans) between 75%-78% of
labour time devoted to rice transplanting and harvesting was
of hired labour.

For multi-purpose and more intensively employed machinery,
such as tractors and pumps, it is clear that there is no
longer a need for a demonstration effect while the rental
price, given the increased supply of custom hire machinery in
the private market, will tend to fall. To this extent,
current stocking practices for the Mechanisation Centres
appear to be ill-conceived. At the same time, the limited
stock of such standard machines implies that the effect of
sub-market rental charges on the general rental price will be
weak. Rather, evidence from the Sharkiya village suggests
that it is the large farmers in the village who are the principal beneficiaries - the very people who claim, not without
foundation, to have arranged for the establishment of the
Centre in the village. It is hardly surprising to find that
when subsidised functions are supply constrained, extra-
economic factors are of the greatest importance in determining
the access to such services.

Current Levels of Mechanisation: Evidence from the 1984 Survey

Mechanisation in Egyptian agriculture has been limited and of
relatively recent duration.   An intensive village survey in
Minoufiya, for example, demonstrated that the two principal
mechanical devices - the tractor and thresher- had largely
been introduced in the decade between 1965 and 1975.[26] In the
mid-1960s between 6% and 9% of farm households used tractor
power or threshers.   By 1970 this proportion had risen to
25%-32% and five years later between 66% and 81% of farm
households used both machines.   A more recent nine-village
survey in Qalyubiya, Sharkiya and Minya found a very low level
of owned-machinery stock but custom-hiring from the private
sector, for a limited range of machinery, was the normal
system in all villages.[27]   Tractor power, water pumping,
threshing, winnowing and limited use of sprayers were the sum
of the machinery available to farm producers. With the exception of rice transplanters and small combines partially
available through the Agricultural Mechanisation Centre in the
Sharkiya village, the stock and usage of machinery appears to
have undergone relatively limited change.   In the decade since
1975 the pattern of mechanisation can best be described as a
consolidation and widening of the use of the existing choice
of machinery.

The expanded demand for mechanical services has been associated with a somewhat broader pattern of ownership.   As is
made clear in Chapter 8, this is closely linked to the profitability of custom-hiring and the relaxation of credit
controls for farm machinery acquisition.   At the same time,
government policy in the recent past has consistently
downgraded the role of the co-operatives; this has been
reflected in the increasing role of the private sector in the
provision of mechanical services.   The 1976/77 Farm Management
Survey indicated that for tractor power over 86% of available
horsepower was provided by co-operatives.[28] Current evidence
suggests that over nine-tenths of available mechanical power
is owned and provided by the private sector.[29]   Even the
recent Mechanisation Centres are projected at their peak to
cover no more than 10% of the cultivated area. This suggests
that further mechanisation will be determined by the response
of the private sector, albeit with substantial explicit or
implicit subsidies from the state.

Apart from traditional farming implements - hoes, spades etc.
- the ownership of mechanical farm implements remained limited
in the three sampled villages. At the same time, ownership
was strongly correlated with farm size - particularly for
tractors. In the case of irrigation pumps, a broader spread
was discernible. Save for the largest farms (above ten feddans) custom-hiring of owned machinery was the norm and this
had major implications for the size and distribution of household income. Tractor, pump and thresher ownership currently
offers a high rate of return through leasing, irrespective of
any possible productivity gains through more timely use of
such machinery on owned land.

Longitudinal data was available only for the Sharkiya village.
In 1972 the village had a stock of nine tractors and irrigation pumps, all privately owned. By 1982 the numbers had
risen to fourteen, of which, in the case of the tractors,
twelve were custom-rented.[30] The village stock of twelve
threshers and nine chisel ploughs in 1972 had remained
constant in the first case and had risen to fourteen in the
latter case.

By 1984 the stock of tractors in the village had grown at a
very rapid pace. Thirty-six tractors were currently in
working condition in the entire village (including the
ezbahs). The great majority were Nasr 65hp machines. The
stock of irrigation pumps had remained constant, this being
attributable to a continuing preference for saqia irrigation
in this village. In addition, fifteen threshers, six large
sprayers (all operated by the Co-operative), 31 small sprayers
and at least ten pick-up trucks were at work in the village.
The nearby Mechanisation Centre also had a functioning stock
of sixteen tractors, nine of which were the standard 65 or
77hp variety. If these are taken into account, the 1984 population of tractors per 1000 feddans of crop area exceeded the
average for Sharkiya by over four times. This assumes, of
course, that the tractor stock was used entirely within the
village. This was unlikely to be the case, particularly for
the Mechanisation Centre tractors. However, even disregarding
these, the tractor/crop area ratio exceeds the Ministry of
Agriculture defined optimum by at least 250%. Nevertheless,
the private financial rate of return clearly remained significantly positive for machine owners despite the recent sharp
growth in tractor acquisitions. Apart from widespread use for

ploughing, levelling and threshing, tractors were also used
for transporting crops from the field, in just under a third
of all cases, as well as non-farm work.

The current stock of machinery in the other villages was more
restricted. In the Gharbiya village, the principal stock of
tractors was owned by the proprietor of the village brick factory. In all, there were five privately-owned tractors, as
well as eight small powered transporters with trailers. In
addition, there were three standard threshers, twenty small
sprayers, ten irrigation pumps and eight pick-up trucks. The
latter were commonly used as country taxis as well as for
transporting agricultural produce. No gamiya-provided machine
services were available nor was the nearest Mechanisation
Centre (some six kilometers away in Santa) of use to village
producers. One consequence of this was that no new types of
agricultural machinery had been demonstrated in the village.
The Extension Service appeared to be entirely non-functional.

In the Dakhaliya village, although the nearest gamiya did
possess a couple of tractors and threshers, most farmers were
reluctant to rely on them because of their poor maintenance
and unreliable service. As in Gharbiya, the nearest
Mechanisation Centre was too distant and this likewise meant
that acquaintance with technology other than the standard
equipment was almost non-existent. The stock of tractors in
the village was put at eighteen. In other words, the
tractor/crop area ratio was slightly above the norm for the
governorate. Village ownership of irrigation pumps (where the
stock was put at seven) was well below the norm. This may
partly be explained by the fact that many households could
take irrigation water through gravity because of their proximity to the primary canal. The absence of threshers and
pick-up trucks in the village, together with the limited
ownership of sprayers (eight), suggested that this village was
under-mechanised when compared with the other two sampled
areas and the governorate as a whole.

In common with the other two sampled cases, no repair facilities existed in the Dakhaliya village for agricultural machinery. In the Sharkiya village, there was one part-time
mechanic who specialised in car and truck repairs; all agricultural machines had to be taken to the neighbouring town.
In all three cases this would have involved a journey of bet-

ween 6-10 kms.   It was generally thought that adequate maintenance and spare parts were available in these towns, but the
promptness of service was not always satisfactory.   Likewise,
manufacture and repair of more traditional farm equipment -
such as the saqia - was only available in the local town.

Despite the wide variation in the stock of machinery and price
of machine services, the level of machine adoption across the
villages for tractors and threshers was fairly uniform.   This
suggests that the market for custom-hire machine services,
though predominantly satisfied by local village suppliers,
also involves machine operators from neighbouring villages.
This is hardly surprising given the relatively small distances
between villages in all these governorates.   Adoption of pump
technology varied to a far greater extent and was dependent on
competing technology - saqia or gravity - available in each
village.

Table 9.9 indicates the scale of machine adoption in terms of
particular crop operations, disaggregated by farm size.   Most
striking is the almost total displacement of traditional land
preparation techniques by tractor power.   This extended across
all farm-size classes.   With tractorised ploughing achieving
comparable coverage to the traditional draught animal-drawn
plough in a sixth of the time and with no negative productivity implications, such substitution is not difficult to
comprehend.[31]   However, tractorised tillage still almost
entirely involves use of chisel ploughs.   The aim of the Five
Year Mechanisation Plan to increase the use of disk and rotary
ploughs, supposedly more suitable for Egyptian heavy clay
soils, appears to have made little progress.   At the same
time, it is important to note that planting remains almost
entirely unmechanised.   This means that hand sowing, rather
than grain drill use, remains the norm.[32]   In the case of
rice, hand sowing and transplanting was also customary.

A recent study of relative wheat productivity under normal
conditions of hand broadcasting and seed drill use concluded
that, in the case of wheat, potentially significant productivity gains could be made by the substitution of the latter
for the former.   An increase in grain yields of over 28% and
straw-yield gains of nearly 21% were estimated from such a
switch.   Financial returns per feddan (using 1983 prices) were
computed at over £E80, with net economic returns exceeding

Table 9.9:   Use of Machinery by Operation and Farm Size, 1984
             (% of observed cases)

Operation	--------Farm Size (feddans)--------				
	0-1	1-3	3-5	5-10	>10
Manuring	3.6%	9.3%	22.2%	52.4%	50%
Ploughing	97.6%	98.2%	96.2%	91.9%	100%
Irrigation	61.9%	71.3%	83.0%	100.0%	100%
Pest Control	44.0%	69.4%	91.7%	100.0%	100%
Harvesting	--	--	--	--	--
Threshing	96.2%	97.2%	100.0%	100.0%	100%
Crop Transportion	3.0%	17.3%	40.7%	47.6%	28.6%

Source: ODI/Zagazig Survey, 1984

£E184 per feddan.[33]   Both calculations, however, treat wheat
straw as a tradeable and straw's use as an animal feed was
priced, having estimated the total digestible nutrient content, in terms of an internationally-traded proxy.   This may
have inflated the level of societal gain that could result
from such a shift in cultivating practice.   At the same time,
the yield increments involved may have been over-estimated by
the plot selection procedure and the 'best practice' conditions under which seed drill use was applied.

While primary tillage was entirely mechanised, with two passes
using a standard chisel plough and a further pass with a
simple kasabiya (harrow), sowing and harvesting (for all
crops) has been untouched by mechanical energy.   Even where
primary tillage was effected by tractor, secondary tillage was
performed by use of the traditional draught animal-drawn
plough in over 17% of cases.   This conforms to the general
trend where tractorisation has recently occurred.[34]

Perhaps the most striking feature revealed by Table 9.9 is the
relative stability of tasks performed by machines and the
choice of machinery currently available to Egyptian farmers.
Although it is quite obvious that the coverage of such machinery has become much wider, encompassing all farm-size categories, it is also important to note that even in the case of
current irrigation technology, between 14%-30% of all irrigation activity on farms of less than five feddans is done
either by saqia or by gravity flows.   Indeed, in the Sharkiya
village in particular saqia irrigation was employed in over
58% of cases for farms of below five feddans.   This can be
explained not in terms of a shortage of available equipment
but as an explicit choice of technology.   Yet, most recent
analysis has argued that in both financial and economic terms
pump technology offers a relatively high rate of return, even
with no productivity effect.   Dyer & Imam's study suggests
that in financial terms by 1981 the cost of saqia irrigation
per feddan was 80% higher than with the use of pump
technology.[35]   However, as a result of energy subsidies, the
economic cost structure was reversed, with saqia use incurring
costs 15% below pump costs.   All attempts at deriving such
comparative cost figures have involved estimation of the
respective milk and meat losses to the livestock involved in
saqia pulling.   Estimates of such loss commonly comprise between 60%-80% of financial and economic costs of saqia use.[36]

Shepley, for example, arrives at figures of £E6.26 and £E7.39 as the net financial and economic benefit per feddan of pump use, largely on the basis of imputed losses for milk, meat and calf production. When these three elements are removed from the calculation, the saqia has a net advantage of £E1.58 in financial terms and £E4.96 in economic terms.[36]

Recent work by Soliman regarding the effect of saqia pulling on milk and calving productivity of draught animals suggests that there is no measurable negative effect.[38] Indeed, most livestock holders considered that relatively light work, such as saqia pulling, had a beneficial effect, at least with regard to milk output. El Tambadawy's detailed survey results showed that if the animal was worked less than four hours a day in relatively light work, such as saqia pulling, there was no loss in milk yield. If the animal was made to work for over four hours the milk loss was estimated at between 1-2kgs.[39] Ploughing work had a particularly adverse effect on milk production, but draught animals are rarely used for heavier ploughing. While a higher proportion of farm house-holds with holdings of less than five feddans owned a cow or cows rather than buffalos, in over 75% of cases in which ani-mal power was used to pull the saqia, a buffalo was employed. As these are the major milk producers on small farm households this would tend to support the view that saqia pulling does not have a negative effect on milk and calving productivity. In addition, it should be noted that the average time per operation using the saqia was 3.6 hours. This gives addi-tional support to the argument.

There is little argument regarding the neutral yield effect of the adoption of irrigation pump technology when compared with saqias. This was also confirmed by the 1984 survey which found no meaningful association between yields and the type of irrigation technology in the regression analysis. However, the effect of the adoption of mechanical technology on the cost structure and the mix and volume of inputs, both of ani-mal and human energy, has been far less well-explored. Irrigation practices provide a particularly interesting instance as it is possible to compare two co-existing tech-nologies. Clearly, the most obvious effect of the introduc-tion of mechanical power in irrigation has been diminished demand for draught-animal power. Since land preparation is now almost completely mechanised, the use of draught animals has clearly been increasingly restricted.

This role has been supplanted by pump technology on the larger farms, and use of the saqia is principally restricted to the smaller farm units.   In terms of the labour substitution effect, for those farm-size classes where comparison can be made, it is very clear that saqia use involves far higher levels of labour time.   By far the greatest share of this labour-time is accounted for by male labour.   In smaller farms, this was household male labour, whereas hired male labour predominated in the larger units.   To that extent, the shift in technology has resulted in a decline in the volume of male labour inputs.   On average, labour inputs using pump technology were around 40% of the level associated with saqia use.   This demonstrates that a shift in irrigation technology has been associated unequivocally not only with the substitution of draught animal energy but also of human labour and, principally, male labour.   This substitution effect is clearly now wide-ranging, with between 70%-79% of irrigation observations for the two smallest farm size classes being achieved with pumps.

The shift to pump technology can be explained in terms of various factors.   In one of the villages sampled, proximity to the main canal and the water level had meant that the saqia was a relatively inefficient system for distributing water. At the same time, there was some evidence to suggest that the length of waiting time and other periodic problems associated with the system of saqia rings,[40] favoured the adoption of individualised pump hire services.   Around 80% of irrigation operations where pumps were used involved custom-hire services.   By contrast, in nearly two-thirds of cases where saqias were employed, shared ownership - the saqia ring - was the norm.

The labour-saving properties of pump technology, given the continuing predominance of male labour for this activity, also appear to have been a major factor behind the change in irrigation practice, and this has been reflected in the comparative cost structure of the two techniques.   Table 9.10 indicates the cost differential where shadow rates are imputed for household labour.   In the case of pumps the standard village hire rate was used.   When saqia technology was employed, the opportunity cost of animal inputs was calculated in terms of the prevailing hire rates for draught animals. Although this is a limited market, a market does exist and

Table 9.10:   Irrigation Technologies: Costs and Inputs per Feddan: 1984

| Variable | \---Farm Size--- | | | | | |
	0-1	1-3	3-5	5-10	>10	All
Labour Inputs[1]						
Saqia	116	105	76	--	--	107.3
Pump	51	42	33	37	52	43.5
Animal Inputs[2]						
Saqia	64	47	39	--	--	--
Hired Labour[3]						
Saqia	3.9%	8.5%	39.8%	--	--	8.2%
Pump	16.9%	24.7%	31.8%	65.5%	98%	28.0%
	\---£E---					
Economic Cost [4]						
Saqia	295	236	159	--	--	256
Pump	74	51	49	46	53	57
Financial Cost[5]						
Saqia	4.5	7	24	--	--	--
Pump	37	26	25	24	39	--
Animal Economic Cost[6]						
Saqia	213	156	132	--	--	--

1. = Total labour inputs in equalized man-hours
2. = Animal hours for Saqia pulling
3. = Hired labour hours as a share of total labour hours
4. = Total economic cost for irrigating one feddan (£E)
5. = Total financial cost for irrigating one feddan (£E)
6. = Economic cost for draught animal inputs in irrigating one
      feddan (£E)

Source: ODI/Zagazig Survey, 1984

this price appeared to be a simpler and as accurate a shadow
rate as the more convoluted and tendentious assumption of milk
and meat production losses. However, neither saqia nor pump
shadow costs include a depreciation component.

When shadow rates were imputed for labour and animal power,
the cost differential proved to be very significant. For
farms of below five feddans, saqia costs per feddan were over
four times those incurred with the predominant pump technology. Using nominal costs as the appropriate measure, pump
custom-hiring implied cash charges of between four and eight
times those generated by the use of a saqia. However, in
farms of between 3-5 feddans, where the hired/household labour
mix was broadly comparable for both types of technology, nominal charges were equalised. This suggested that the continuing importance of the saqia for the smallest farm
households could principally be explained in terms of the far
lower direct cash costs associated with that technology. At
the same time the availability of household labour for this
task remains an important factor in the selection of technique.

What is more problematic is the significance of the availability of draught animal power in this choice. In the Dakhaliya
village, the absence of saqias was accompanied by relatively
restricted livestock holdings. However, this cannot be attributed simply to substitution effects achieved in recent years
by mechanical technology, particularly given the structure and
ratio of crop and meat prices. This was clear in both the
Sharkiya and Gharbiya villages, where livestock holdings, when
tested statistically, demonstrated no meaningful association
with the choice of technique in irrigation. Indeed, as in the
Delta, the substitution of mechanical for animal energy has
not achieved a reduction in the level of livestock holdings.
With milk and meat sales important components of household
income, the trend may have been towards increasing animal
stocks. However, this effect was obviously contingent on the
current structure of relative prices.

The 1984 Survey demonstrated that, apart from a broadening in
the level of adoption, the stock and range of farm machinery
available to producers was extremely limited. This suggests
that the last decade has been one of consolidation of existing
technology rather than the introduction of new types of

Table 9.11: <u>Irrigation Technology: Proportion of Cases Where Pumps</u>
<u>Used: 1984</u>

Farm Size	Proportion
0-1	70%
1-3	79%
3-5	86%
5-10	100%
>10	100%

machine. This has resulted in an almost complete mechanisation of seedbed preparation, threshing/winnowing and, in some
villages, irrigation. The principal agricultural machine -
the tractor - is relatively widely used for crops and general
purposes, such as brick transportation.

The limited scale of machine substitution can be further seen
when the data are disaggregated by crop (Appendix Tables 9B
and 9C). The crop most substantially mechanised to date has
been wheat, but even there machine hours as a proportion of
total production time averaged 14%. For cotton, most particularly, the absence of any mechanisation apart from the use
of tractors for seedbed preparation, was demonstrated in the
very low proportion - circa 5% - of production time accounted
for by mechanical energy inputs.

These tables allow for some understanding of the relationship
between machine and animal inputs and farm size. This relationship was, in addition, explored through regressions.
Except in the case of wheat, where a significant negative
association between machine hours and farm size was estimated,
regressing machine hours on farm size by crop yielded no
meaningful association. This is confirmed by Table 9C
(Appendix) where it can be seen that the largest farms (over
ten feddans) had the highest labour share in total inputs, but
that there is no definite trend for the other farm size
classes. Indeed, the relative equalisation of machine inputs,
when calculated as a proportion of total inputs to production,
is quite striking.

If the adoption of available machinery was fairly homogenous
for all farm-size categories, in type and use patterns, this
was definitely so for the use of draught animal power. Except
for birseem, a clear negative association was estimated,
significant at the 1% level, between animal inputs and farm
size. This reflects the continuing importance of animal power
for saqia pulling, particularly for small farms, bringing fertiliser to the fields and for lifting the crop from field to
store. With the exception of saqia work, the other two tasks
were normally performed by donkeys and camels; the latter
being commonly hired for crop transportation.

The principal effect of machine adoption has clearly been to
substitute mechanical for animal energy. This displacement

has occurred largely because of the mechanisation of ploughing and irrigation operations. While both technical shifts have had labour substituting properties, the principal labour-intensive tasks have been untouched by mechanisation and this is reflected in the distribution of time shares in production by type of input.

The relationship between machine, animal and human inputs was further considered in terms of relative complementarities. This was particularly apt in the case of animal inputs. Here, animal labour time as a proportion of human labour time was regressed on farm size for all crops and for individual crops. As expected, there was a general highly significant negative relation, except in the case of birseem. Although earlier analysis has suggested that no consistent inverse relationship exists between labour inputs and farm size, it seems that in total crop production there is complementarity between animal and human labour. When machine time as a proportion of total labour time was regressed on farm size, the coefficient was generally positive but not statistically significant. In other words, it would seem that while the substitution of mechanical for animal energy has potential for parallel labour displacement, the current technical mix has not had any uni-form impact on labour-use patterns, save with regard to the hired/household labour ratio. This can simply be explained as a function of the custom-hire market, where machine rental implies the hire of the operator both in the case of tractors and irrigation pumps. However, this shift needs to be con-sidered in the light of broader labour allocation decisions made at the household level where non-farm employment oppor-tunities are a crucial variable.

The displacement of draught animal inputs by machinery is best understood as an outcome of the combination of relative factor and output prices. Clearly the rising real wage trend for male labour has stimulated the adoption of machinery for the current range of tasks. These are operations where male labour has been and is predominant. The limitation of draught animal inputs has also been particularly attractive given recent milk and meat prices, and mechanical energy adoption has been heavily subsidised, principally through low fuel costs. Furthermore, in a context where household labour - particularly male labour - can realistically be said to have an opportunity cost either in non-farm employment or educa-

tion, shorter working periods have been a major attraction.
In addition, the release from drudgery should not be
overlooked as a factor, if only because it was commonly cited
by farmers themselves as a reason for machine preference.
Primary tillage with an animal-drawn plough requires eight
times more labour than the same operation done with a tractor.
Such technical shifts clearly imply not only a diminution of
labour costs, but also a release of labour from crop-
associated work.

Available time-series data regarding the share of machine
costs in total costs indicate that over the last decade
machine costs have risen slightly. The most pronounced increment has been for wheat, while in the case of rice and cotton
the machine cost share has remained roughly constant. In all
cases the share of animal costs has fallen.

By 1984 machine costs ranged from around 23% of total shadow
costs for wheat production to around 10% for cotton. However,
no rental element was imputed in this calculation. When this
is taken into account and the data from the 1984 survey are
set alongside the time-series data from the Ministry of
Agriculture, machine costs as a share of total costs have
risen very gently since the early 1970s and remained broadly
constant over the last three years. However, as the detailed
analysis in Chapter 8 has demonstrated, the overall cost of
production for major field crops has increased at a rate
higher than that of the rate of inflation and the growth in
producer prices. This can largely be explained as a function
of the wage trend in agriculture. To this extent, it is clear
that machine adoption has not had a major depressing effect on
farm costs.

The limited impact of machine use on production costs has been
variously explained. One obvious factor has been the range of
tasks performed by the available machinery, further linked to
the fact that the most labour-intensive tasks have as yet been
unmechanised. In addition, it has commonly been argued that
the cost-saving properties of mechanisation have been weakened
by the excessive cost of machine-hire services. Indeed this
provided one important rationale for the state's most recent
foray in machine provision - the Mechanisation Centres with
their half market-price hire services. Yet, a comparison of
tractor rental charges for the period 1977-1984 suggests that

this argument is a weak one. Table 9.12 demonstrates that the cost of tractor hire fell in real terms by around 9% in this period.

Table   9.12:   Tractor   Rental   Rates: Delta,   1977-1984

Year	Rate per hour (£E)	Index	Cost of Living Index (Rural)	Real Hire Cost Index
1977	1.35	100	100	100
1984	3.58	265	90	91

But it should also be noted that there was a very wide spread of charges for machine services across villages. Thus, for the 1984 sample, tractor hire charges in the Gharbiya village were over double the rates for the two other villages. By contrast, in the Sharkiya village where the ratio of tractors and pumps to the cultivated area was highest, machine rental rates were very appreciably lower. Indeed, comparing the 1977 FMS data for Sharkiya with that collected in 1984 it appears that tractor rental rates declined by over 40% in real terms in the period from 1977 to 1984. Clearly this has been a direct function of the supply of such machinery.

Conclusion

Mechanisation in Egyptian agriculture has so far been largely concentrated on power-intensive operations. As yet, there has been little shift towards mechanisation of control intensive operations, despite the rise in the labour factor share.

There is conflicting evidence of the mechanisation productivity relationship. The 1984 survey was only able to compare output for different irrigation technologies, and no significant, positive relationship was found. However, Shepley has suggested that fairly substantial cotton yield increments occur with the adoption of mechanised seedbed preparation and water lifting. It is argued that, when combined, this technical shift allows for yield increments of just under 2 qantars per feddan. At 1984 prices, this would yield an additional financial return of £E118 per feddan.[41] But these estimates were based on a very limited sample and systematic investigation of this relationship for other countries has not provided satisfactory evidence of direct productivity gains.[42] Moreover, if the technical mix were assumed to be broadly

yield-neutral or slightly positive, net revenue would fall by
as much as 60% in financial terms. This then, obviously begs
the question: Why would farmers switch technologies in the
absence of gains in value-added?

Here, a distinction must be drawn between machine ownership
and use, as well as attention drawn to the wider set of uses
for tractors, in particular, in the rural economy. This
chapter has demonstrated that while ownership of farm machinery remains very limited, use of the available machine stock
is now widespread, cutting across all farm-size classes. This
means that for certain operations - seedbed preparation,
threshing and, to a lesser extent, water lifting - the shift
to mechanical power has already taken place. There is an
extremely well-developed rental market for machinery with wide
dispersion of prices in the hire charge. Recourse to this
market clearly has to be explained in terms of, firstly, the
cost implications of machine use and the structure of crop
profitability, and secondly, the implications for alternative
utilisation of farm resources resulting from the combined
time-saving properties of machine use.

In the first case - that of costs - there is relatively wide
divergence between the financial and economic costs associated
with the available technology. Apart from the very substantial subsidisation of capital - interest rates for machine
acquisition have been at least 15% below the rate of inflation
on an average annual basis - the other major divergence between private and societal costs has been in the price of
energy itself. By 1984, domestic fuel prices were just 12% of
the international price, one implication of which was that
economic tractor operating costs were between 217% and 287%
higher than financial operating costs, depending on the level
of use through the year. Most of the private gains therefore
derive from a redistributive, rather than direct productive,
effect. Clearly, this divergence has been a major factor in
stimulating the acquisition of farm machinery and its subsequent, wider adoption through the rental market.

At the farm level the factors determining adoption, through
custom hiring, are complex. Despite the undoubted direct
labour-substituting properties of both tractors and irrigation
pumps, the scale of such substitution has been relatively weak
and temporally condensed. Additionally, machine use has been

associated with a higher level of <u>hired</u> labour use for those
operations. This could, of course, reflect the labour-
disposition conditions that gave rise to the adoption decision
itself, or equally, could be an outcome of the actual basis on
which custom-hiring takes place. This is because tractor or
pump hiring involves the conjoint hire of labour to run the
machine. Yet given the strong diversification of employment
in the rural sector (See Chapter 7) and the growth in the
overall share of hired labour in total crop-labour time across
all farm-size categories, this shift should probably be
interpreted as a function of the decreasing overall involvement of household <u>male</u> labour in farm work. This implies
that, <u>ceteris paribus</u>, machine adoption becomes an attractive
proposition when the choice is not simply a <u>reduction</u> in
labour inputs (itself a function of the wage trend) but a
reduction in the aggregate cost per task where <u>hired</u> labour
inputs are predominant. Tractorisation, in particular, should
be construed as a mechanism for releasing male family labour
from intensive crop-related tasks in a context where supervision costs and time are minimised. At the same time the
release of household livestock from heavy draught work has a
positive effect on milk and meat yields. Thus, private profitability derives from a combination of factors where, with
rising wage rates and employment diversification, the adoption
of mechanical technology achieves a given input with a lower
level of <u>hired</u> labour time and limited supervision costs. As
financial costs - given the labour mix on small farms - are
heavily weighted in favour of 'traditional technology', this
suggests that the question needs to be viewed dynamically,
where - in the small farm sector- household labour allocation
is increasingly guided by the availability - for males - of
non-farm employment.

From the point of view of the tractor and pump owner, rates of
return have been high in financial terms. One estimate
suggests a marginal return of 376% for tractors on the assumption of more than 1000 operating hours per annum and a tractor
life of around 8000 hours.[43] This estimate is likely to be on
the high side. However, the earnings from machine hire per
annum, the details of which are presented in Chapter 8,
suggest that for both tractor and pump ownership, the rate of
return is significantly positive. This derives not only from
hiring out for crop-related activity, but also, in the case of
tractors, from their use in non-agricultural work. Such wider

consumption benefits have been noticed in numerous other cases where tractorisation has occurred and Egypt is no exception. Yet, this is particularly true for Egypt because of the very low cost of diesel fuel and it has been a major factor in broadening tractor ownership beyond the larger farm households.

The importance of non-agricultural benefits for tractor owners rather reduces the requirement for public subsidisation of machine acquisition and use. This is particularly true for tractors where current stocks are estimated to be near the optimal level. Insofar as energy costs have been raised towards the border price level, this would imply, in the short run, a possibly substantial upward twist to crop production costs which would have economy-wide inflationary implications in the absence of further state interventions in the pricing and distribution of food items. The effect would be transmitted through the price of wage goods to be the wage rate itself. This might lead in the medium term to a new equilibrium point where a rising labour factor share could again rationalise the adoption of the available technology. However, this would depend very strongly on the trend in the agricultural labour force, the participation rate and the absorptive capacity of the non-agricultural and overseas labour market.

The longer-run implications of farm mechanisation in Egypt are of obvious and central importance. It is clear that the present policy of government and donors places more emphasis on the current state of the agricultural labour market than on any projected change in those conditions. This is understandable when it is remembered that the types of technology now being tested have far more labour-displacing potential than the limited range of mechanical technology available until now. Already, the highly labour-intensive task of cotton pest-control - a task normally done by children and household women - is being supplanted by a growing use of aerial spraying, where consolidated cropping allows for such a shift. The major labour-supervising tasks of weeding, transplanting and harvesting are still untouched by machinery. One key constraint has been the excessive fragmentation of farm holdings and the general lack of crop consolidation, save for cotton.

While real wages for agricultural workers, particularly male workers, have consistently risen over the recent period, the high 'innovation costs' associated with harvesting and rice transplanting technology have restricted private adoption of such machinery. The very limited ownership of small combines must, for example, be attributed not only to the relatively high-capital cost and current supply constraints, but also to the limited functions of such machinery. Tractor 'fungibili-ty' has been one major reason for the growth in domestic con-sumption of such machines; this capacity is absent for the technology now being tested - largely for the 'demonstration effects'- by donor-funded projects and the government's Agricultural Mechanisation Centres.[43] In addition, the fami-liar scale economies that have stimulated the adoption of such machinery in other countries are largely absent in Egypt. While the 1984 survey provided evidence that, in the Sharkiya village, the major large farmers preferred to substitute rice transplanters and combines for the current production process, even at the highly subsidised rates offered by the Mechanisation Centres relative costs still favour the tradi-tional labour-intensive process.   Furthermore, technical problems appear to have reduced, or nullified, any output gains from adoption. On the assumption that these will be eliminated, it is nevertheless instructive to look at the implications for labour requirements if the role of such machinery was to be successfully generalised.

Although mechanisation of the most labour-intensive task - cotton picking - is unlikely in the short or medium term, rice transplanting and harvesting are currently subject to field tests. It seems likely that increased imports, and to some extent grants, will augment the present limited stock of such machinery. In the longer run, licensed production seems to be one possible outcome. Assuming that the diffusionary process is accelerated, both machines would have highly significant labour displacing properties. Current labour inputs for rice transplanting average around 25 man-hours (equalised) per fed-dan while for harvesting, the figure stands at around 57 man-hours per feddan. By contrast, mechanised rice transplanting can achieve the same coverage with a labour input of between 8% and 16% that of the traditional process. For rice har-vesting, the labour input would be between 7% and 14% of the level of current requirements, implying a displacement of hired labour and male hired labour in particular.   For transplanting, it would be largely family labour that was substituted.

Similar levels of labour saving could be expected with the introduction of wheat harvesting through mower binders, or multi-purpose combines. However, at current relative-factor costs, investment in such machinery would yield a negative social rate of return because of the size of the initial investment and the level of operating costs. For small combines, labour savings, when measured in hours, could be as high as 80% but the area requirements sufficient to generate positive returns would be concomitantly high. Indeed, a minimum of around 15 feddans would be required and use of such machinery on a smaller area would yield highly negative rates of return. With less than 2.3% of farm units exceeding 15 feddans and with little move towards effective consolidation of holdings, the introduction of such machinery seems unlikely in the near future.

Mechanisation of harvesting runs into further difficulties because of the premium placed by cultivators on straw as against grain output. Where - as with birseem - output is integral to on-farm livestock feeding, the introduction of mower binders tends to conflict with piece-meal cutting for current requirement, as well as on-field grazing, the present preferred practice. On small farms, in particular, birseem cutting is done by male household members. Where hired labour is employed, as on the larger units, it is normally male labour. With labour savings, in terms of hours, of as much as 75%, it is clear that such technology could be attractive for the larger units where hired labour predominates and where piece-meal cutting is not the dominant practice. This confirms the general, historical experience that further mechanisation, beyond seedbed preparation and water-lifting, will tend to be biased towards the needs of the larger farm households.

Footnotes

1. IBRD, Agricultural Development Project, Minoufiya-Sohag, 1977 and 1979.
2. IBRD, Egypt: Second Agricultural Development Project, Appraisal Report 5342a-EGT, Washington, 1985.
3. See, for instance, Rice Mechanisation Project, Annual Report, 1982/3.
4. Agricultural Mechanisation Project, Inception Report, 1981
5. Agricultural Mechanisation Plan, 1982/3.
6. Hopkins, et al., 1982.
7. ERA2000 Report, 1979.
8. Binswanger, 1978; Agarwal, 1984, pp290-302.
9. Binswanger, 1984, pp5-7; David, 1975.
10. ERA2000, 1979.
11. Binswanger, 1978.
12. Agarwal, 1984.
13. Abdel-Fadil, 1975, pp31-33.
14. Hopkins, 1985.
15. Hopkins, et al., 1982, pp158-167.
16. ERA2000, 1979, ppX14-X16.
17. Hopkins, et al., 1982.
18. Binswanger, 1984, pp12-13.
19. Dyer and Gotsch in Richards and Martin, 1983, pp214-222.
20. Hopkins, et al., 1982, pp158ff.
21. Imam and Khalil, 1983.
22. The following section is based on information given by Abdel Qadir Abdel Wahid, Deputy Chairman, PBDAC, Cairo, in September 1984.
23. IBRD, 1983(a), pp69ff; Dervis, Martin and van Wijnbergen, 1984.
24. Data collected at Mashtoul and Minyet-el-Qam markaz Mechanisation Centres.
25. Abdel-Maksoud, 1977,pp102-3.
26. El-Kholy and Abbas, 1982, pp61-66.
27. Goueli et al., 1980, Tables 5 and 8.
28. Hopkins et al., 1982, pp158ff.
29. Reiss, Lutfi, et al., 1982, pp31ff.
30. Shepley, Wissa and El Haddad, 1982.
31. Shepley, Gaiser and El Haddad, 1983.
32. Shepley, Wissa, El Din Nasr, 1984.
33. Binswanger, 1984, pp19-20.
34. Dyer and Iman, in Richards and Martin, 1983, pp159-180.

35. eg Dyer, 1982.
36. Shepley,   Shoukry   and   Wissa,   1983,   pp22-24.
37. Soliman, 1984, pp11-13; Soliman and El-Shenawy, 1983.
38. El Tambadawy, 1979.
39 Mehanna, Huntingdon et al., 1983, pp14-17; Knap, Sallam,
    et al., 1982.
40. Shepley, 1984, pp33ff.
41. Binswanger, 1978.
42. Shepley, Wissa, El Haddad, 1982 pp11ff.
43. For instance, the Japan-Egypt Technical Cooperation
    programme which has developed the Rice Mechanisation
    Project in Kafr-el-Sheikh.

CHAPTER TEN

Conclusion

In little over a decade the Egyptian economy has undergone a series of highly significant shifts, in terms of its external trade framework and with regard to the distribution of its national product. Concomitantly, it is widely believed that the set of policies that have come to be known as Infitah have been associated with, on the one hand, relatively high rates of economic growth and, on the other hand, regressive income distributional consequences, not to mention political and economic clientage. Whatever the precise interpretation of recent events, it is very clear that the combination of accelerated growth, fueled by liberalisation of controls, trade and investment and a rather restricted spread of rewards flowing from that particular growth path is a potentially explosive mixture.

While the depiction of Infitah as an era of unparalleled prosperity for the new entrepreneurial class - or, perhaps, more exactly, the new speculative class - may rather ignore the very substantial gains for the economy as a whole that have occurred in this period, the image of Infitah as an inequalising - and hence socially polarising - set of policies has an exceptionally wide currency. As the Egyptian economy moves yet again into a more resource constrained period this very image - and the material environment that it has spawned - necessarily makes the process of economic adjustment to the modified environment a particularly hazardous operation. This is only likely to be made more complex and fraught by the limitations of the political process and the character of the Egyptian state.

Acceleration in the rate of economic growth since 1973 can obviously be attributed to a range of factors. Most prominent amongst these were: firstly, the inflow of co-opted resources earned outside the real economy; secondly, the political effects of the cessation of hostilities with Israel and an apparently extended horizon of mutual tolerance - if not genuine amity; and thirdly, the greatly enhanced handle on concessional transfers associated with these dual policy shifts. By 1985/86 the crucial revenue sources which fueled

this growth path were either subject to downward pressure or
remained stagnant.   However political and military rents
levied by the Egyptian state from the USA alone amounted to
around $2.6bn - of which half was allocated for military pur-
poses - and are likely to remain substantial.   At the same
time, strong domestic consumption propensity, stimulated by
the inflow of resources and the parallel policy measures
implemented by the state, had not yet been successfully dam-
pened.   This has given rise to a difficult political and economic   environment   in   which   necessary   constraints   on
consumption have come to be indissociably linked to major,
highly visible curbs on the state expenditure programme.

As expected, the main source of economic pressure derives from
the underlying trend in the balance of payments.[1]   The price
of oil on international markets has declined by two-thirds
since the peak in 1980 and this sharp fall in the unit value
of Egypt's principal visible foreign exchange earner has also
been accompanied by increased volatility and longer term
doubts concerning the inflow of resources from migrant workers
in the Gulf and other Arab states.   In the recent period,
remittances have contributed more than oil to the balance of
payments.   Yet these levels will be hard to sustain.

At present rates of exploitation, Egypt will cease to be an
oil exporter by the end of the 1990s or thereabouts.[2]
Secondly, remittance income clearly remains critically dependent on the level of economic activity sustained in the oil-
rich economies to which most Egyptian migrants have gone.
Falling oil revenues and a problematic overall economic
environment have already resulted in Libya expelling a
substantial number of Egyptian workers.   Although precise
figures are unavailable, the stock of Egyptian migrant workers
in Libya appears to have fallen from around ˙00,000 to 60,000
between January 1985 and January 1986.   Present trends in the
oil market, as well as projections for the coming decade,
point to further pressure on the principal revenue earning
resource of the economies to which Egypt has despatched its
workers.   As oil accounts for, on average, between 40-50% of
GDP for Saudi Arabia and the Gulf economies, the direct link
to the general level of economic activity is clear.   In the
case of Iraq - the main current source of demand for Egyptian
migrant labour - certain special conditions apply, principally

the continuing war with Iran and its effects on the domestic labour force.

The most recently available estimates for the flow of remittances suggest that between 1984 and 1986 they fell by 25% in nominal terms. Tourism revenues have fluctuated substantially in recent years. In 1985/86 they declined by over 20% because of perceived domestic instability. Suez Canal receipts have failed to increase in the most recent period. Thus, all the principal components of the growth in exogenous resources available to the economy in the mid-1970s have either declined or are likely to prove relatively inelastic in the longer run. Not surprisingly, it was estimated that GDP growth fell to 5-6% per annum in the eighteen months after mid 1985.

A decade after the turn to Infitah, the Egyptian economy is characterised by a number of major imbalances. In the first place, the current account remains precarious. Exports have not held up well, partly because of a 50% appreciation in the weighted real exchange rate index since 1979. Falling petroleum exports, in particular, and a sharp increase of over 20% in imports between 1981/82 and 1984/85, have widened the trade deficit. Moreover, external liabilities had exceeded $38bn by mid-1986. For 1985/86, debt servicing accounted for nearly 53% of current account receipts, having risen sharply from a level of 37% in 1981/82. At the same time, government expenditure and commitments have only been partially restrained. Interventions in the pricing and delivery of basic commodities, especially energy and foodstuffs, have placed the government budget under pressure.

Since 1984 the government has instituted a range of measures designed to reduce the level of subsidy. The domestic price of petrol for example, has been raised to more than 75% of the international price, but this has largely been a consequence of the general fall in oil prices. Local prices of the main subsidised food commodities – sugar, meat, rice, flour, oil and tea – were revised upwards in December 1985. Direct subsidies – the third largest expenditure item – have fallen as a share of GDP and total expenditure, but this has been attributable to the General Authority for Supply Commodities, the principal agency, increasingly having to finance its operations from commercial borrowing rather than through direct budgetary transfers. Total government expenditure has fallen

relative to GDP between 1981/82 and 1985/86 but this reduction
has been achieved almost entirely at the expense of the
investment budget.   Egypt's investment ratio, which exceeded
30% of GDP in the early 1980s, consequently fell to around 20%
by 1985/86. On the revenue side, recent performance has been
very weak. Tax revenues have declined steadily.

With the failure to reform the structure of the public finance
system and to curtail expenditures, except in the investment
budget, the overall deficit has remained high.   Table 10.1
indicates the share of government expenditures in GDP as well
as the magnitude of the deficit. With substantial domestic
financing, this has tended to exert a strong upward pressure
on the price level.   Although the official consumer price
index points to an average inflation rate of around 15.5% between 1980/81 and mid-1986, the true rate may have been at
least 5-6 percentage points higher.

The combination of a substantial inflow of co-opted earnings
and an increased level of state intervention in the economy
has had a number of consequences, posing significant barriers
to more efficient long-term management of the economy.

Firstly, commodity pricing policy has not only led to an
entrenched commitment to the provision of subsidised food and
energy but has also more generally resulted in the shifting of
resources away from tradeables output to services.   At the
same time, manufacturing investment, whether for the domestic
or export market, has fallen back.   One result has been that
the value of industrial exports has remained roughly constant
over the last decade.

Secondly, investment policy - hinged on attracting foreign
capital - has been generally unsuccessful.   Indeed, investments made under Law 43 may have actually been a drain on
foreign exchange reserves rather than providing the antici-
pated inflow of resources. The current policy of extending
the tax holiday for investment under this title from five to
ten years is unlikely to achieve a major change.

Thirdly, despite the apparent emphasis on encouraging private
sector investment, the last decade has seen a further consolidation of the state sector, and a striking growth in state
employment.   This has resulted in a chronically over-staffed

Table 10.1: <u>Government Budget (as percentage of GDP)</u>

Govt Budget	1981/82	1982/83	1983/84	1984/85	1985/86
Revenue*	41.0	39.3	37.2	34.8	31.1
Expenditure	65.3	58.5	60.3	56.8	54.6
Budget deficit	-24.3	-19.1	-23.1	-22.1	-23.5
Domestic financing	(12.7)	(8.1)	(10.1)	(8.5)	(13.0)

* = excludes foreign grants

Source: IMF

bureaucracy and relatively inefficient public sector economic enterprises. These inefficiencies have been compounded by the current policy of enforcing wage restraint without manpower reorganisation. This has, in turn, ensured that a substantial number of state employees hold other employment contemporaneously, further lowering productivity in their formal employment while doing little to address the government's real budgetary problems.

Intervention by the state in the economy has had a very long and sustained history in Egypt, particularly with respect to the administration of agricultural prices and the system of forced deliveries. But, since the late 1950s this has been complemented by a growing commitment to the provision of employment, irrespective of the productive needs of the economy. Indeed, the growth of state employment - and particularly that in government administration - may actually have been the most lasting feature of the Nasser epoch. In a well-turned phrase, Hansen and Marzouk, writing in the mid-1960s, pointed out that not only was the Lewis model unworkable in the Egyptian context but that 'if zero-productivity was to be found anywhere in Egypt, it was most probably in government administration'.[3]

Between 1962 and 1970 the number of people employed by the administration (excluding companies) rose from around 770,000 to 1.3m.[4] Although reliable statistics are hard to come by, it seems that by 1980/81 more than 3.5m people were employed in the state sector, nearly three-quarters of whom were in administrative departments.[5] As much as a third of the labour force were probably directly employed by the state and an estimated 92% of the population had access to subsidised commodities through possession of a ration card.[6] Measures to restrict the government budget deficit - inextricably linked to rationalisation of the subsidy system and modification of the state's profile in the labour market - will therefore directly touch upon the interests and welfare of the great majority of Egyptians. This largely accounts for the government's apparent prevarication in implementing any sustained adjustment measures.

Such prevarication is not a novelty. There has been a very recent historical precedent. The post-1960 period was increasingly characterised by a substantial domestic savings gap and the over-commitment of state resources. Rather than implement potentially difficult policy measures at home, the government avoided austerity by reliance on concessional transfers from the socialist bloc and other Arab states. While the reliance has now been switched politically, it is true to say that in the recent period aid transfers have again provided a means for postponing the adoption of more structural measures.

The complex and drawn-out dialogue between the Egyptian government and the donor agencies about the possible substance of any adjustment programme has at times appeared like a dialogue of the deaf. However, the very size of Egypt's external obligations, let alone the crucial political role of the country in the region, has meant that some flexibility has entered into the discussions of the feasible range of policy options. Altogether more problematic is whether such flexibility exists, so to speak, on the ground.

Even in the relatively recent past, it could be said that the effective political forum, bearing in mind the somewhat circumscribed means for expressing political dissension, was almost entirely urban. Indeed, if the political economy of Nasserism has been depicted in terms of a Kaleckian intermediate regime, the predominantly lower middle-class nature of the regime was directly reflected both in its structure and the location of employment.[7] The Infitah years have obviously modified this configuration by changing some of the key rules of the game and, as this study has demonstrated, this has been accompanied by a significant diffusion of benefits - economic and social - through the economy.

The impact of recent trends on the agricultural sector has been most striking. Two features stand out - emigration of rural sector workers to urban areas or to other Arab states and secondly, the growth of state employment in rural areas. The magnitude of these direct effects on the labour market has been accentuated by a parallel growth in aspirations. An increasing number of children stay longer in education, and there has been a less easily defined, but nonetheless important, change in attitudes to agricultural work. For male labour, employment in the state sector has emerged as a key feature of the rural labour market. Although for male members of small farm households, this has tended to be combined with on-farm agricultural work, some contraction in the supply of

male labour to the agricultural labour market has apparently
resulted.

Yet it would be wrong to suppose that the accelerated pace of
change and diffusion of economic benefits of the last decade
has simply been a function of economic liberalisation and the
fortuitous availability of external resources. Rather, economic progress in rural areas has to be understood in relation
to earlier developments in the Nasser epoch. It was then that
the structural preconditions - land reform and the establishment of the gamiya system - were laid. However, even though
the land reform programme in Egypt was genuinely more radical
than elsewhere, it is important to note that the dismantling
of the large estates often left untouched the smaller, yet not
insubstantial, holdings of the village based elites. Thus,
despite the fact that land reform broadened the ownership base
in Egyptian agriculture and hence had a fairly marked
equalising effect, substantial inequalities in asset control
and income remained. As the Sharkiya case study has
demonstrated, this has had important longer-run implications,
allowing for, amongst other things, the village elite families
to consolidate their political and economic positions.

While Infitah has commonly worked to the benefit of asset-
endowed households, it would be quite false to suppose that
this has necessarily been at the expense of poorer landed
households, let alone the landless section of the rural population. The principal characteristic of the last decade has
been the emergence of, on the one hand, income-generating
opportunities outside the rural sector and, on the other hand,
the growth and consolidation of subsidised services to rural
households. Apart from the growth in employment opportunities, rural-sector incomes have been directly affected by
the growth in input subsidies, the substantial subsidisation
of capital and energy and by the increased provision of consumer subsidies in rural areas. Thus, although implicit taxation of farmers has continued through administered pricing,
other types of subsidy - particularly for inputs - have
weakened the overall rate of taxation on the sector.

The very scale of state interventions in markets and the
interlinked nature of these interventions, not only points to
the political problems related to any systematic move to
reduce the level of subsidy but also suggests that any

restructuring or elimination of subsidies would have highly
significant implications for farm household incomes. Allowing
producer prices for controlled crops to converge with international prices, while at the same time reducing the subsidy
on inputs, would probably result in a small welfare gain for
producers. But reductions in energy subsidies and an end to
negative interest rates, coupled with cuts in the government
sector's labour force, would have major adverse consequences
in the short and medium term. Moreover, an upwards shift in
the price of energy and capital would run strongly counter to
recent government agricultural sector policies. In the context
of falling non-farm employment, brought about by declining
state-sector employment and falling demand for Egyptian
unskilled labour in the Gulf, there would be a radical change
in the availability of labour and, by implication, in the
level of demand for mechanisation.

One central aim of this study has been to demonstrate how
current policy characterisations of the agricultural sector
have been false, or at least inexact, in most crucial aspects.
It has been widely accepted that Egyptian agriculture has
moved in the last decade from a position of relative labour
availability to one in which the labour market has been
characterised by scarcity. This in turn has led to the promo-
tion of mechanisation programmes.

But detailed investigation of the condition of the labour
market has suggested that while a generalised tightening of
the market for male labour has undoubtedly occurred, consequent on the growth in non-farm employment, this has neither
led to significant diminution in the volume of labour inputs
committed to crop production, nor to pronounced negative consequences for productivity. This has, in part, been a function of the substitution of female and child labour for male
labour.

At the same time, the last decade has seen an acceleration in
the adoption of available machine technology. This has principally implied the use and diffused ownership of tractors,
irrigation pumps and threshers. In the highly labour-
intensive tasks associated with harvesting there has not been
any substitution of mechanical for human energy. To that
extent, the demand for labour in agriculture has retained its
characteristically fluctuating yet periodically bunched pro-

perties. These have been magnified by the segmented nature of the agricultural labour market and the restricted role historically played by women in the labour market.

Although under the impetus of the declining availability of adult male labour for agriculture, this segmentation has weakened, it is still the case that task limitation by sex remains a major feature of the labour profile in agriculture. The fact that the dissolution of such segmentation has not proceeded further suggests that the degree of male labour scarcity has been over-estimated and that social attitudes towards female labour market entry have considerable resilience.

The response of the state to the apparent shift in the structure of the labour market has been both interventionist and short-sighted. An elaborate and costly programme of subsidised mechanisation has been set up. But at present the state's Agricultural Mechanisation Centres appear only to duplicate existing technology offered by the private market while promoting the introduction of technology that if adopted on a widespread basis, would markedly depress the labour-absorbing capacity of the agricultural sector. However, adoption of such technology, let alone a diffusionary ownership process, would be strictly contingent on the maintenance of the current range of subsidies. Furthermore, it is clear that adoption of such technology at the farm level would not only be a function of relative costs but also of actual labour dispositions on-farm.

Analysis presented in this study suggests that the labour force will continue to grow at a high rate for the foreseeable future. If major labour-substituting policies are implemented the result will be even higher burden of absorption on the government sector, which would have harmful consequences for the economy as a whole.

Although the scale of reduction in the availability of agricultural labour has been over-stated, it is nevertheless true that evidence has indicated that economy-wide cost inflation has had repercussions for agriculture. In particular, this study suggests that labour factor shares have significantly increased during the last decade. However, real wages for agricultural male labour fell in real terms in 1986, possibly pointing to a reversal of recent trends. Given the limited range of mechanical services available for cultivation and the high level of subsidisation of inputs, the wage trend has reflected inflationary pressures in the economy. To the extent that the trend in real agricultural wages has mirrored trends in other sectors, albeit with a lag, the issue at hand is as much to do with the structure of product prices facing producers as the price of labour.

The wholesale abolition of subsidies and price intervention is unlikely and probably undesirable, given the path on which the economy has been placed over the last three decades. The key to weakening the cost constraints on Egyptian farm enterprises lies more through restructuring price interventions than in attempting to modify radically demand for labour in the sector. Abolition of graduate employment guarantee schemes, together with constraints on the overall supply of government-sector employment would have significant repercussions for the availability of male labour in agriculture, but some of this effect could be achieved through the abolition of forced deliveries and the consequent increments to farmgate prices.

Deregulation of producer prices would yield positive income benefits for farm households and permit greater regional specialisation in cropping patterns, while tending to lessen the private financial attractiveness of fodder cultivation. A shift out of fodder cultivation would not only yield a positive societal return but would also have implications for the level of labour demand in agriculture. In other words, use of the product pricing mechanism could secure adaptation in the labour market which would, in the medium term, ease the supply of labour to the agricultural sector, while also raising farm incomes.

Between a quarter and a third of small farm households generate incomes on or below an estimated poverty line. Thus, the major changes witnessed over the last decade in the range of employment opportunities open to male members of agricultural households, have not necessarily been associated with a substantial and sustained improvement in income. If current government policies on employment and the choice of agricultural technology are continued in the long term, there will be no improvement in the income levels of a significant proportion of farm households. In short, the next phase of

Egyptian history will be characterised by the socially divisive consequences of unemployment.

Footnotes

1.   Egypt: Balance of Payments, 1978-1984 (US$ million)

	1978	1979	1980	1981	1982	1983	1984
Current account	-1220	-1542	-438	-2136	-1852	-411	-2451
Merchandise exports	1939	2424	3854	3999	4018	3693	3864
Merchandise imports	-4743	-6002	-6814	-7918	-7733	-7515	-9250
Trade balance	-2804	-3578	-2960	-3919	-3715	-3822	-5386

Source: IMF, International Financial Statistics, 38,12, 1985.

2.   IBRD, 1983(a), p.22.
3.   Hansen and Marzouk, 1965, p.298.
4.   Abdel-Fadil, 1980, p.10: Waterbury, 1983, p.242.
5.   Waterbury, 1983, p.243.
6.   Alderman and von Braun, 1984, p.9.
7.   Abdel-Fadil, 1980, p.106.

Table 7A

Primary Occupation (Males & Females):
Distribution of Employment, by Farm Size, 1984

Primary Occupation	0-1	1-3	3-5	5-10	>10	All	
1. Government	8%	5.1%	7.5%	6.8%	–	6.6%	(52)
2. Public Sector	2.1	2.1	1.9	–	25	2.1	(17)
3. Cooperative	–	0.3	0.9	–	–	0.3	(2)
4. Police/Army	4.2	4.2	2.8	3.4	12.5	4.0	(32)
5. Farmer	15.3	13.6	17.8	13.6	25	14.9	(118)
6. Agric. Labourer	8	8.2	2.8	–	–	6.7	(53)
7. Construction	0.4	0.6	–	–	–	0.4	(3)
8. Services	1	1.2	2.8	1.7	–	1.4	(11)
9. Working Abroad	1	0.3	–	1.7	–	0.6	(5)
10. Retired	2.8	1.2	–	1.7	–	1.6	(13)
11. Housewife	31.9	34.7	26.2	25.4	25	31.8	(252)
12. Student	22.9	26.3	35.5	39	12.5	27.1	(215)
13. Disabled	–	0.3	–	–	–	0.1	(1)
14. Unemployed	–	0.3	–	–	–	0.1	(1)
15. Carpenter	–	–	0.9	–	–	0.1	(1)
16. Driver	0.4	–	0.9	1.7	–	0.4	(3)
17. Waiting for Work	0.4	–	–	–	–	0.1	(1)
18. Weaver	0.7	1.2	–	–	–	0.8	(1)
19. Trader	–	0.3	–	1.7	–	0.3	(2)
20. Other	1	–	–	3.4	–	0.6	(5)
No. of Observations:	288	331	107	59	8	793	

Farm Size (feddans)

( ) = No. of Observations

Table 8A

Production Costs Disaggregated: Major Field Crops 1972-1983: All Egypt

Crop	1972/3	1973/4	1974/5	1980/1	1981/2	1982/3	1983/4	1984/5
Cotton								
Rent	33.0	30.0	25.2	20.2	17.2	14.8	10.7	9.9
Wages	31.9	35.6	39.3	50.8	54.4	56.0	59.3	60.0
Draught Power	3.5	3.9	3.2	2.5	2.2	2.4	1.5	1.3
Machinery	6.5	6.4	6.3	6.1	8.0	7.2	8.7	8.3
Material								
Inputs	23.6	22.7	24.0	17.9	15.4	16.6	15.5	15.5
Other Costs	1.5	1.4	2.0	2.5	2.8	3.0	4.3	5.0
Wheat								
Rent	36.8	35.9	28.8	34.3	29.9	25.9	19.6	14.9
Wages	17.2	17.0	22.3	26.7	27.5	29.1	38.1	41.1
Draught Power	8.7	8.5	5.9	6.8	6.8	5.3	5.0	5.2
Machinery	10.6	10.8	16.2	13.0	14.4	16.3	15.6	17.7
Material								
Inputs	25.1	25.6	24.2	16.5	18.4	19.0	15.8	16.3
Other Costs	1.6	2.2	2.6	2.7	3.0	4.4	5.9	4.8
Rice								
Rent	23.4	23.0	21.1	16.9	14.0	12.6	11.6	10.0
Wages	26.2	27.9	31.3	34.8	40.0	46.0	45.5	48.6
Draught Power	8.3	7.0	7.3	10.1	8.5	5.7	3.6	5.6
Machinery	14.5	15.0	14.8	14.0	12.8	13.6	19.0	14.6
Material								
Inputs	26.9	25.6	22.6	20.5	20.3	17.6	15.1	13.4
Other Costs	0.7	1.5	2.9	3.7	4.4	4.5	5.2	7.8
Maize								
Rent	27.9	26.0	25.2	19.9	17.3	17.1	12.8	11.8
Wages	25.2	26.7	30.6	37.5	40.8	41.8	45.1	47.9
Draught Power	8.5	8.5	7.5	6.4	5.5	4.9	3.3	0.9
Machinery	5.8	6.9	6.7	8.5	9.0	10.4	14.3	15.2
Material								
Inputs	31.4	30.1	28.0	22.3	22.4	21.0	20.4	20.1
Other Costs	1.2	1.8	2.0	5.4	5.0	4.8	4.1	4.1

Material Inputs = seeds, organic/chemical fertilizer and pesticides

Source: Ministry of Agriculture, A.R.E.

Table 8B

Labour Costs as Proportion of Total Costs: Nominal and Shadow, 1984

| Crop | ----------Farm Size---------------------- | | | | |
	0-1	1-3	3-5	5-10	>10
Wheat					
Nominal	30.1	36.5	39.8	44.6	41.4
Shadow	47.8	49.3	46.2	44.9	40.2
Long Birseem					
Nominal	24.2	32.5	37.8	46.2	59.8
Shadow	45.9	52.5	49.9	49.2	53.0
Cotton					
Nominal	56.8	67.9	67.1	70.9	88.1
Shadow	59.8	67.4	68.6	71.4	78.1
Rice					
Nominal	42.6	48.6	55.2	60.5	60.7
Shadow	53.5	58.7	55.9	58.1	57.0
Maize					
Nominal	44.5	47.4	52.3	59.9	65.8
Shadow	56.1	54.0	57.2	59.1	63.1
Short Birseem					
Nominal	18.3	22.8	27.3	32.4	51.8
Shadow	43.3	45.6	36.9	34.9	45.4
Standard Two-Season Rotation					
Nominal	42.9	47.7	52.7	57.3	61.0
Shadow	54.5	56.2	56.6	57.1	58.4

Source: ODI/Zagazig Survey, 1984

Table 8C

Mean Value of Material Inputs per Feddan: By Crop and Farm Size, 1984

Crop	----------Farm Size (feddans)-----				
	0-1	1-3	3-5	5-10	>10
Wheat	16.6	18.0	14.9	17.6	20.0
Short Birseem	19.2	17.6	17.1	16.7	25.0
Long Birseem	18.0	15.8	18.6	15.3	22.3
Cotton	24.0	23.4	25.1	22.8	27.0
Rice	18.9	21.0	21.0	23.2	21.8
Maize	20.2	23.5	20.3	20.3	21.5

Table 8D

Average Crop Value per Feddan per Annum, 1984

Farm Size	Mean	Index
	£E	
0-1	1665	100
1-3	2176	131
3-5	2203	132
5-10	2634	158
>10	2499	150

Table 8E

Average Non-Agricultural Income per Annum: Breakdown by Source, 1984

	Rental	Dairy	Agric Wage	Non-Agric Wage	Remit-tances	Trade	Sale of Livestock	Other Income	Total Income
Mean	957	293	740	929	1167	933	139	995	1231
Obser-vations	38	98	38	87	3	7	75	6	163

Table 8F

Average Value of Crop Output (primary and secondary) by Farm Size, 1984

Village	Farm Size (feddans)				
	0-1	1-3	3-5	5-10	>10
Sharkiya	757.6	1658.4	2752.9	6505.5	19941.5
Gharbiya	457.6	1144.7	2441.8	3514.0	—
Dakhaliya	496.8	1204.5	2295.7	4571.6	8729.0
All Villages	546.8	1340.8	2498.7	5239.4	16204.0

Source: ODI/ZAGAZIG Survey, 1984

Table 8G

Average Non-Crop Income: By Farm Size, 1984

Village	Farm Size (feddans)				
	0-1	1-3	3-5	5-10	>10
Sharkiya	1043.4	1035.0	2001.4	4037.5	7416.5
Gharbiya	924.9	623.9	2610.0	530.0	—
Dakhaliya	532.9	989.7	1028.3	2617.0	1200.0
All Villages	918.0	994.0	1583.0	2977.0	5344.0

Table 8H

Average Gross Income: Farm and Non-Farm Combined: By Farm Size, 1984

Village	Farm Size (feddans)				
	0-1	1-3	3-5	5-10	>10
Sharkiya	1801.0	2693.4	4574.3	10543.0	27358.0
Gharbiya	1382.5	1768.6	5051.8	4044.0	—
Dakhaliya	1029.7	2194.2	3324.0	7188.6	9929.0
All Villages	1425.5	2267.1	4072.2	8215.9	21548.0

Table 9A

Current Population of Tractors and Agricultural Equipment per 1000 Feddans of Crop Area, by Governorate: 1982/83

Governorate	Tractors	Ploughs	Pesti-cide Sprayers	Threshing machines	Agricul-tural trailers	Mechanical power for irrigation hp
Alexandria	6.3	1.3	0.8	0.2	0.4	73.6
Behera	7.1	5.6	0.2	1.0	1.1	133.3
Gharbiya	9.4	11.2	4.4	2.1	6.4	114.3
Kafr El Sheikh	5.9	6.4	3.4	1.1	1.1	115.3
Dakhaliya	8.3	10.7	4.5	1.2	4.8	191.2
Damietta	8.3	5.5	2.9	0.4	1.9	393.1
Sharqiya	6.8	7.0	3.2	1.2	4.8	73.7
Ismailia	9.7	8.9	1.4	0.7	6.5	180.3
Suez	12.7	11.8	1.5	1.5	3.7	379.1
Port Said	-	-	-	-	-	-
Menufia	6.3	5.9	1.7	2.3	1.7	139.8
Qaliubiya	7.3	8.6	2.7	2.3	6.0	127.4
Cairo	4.4	3.9	0.4	-	1.4	139.8
Giza	7.7	1.6	0.6	1.5	0.7	129.9
Beni Suef	4.5	1.2	0.4	0.5	0.1	104.6
Fayoum	7.0	5.0	1.1	0.1	2.3	13.5
Minya	6.8	4.2	3.8	1.7	2.1	162.5
Assiut	7.7	10.8	0.2	2.3	9.3	309.5
Sohag	7.7	6.8	0.9	3.1	4.1	266.6
Qena	10.6	7.6	0.4	3.1	4.3	610.0
Aswan	4.3	2.03	0.1	0.1	0.5	30.6
Matruh	-	-	-	-	-	-
New Valley	6.2	1.03	-	0.4	-	139.1
North Sinai	-	-	-	-	-	-
Average	7.3	6.8	2.4	1.5	3.37	163.9

Source: Egyptian Agricultural Mechanisation: Five Year Development Plan, 1982/83-1986/87, Ministry of Agriculture, Cairo, 1983, p.5

Table 9B

Machine and Animal Inputs per Feddan: By Farm Size & Crop, 1984

Crop	-------------------------Farm Size (feddans)-------------------------				
	0–1	1–3	3–5	5–10	>10
Wheat					
M	32.8	29.7	21.1	21.7	28.4
A	25.5	17.1	10.7	3.7	9.5
Long Birseem					
M	23.6	18.4	27.1	23.8	12.8
A	17.6	24.3	28.3	12.8	12.2
Short Birseem					
M	12.8	14.5	13.5	14.7	7.5
A	16.1	14.4	19.7	3.0	0
Cotton					
M	41.3	33.4	38.0	37.4	29.0
A	64.4	40.5	15.9	9.1	0
Rice					
M	63.1	94.2	77.6	88.8	35.9
A	51.8	49.6	23.4	4.8	11.7
Maize					
M	40.3	35.7	30.4	31.3	18.6
A	63.5	41.6	21.1	14.4	6.9

M = Machine Hours

A = Animal Hours

Table 9C

Machine and Animal Hours as Proportion of Total Hours:
By Crop & Farm Size,   1984

Crop	---Farm Size (feddans)---				
	0-1	1-3	3-5	5-10	>10
	%	%	%	%	%
Wheat					
M	15.4	14.8	13.0	14.7	10.1
A	11.9	8.5	6.5	2.5	3.3
Long Birseem					
M	9.4	7.5	9.4	12.5	8.5
A	7.0	9.9	9.7	6.8	8.1
Short Birseem					
M	10.5	11.6	10.5	15.7	8.8
A	13.2	11.5	15.4	3.2	0
Cotton					
M	5.7	4.3	5.8	5.6	2.8
A	8.8	5.3	2.3	0.8	0
Rice					
M	11.8	15.7	16.6	20.8	9.0
A	9.7	8.3	5.0	1.1	3.0
Maize					
M	8.6	9.0	7.8	8.5	4.4
A	13.4	10.5	5.3	4.0	1.6

M = Machine Hours as Proportion Total Hours
A = Animal Hours as Proportion Total Hours

Table 9D

Labour Use in Irrigation: By Type and Farm Size, 1984
(As Proportion of Total Labour Inputs-Equalized Man-Hours)

Type	Farm Size				
	0-1	1-3	3-5	5-10	>10
	%	%	%	%	%
Household Male	73.3	69.1	63.5	27.5	—
Household Female	11.8%	8.3%	—	2.4%	—
Household Child	4.0%	3.1.%	3.2%	3.5%	1.1%
Hired Male	10.9%	18.2%	30.1%	66.6%	98.9%
Hired Female	—	0.2%	—	—	—
Hired Child	—	1.1%	3.1%	—	—

Source: ODI/Zagazig Survey, 1984

Table 9E

Agricultural Machinery, 1972-1982 (23 Villages)

Type	1972		1982	
	Private	Cooperative	Private	Cooperative
Tractor	95	19	339	23
Pump	118	—	637	—
Drum Thresher	52	18	233	15
Chisel Plough	83	18	319	22

Source: Agricultural Mechanisation Project, Working Paper No.6:
         P. Reiss et al., Village Profile. Cairo, December 1982, p33.

Table 9F

Tractor Use: Source: By Farm Size, 1984

Source:	0-1	1-3	3-5	5-10	10	All
				Farm Size (Feddans)		
1	253	321	101	53	12	740 (72.3%)
2	44	113	24	2		183 (17.9%)
3		2				2 (0.2%)
4		1	4			5 (0.5%)
5		4	7	6		17 (1.7%)
6	18	1	13	28	16	76 (7.4%)
7			1			1 (0.1%)
	315	442	150	89	28	1024 (100%)

Source Code: 1 = From Other Farm   3 = Rental Shop   5 = Cooperative
            2 = Trader   4 = Relation   6 = Own Farm
                                                   7 = Other Source

Table 9G

Irrigation Pump Use: Source: By Farm Size, 1984

Source	0-1	1-3	3-5	5-10	10	All
1	192	250	71	57	8	558 (72%)
2	19	25	5			49 (6.3%)
3			3	4		7 (0.9%)
4		1	2			3 (0.4%)
5						0 (-)
6	19	82	25	19	9	154 (19.9%)
7		2	1	1		4 (0.5%)
	230	360	107	61	17	775 (100%)

Source Code: 1 = From Other Farm   3 = Rental Shop   5 = Cooperative
            2 = Trader   4 = Relation   6 = Own Farm
                                                   7 = Other Source

Agricultural Development in Egypt since 1973

Table 9H

Saqia Use: Source: By Farm Size, 1984

Source	0-1	1-3	3-5	5-10	10	All
1	43	26				69 (32.7%)
2	1	1				2 (0.9%)
4	6					6 (2.8%)
6	49	67	17			133 (63%)
7			1			1 (0.5%)
	99	94	18			211 (100%)

Source Code: 1 = From Other Farm   3 = Rental Shop   5 = Cooperative
            2 = Trader   4 = Relation   6 = Own Farm
                                                                                    7 = Other Source

Table 9I

Tractor and Irrigation Pump Hire Costs per Hour: by Farm Size and Source, 1984

Farm Size & Village	----------Tractor (£E)----------			--------Pump (£E)--------		
	1	2	5	1	2	3
0-1 A	1.97	1.93		1.54	1.56	
B	4.47			1.05		
C	2.59			0.77		
1-3 A	1.94	1.84		2.00	1.58	
B	5.33			0.94		
C	2.81			0.68		
3-5 A	2.22	1.48		2.00	2.04	
B	5.64					
C	3.10			1.12		
5-10 A			2.5			2.25
B	(9.2)					
C	4.03			0.67		
> 10 A						
B						
C	3.44			0.82		

Source: 1 = From other Farmer   Village: A = Sharkiya
       2 = Trader   B = Gharbiya
       3 = Rental Shop   C = Dakhaliya
       5 = Cooperative

Bibliography

Abdalla, A., The Student Movement and National Politics in
    Egypt, London:Al Saqi, 1984.
Abdel Al, F. and Skold, M., Farm record summary and analysis
    for study cases at Abyuha, Mansuriya and Abu Raya sites,
    Egypt Water Use & Management Project Technical
    Report 23, Cairo 1982.
Abdel-Fadil, M., 'Economic development in Egypt in the New
    High Dam Era', L'Egypte Contemporaire 65(356):1974,
    pp.247-73.
  -   Development, Income Distribution and Social Change in
    Rural Egypt 1952-1970, Cambridge University Press, 1975.
  -   The Political Economy of Nasserism: A Study in
    Employment and Income Distribution in Urban Egypt,
    1952-1972, Cambridge University Press, 1980.
  -   'Educational expansion and income distribution in Egypt,
    1952-1977', in Abdel Khalek and Tignor, op cit., 1982,
    pp.351-374.
  -   Informal Sector Employment in Egypt, Geneva:ILO, 1983.
  -   Abdel-Hai Salah, M. and Osada, M., The Transition of the
    Egyptian Economy under the New Open-Door Policy
    (1973-83), Tokyo:United Nations University, 1984.
Abdel-Fathah, F., The Contemporary Village: Between Reform and
    Revolution, 1952-1970, Cairo 1975.
Abdel-Khalek, A.R.Z., 'Production and Distribution of Milk and
    Dairy Products in Egypt: Towards a Crop System',
    University of Stockholm, 1981.
Abdel-Khalek, G. and Tignor, R., The Political Economy of
    Income Distribution in Egypt, London:Holmes & Meier,
    1982.
Abdel-Khalek, M., 'Agrarian reform in Egypt: a field study
    of the agrarian reform in two typical areas during the
    period 1953-73', PhD thesis, University of London, 1971.
Abdel-Maksoud, B.M., 'Social and psychological aspects of
    innovation among Egyptian farmers', PhD thesis,
    University of Reading, 1977.
Abdel-Malek, A., Egypt: Military Society, New York: Random
    House,1968.
Abdou, D., Gardner, D.B. and Green, R., 'The economic implica-
    tions of enforcing agricultural laws in Egypt',
    Agricultural Development Systems DS Paper 144, Cairo,
    1983.
Adams, R.H., 'Development and structural change in rural
    Egypt, 1952-1982', World Development, 13(6): 1985, pp.
    290-302.
Agarwal, B., 'Tractors, tubewells and cropping intensity in
    the Indian Punjab', Journal of Development Studies,
    20(4):1984, pp.290-302.
Agricultural Mechanization Project, Inception Report, Ministry
    of Agriculture, Cairo, 1981.
  -   Activity Reports 8 and 9, Cairo, 1983.
  -   'Egyptian Agricultural Mechanziation: Five Year

Development Plan, 1982/3-1986/7', Cairo, 1983.
Ahmed, I., 'Wage determination in Bangladesh agriculture',
    Oxford Economic Papers, 33(2):1981, pp.298-322.
  - 'Farm size and labour use: some alternative explana-
    tions', Oxford Bulletin of Economics and Statistics,
    43(1): 1981, pp.73-88.
  - 'Unemployment and underemployment in Bangladesh agri-
    culture', World Development, 6(11/12):1978,
    pp.1281-1296.
Ahmed, S., Public finance in Egypt: Its structure and trends,
    World Bank Staff Paper 639, Washington 1984.
  - Bhattacharya, A. Grais, W. and Pleskovic, B., Macro-
    economic effects of efficiency pricing in the public
    sector in Egypt, World Bank Staff Paper 726, Washington,
    1985.
Al-Ayubi, N., Bureaucracy and Politics in Contemporary Egypt,
    London:Ithaca Press, 1980.
Alderman, H. and von Braun, J., The effects of the Egyptian
    food ration and Subsidy System on Income Distribution
    and Consumption, Washington:IFPRI, 1984.
  - von Braun, J. and Sakr Ahmed Sakr, Egypt's food subsidy
    and rationing system: a description, Washington, 34,
    October 1984.
Aly, H.Y. and Grabowski, R., 'Technological change and surplus
    labour in Egyptian agriculture, 1952-72'. Journal of
    Agricultural Economics, 35(1):1984, pp.109-116.
American Embassy, 'Livestock and Poultry Annual 1984', Cairo,
    1984.
Amin, G., Food supply and economic development with special
    reference to Egypt, London:Frank Cass, 1966.
  - 'Income distribution and economic development in the
    Arab world', L'Egypte Contemporaire 64(352):1973,
    pp.5-37.
Amin, G. and Awny, E., International migration of Egyptian
    labour. A review of the state of the art.   IDRC Report,
    Ottawa, May 1985.
Ammar, A., A demographic study of an Egyptian province
    (Sharqiyya), London:Lund Humphries, 1944.
Antle, J. and Aitah, A.S., Agricultural technology and policy
    in Egypt, 1976/77-1982/82, ADS Paper 143, Cairo 1983.
Arman, I.M.I., Manpower and employment in Egypt, 1980-2000,
    Institute of National Planning, Memo 1320, Cairo, 1982.
    Labour migration and its impact on the Egyptian labour
    market, INP Memo 1385, Cairo 1983.
Artin, Y., La Propriété Foncière en Egypte, Cairo, 1883.
Ayalon, D., Mamluk military society, Amsterdam:North Holland
    Press, 1979.
Ayrout, H.H., The Egyptian peasant, Boston:Beacon Press, 1963.
Baer, G., A history of land ownership in modern Egypt,
    1800-1950, Oxford University Press, 1962.
  - Fellah and Townsmen in the Middle East, London:Frank
    Cass, 1982.

Baker, R.W., Egypt's Uncertain Revolution, Harvard University
    Press, 1978.
Ball, J., Contributions to the gGography of Egypt, Cairo, 1939.
Bardhan, K., Economic Growth, Poverty and Rural Labour Markets
    in India, ILO World Employment Programme Paper
    10-6/WP54, Geneva 1983.
Bardhan, P., 'Size, productivity and returns to scale: an ana-
    lysis of farm-level data in Indian agriculture',
    Journal of Political Economy, 81:1973, pp.1370-1386.
  - 'On measuring rural unemployment', Journal of
    Development Studies, 14(3):1978, pp.342-351.
  - Land, Labour and Rural Poverty, Essays in Development
    Economics, New York:Oxford University Press, 1984.
Barnum, H.N. and Squire, L., A Model of an Agricultural
    Household Theory and Evidence, Washington:Johns Hopkins
    Press, 1979.
Berry, A and Sabot, R.H., 'Labour market performance in deve-
    loping countries: a survey', World Development,
    6(11/12):1978, pp.1199-1241.
Bharadwaj, K., Production Conditions in Indian Agriculture,
    Cambridge University Press, 1974.
Binder, J.L., In a Moment of Enthusiasm, Chicago University
    Press, 1978.
Binswanger, H.P., The Economics of Tractors in South Asia - An
    Analytical Review, New York:Agricultural Development
    Council, 1978.
  - Agricultural Mechanization: a Comparative Historical
    Perspective, World Bank Staff Paper No.673, Washington
    1984.
  - and Ruttan, V.W., Induced Innovation, Baltimore:Johns
    Hopkins Press, 1978.
Birks, J.S., et. al., 'Who is migrating where? An over-
    view of international labour migration in the Arab
    world', in Richards and Martin, 1983 op cit.,
    pp.103-116.
  - and Sinclair, C., International Migration and
    Development in the Arab Region, Geneva:ILO, 1980.
  - Sinclair, C. and Socknat, J.A., 'The demand for Egyptian
    labour abroad', in Richards and Martin (1983) op cit.,
    pp.117-134.
Blaug, M., Education and the Employment Problem in Developing
    Countries, Geneva:ILO, 1973.
Boutros-Ghali, Y. and Taylor, L., 'Basic needs macroeconomics:
    is it manageable in the case of Egypt?', Journal of
    Policy Modelling 2(3):1980, pp.409-436.
Bowen, K.L. and Young, R.A., Allocative Efficiency and Equity
    of Alternative Methods of Charging for Irrigation Water,
    EWUP Report 37, Cairo 1983.
Bliss, C.J. and Stern, N.H., Palanpur: The Economy of an
    Indian Village, Oxford University Press, 1982.
von Braun, J., 'The role of subsidised and rationed food for
    food supply and consumption in Egyptian farm

households', Gottingen University, 1981 (mimeo).
- and de Haen, H., 'Egypt and the enlargement of the EEC', Food Policy, 17(1):1982, pp.46-56.
- and de Haen, H., The Effects of Food Price and Subsidy Policies on Egyptian Agriculture, Washington:IFPRI, 1983.
Braverman, A., 'Credit and sharecropping in agrarian societies', Journal of Development Economics, 9:1981, pp.289-312.
- and Stiglitz, J.E., 'Sharecropping and the interlinking of agrarian markets', American Economic Review, 72(4):1982, pp.695-715.
Bruton, H.J., 'Egypt's development in the 1970s', Economic Development and Cultural Change, 31(4):1983, pp.679-704.
Butzer, K., Early Hydraulic Civilisation in Egypt, University of Chicago Press, 1976.
CAPMAS, Labour Force by Sample Survey, 1975 and 1981, Cairo, 1977 and 1982.
- Family Budget Survey by Sample in the Arab Republic of Egypt, 1958/59, 1964/65 and 1974/75, Cairo, 1961, 1972 and 1978.
- Population and Housing Census, 1976, Fertility and Internal Migration, Vol.II, Cairo 1980.
- Major Features of Temporary Migration for Egypt, Cairo 1980.
- Monthly Bulletin of Consumer Prices, 1984.
- General Indicators Concerning the Economic Open-Door Policy, Cairo, 1982.
- Statistical Yearbook: Egypt 1952-82, Cairo, 1983.
Carr, D.C., Foreign Investment in Egypt, New York:Praeger, 1979.
Choucri, N., 'A new migration in the Middle East', International Migration Review, 11:1977, pp.421-443.
'Construction and development: the effects of labour migration',in Management of the Construction Industry in Egypt, Seminar Proceedings, January 1980, TAP Report 80-6, Cairo, 1980, pp.77-87.
- Migration in the Middle East: Transformations, Policies and Processes, 2 vols, TAP Report, 83 8/9, Cairo, 1983.
- and Lahiri, S., 'Short-run energy - economy interactions in Egypt', World Development 12(8):1985, pp.799-820.
- Eckaus, R. and Mohieldin, A., Migration and Employment in the Construction Sector: Critical Factors in Egyptian Development, Cairo University/MIT, Technology Adaptation Programme, 1978.
Commander, S., 'From labour surplus to labour scarcity? The agricultural labour market in Egypt', Development Policy Review, 4(2):1986.
- The political economy of food production and distribution in Egypt: a survey of developments since 1973, ODI Working Paper No.14, London, 1984.

Cooper, M., 'Egyptian State capitalism in crisis: economic
      policies and political interests, 1967-71'.
      International Journal of Middle East Studies, 10:1979,
      pp.481-516.
   -   The Transformation of Egypt, London:Croom Helm, 1982.
Cuddihy, W., Agricultural price management in Egypt, World
      Bank Staff Paper 388, Washington, 1980.
   -   'Agricultural prices, farm mechanization and the demand
      for labour', in Richards and Martin (1983) op cit.,
      pp.225-236.
Dager, E.Z., Attitudes of Egyptian Farmers Towards
      Mechanisation, Cairo, 1979 (mimeo).
David, P.A., Technical Choice, Innovation and Economic Growth,
      Cambridge University Press, 1975.
Davis, E., Challenging Colonialism, Bank Misr and Egyptian
      Industrialisation, 1920-41, Princeton University Press,
      1984.
Deolalikar, A., Are There Pecuniary Returns to Health in
      Agricultural Work?, ICRISAT Economics Programme, Report
      66, Patancheru, 1984.
   -   and Vivjerberg, W.P., The Heterogeneity of Labour in
      Agriculture: a Test Using Farm Level Data From India
      and Malaysia, Economic Growth Centre Discussion Paper
      444, Yale University, 1983.
Dervis, K., Martin, R. and van Wijnbergen, S., Policy Analy-
      sis of Shadow Pricing, Foreign Borrowing and Resource
      Extraction in Egypt, World Bank Staff Paper 622,
      Washington, 1984,
El Dib, M., Ismail, S. and Gad, O., 'Economic motivation and
      the impact of external migration of agricultural workers
      in an Egyptian village, Population Studies, 11(68):1984,
      pp.27-46.
Dyer, W., The Opportunity Cost of Animal Labour in Egyptian
      Agriculture, ADS Paper 3, Cairo, 1980.
   -   and Gotsch, C.H., 'Public policy and the demand for
      mechanisation in Egyptian agriculture', in Richards and
      Martin (1983) op cit., pp.199-224.
   -   and Imam, S., 'Mechanization decisions in Egyptian agri-
      culture', in Richards and Martin (1983) op cit.,
      pp.159-180.
Eckaus, R.S., El-Din, A.M., Consequences of the changes in
      subsidy policies in Egypt, Department of Economics/MIT
      Working Paper 265, Cambridge, Massachusetts.
El Edel, M.R., 'Impact of taxation on income distribution: an
      exploratory attempt to estimate tax incidence in Egypt',
      in Abdel-Khalek and Tignor (1982) op cit., pp.132-164.
ERA 2000 Inc., Further Mechanization of Egyptian Agriculture,
      New York, 1979.
Eshag, E. and Kamal, M.A., 'A note on the system of rural con-
      ditions in UAR', Oxford Bulletin of Economics and
      Statistics, 20(2):1967.
   -   'Agrarian reform in the UAR', Oxford Bulletin of

Economics and Statistics, 21(2):1968.

Eswaran, M. and Kotwal, A., 'A theory of two-tier labour
   markets in agrarian economies'. American Economic
   Review, 75(1):1985, pp.162-177.

Farrington, J. Abeyratne, F. and Gill, G.J., (eds), Farm Power
   and Employment in Asia, Bangkok:Agricultural Development
   Council, 1984.

Feder, G., Just, R. and Silberman, D., Adoption of
   Agricultural Innovations in Developing Countries: a Survey, World Bank Staff Paper No.542, Washington, 1982.

Fergany, N., Intra-Arab Migration and Development, Oxford, May
   1983 (mimeo).

Field, J. and Ropes, G., 'Development in the Egyptian
   Governorates: a modified physical quality of life
   index'. L'Egypte Contemporaire, 69(354):1978,
   pp.149-161.

Fields, G., 'The private demand for education in relation to
   labour market conditions in ldcs'. Economic Journal,
   84(336):1974, pp.906-925.
   -   'Rural-urban migration, urban unemployment and
       underemployment and job search activity in ldcs',
       Journal of Development Economics, 11 June 1975.

Firebaugh, F.M. et al., 'Increasing agricultural production
   through more effective use of technology: recommen-
   dations for a strengthened agricultural extension
   programme in Egypt', AID Research and Development
   Abstracts, 10(1/2):1982, pp.65-66.

Fitch, J.B., Goueli, A.A. and El Gabely, M., 'The cropping
   system for maize in Egypt: survey findings and
   implications for policy and research', Cairo, 1979.
   -   and Abdel-Aziz, A., Multiple Cropping Intensity in
       Egyptian Agriculture: a Study of its Determinants,
       Micro-Economic Study of Egyptian Farm Systems, Paper 6,
       Cairo, 1980.
   -   and Imam, S., 'An economic re-evaluation of the
       multi-crop thresher system for Egypt', Cairo, 1980.
   -   and Soliman, I., 'Livestock and crop production linkages:
       implications for agricultural policy', ADS Paper 92,
       Cairo, 1982.
   -   and Soliman, I., 'Livestock and small farmer labour supply',
       in Richards and Martin (1983) op cit., pp.45-78.

Gemmell, N., 'The role of the non-market sector in Egypt's
   economic growth, 1960-1976'. Oxford Economic Papers,
   34(1):1982.
   'The growth of employment in services: Egypt,
   1960-1975', The Developing Economies, 23(1):1985,
   pp.53-68.

Ghose, A.K., 'Wages and employment in Indian agriculture',
   World Development, 8(5/6):1980, pp.413-428.

Gilbert, T., 'Changing values in Egyptian agriculture', MA
   Thesis, London University, 1940.

Girgis, M., Industrialisation and Trade Patterns in Egypt,

Tubingen, 1977.

Goueli, A. et al, 'Village institutions, socio-economic characteristics and economic indicators from the 1976/77 Egyptian farm management survey', Cairo, 1980.

- 'Food security programme in Egypt', in A. Valdes (ed), Food Security for Developing Countries, Boulder:Westview Press, 1981, pp.143-157.

- 'Some aspects of agricultural labour in Egypt', Cairo, 1980 (mimeo).

- and Hindy, M.K., 'The Egyptian farm management survey: an approach to understanding a complex agricultural system', Cairo, 1979 (mimeo).

- and Soliman, I., 'The productive efficiency of the broiler industry in Egypt', (unpublished), Cairo, 1984.

Gotsch, C.H., 'Mechanical technology in Egyptian, Indian and Pakistani agriculture: an induced innovation perspective', in Richards and Martin (1983) op cit., pp.265-282.

- and Dyer, W., 'Rhetoric and reason in the Egyptian 'New Lands' debate'. Food Research Institute Studies, 18(2):1982, pp.129-148.

Gubbins, K.E. and Campion, D.G., 'Economic aspects of pheromone trapping techniques for the control of Egyptian cotton leafwork', Outlook on Agriculture, 11(2):1982, pp.62-66.

Habashy, N.T. and Fitch, J.B., 'Egypt's agricultural cropping pattern', Cairo, 1980.

Hadhoud, A.A., 'An economic study of agricultural labour in Egypt', PhD, University of Zagazig, 1982.

Haider, M. and Skold, M., 'Planning irrigation improvements in Egypt: the impact of policies and prices on farm income and resource use', EWUP Report 43, Cairo, 1983.

- Fawzi, G. et al., Farm record summary and analysis, Beni Maghdul (1978-1983), EWUP Technical Report 78, Cairo, 1984.

Handoussa, H.A., Industrialisation in Egypt: Lessons from the Recent Past, Vienna:UNIDO, 1983.

- Public Sector Employment and Productivity in the Egyptian Economy, Geneva:ILO, 1983.

Hansen, B., 'Employment and wages in rural Egypt', American Economic Review, 59:1969, pp.298-314.

- 'Economic development in Egypt', in C. Cooper and S. Alexander (eds), Economic Development and Population Growth in the Middle East, New York:Elsevier, 1972.

- 'Arab socialism in Egypt', World Development, 3(4):1975, pp.201-211.

- 'An economic model for Ottoman Egypt: the economics of collective tax responsibility', in Udovitch (1984) op cit., pp.473-519.

- The Egyptian Labour Market: An overview. Development Research Department Discussion Paper DRD 160, Washington:World Bank, 1985.

- and Marzouk, G., Development and Economic Policy in the UAR (Egypt), Amsterdam:North Holland Publishers, 1965.
- and Nashashibi, K., Foreign Trade and Economic Development: Egypt, New York:National Bureau of Economic Research, 1975.
- and El Tomy, M., 'The seasonal employment profile in Egyptian agriculture', Journal of Development Studies, July 1965, pp.399-409.
- and Wattleworth, M., 'Agricultural output and consumption of basic foods in Egypt, 1886/67-1967/68', International Journal of Middle Eastern Studies, 9(4):1978.

Hanson, J.A., 'Employment and rural wages in Egypt', American Economic Review 61:1971, pp.492-499.

Harik, I., Distribution of Land, Employment and Income in Rural Egypt, Cornell Series on Landlessness and Near-Landlessness, No.5, Ithaca, 1979.
- 'Certainty and change in local development policies in Egypt', in L. Cantori and I. Harik, (eds), Local Politics and Development in the Middle East, Boulder:Westview Press, 1984.
- The Political Mobilisation of Peasants: A Study of an Egyptian Community, Indiana University Press, 1974.

Hassan, A., A Field Study on Crop Rotation in Ten Villages, INP, Cairo, 1974.

Hassanain, T.M., 'Socio-economic characteristics of small farmers in Sharkiya Governorate', MSc, University of Zagazig, 1984.

Hayami, Y. and Ruttan, V.W., Agricultural Development: An International Perspective, Baltimore:Johns Hopkins Press, 1971.

Hebblethwaite, M., 'An economic assessment of Pheronomes in cotton pest control in Egypt', London:TDRI, 1985.

Hindy, M.K., Egyptian Agricultural Development and the Role of Agricultural Intensification, ADS Paper 5, Cairo, 1981.

Hofmann, M. et al, Employment and Migration in an Intermediate Egyptian City: The Role of the Informal Sector in Fayoum City, Berlin:German Development Institute, 1983.

Holt, P.M. (ed), Political and Social Change in Modern Egypt, Oxford University Press, 1968.

Hopkins, N.S., Mechanization Decisions in Egyptian Villages, ADS Paper 47, Cairo, 1981.
- 'The social impact of mechanization', in Richards and Martin (1983) op cit., pp.181-198.
  'Irrigation, mechanized agriculture and the State: the case of an Upper Egyptian village', in B.L. Turner and S.B. Brush, Farming Systems, New York, 1985.
- Abdel-Maksoud, B. et al., Animal Husbandry and the Household Economy in Two Egyptian Villages, Cairo, 1980.
- and Mehanna, S., Egyptian Village Studies, ADS Paper 42, Cairo, 1981.

-   Mehanna, S. and Abdel-Maksoud, B., 'The state of agricultural mechanization in Egypt: the results of a survey, 1982', Cairo, 1982.
Hopwood, D., Egypt, London:Croom Helm, 1982.
El Hossary, A., A Case Study of the Effect of Mechanization on Productivity and Employment in Egypt, Rome:FAO, 1975.
-   'Agricultural mechanization in Egypt', Cairo, 1979.
Howitt, R. Goueli, A.A. and El-Khashen, K., 'An investigation of the pattern of regional specialisation in Egypt', Cairo, 1984.
Huntingdon, R., Mehanna, S. et al, The Introduction of Appropriate Technology to Upper Egyptian Agriculture, Cairo:American University, 1984.
Hussein, H.M., 'Pilot survey of family budgets in Egypt', International Labour Review, 78(3)September 1958.
Hussein, M., Class Conflict in Egypt, 1945-1971, New York:Monthly Review Press, 1973.
Ibrahim, S.E., 'Social mobility and income distribution in Egypt, 1952-1977', in Abdel Khalek and Tignor (1982) op cit., pp.375-434.
-   Internal Migration in Egypt: A Critical Review, Research Monograph No.5, Population and Family Planning Board, 1982.
IBRD, Arab Republic of Egypt: Economic Management in a Period of Transition, (6 vols), Washington, 1978.
-   Arab Republic of Egypt: Domestic Resource Mobilization and Growth Prospects for the 1980s, Washington, 1980.
-   Some Issues in Population and Human Resource Development, Washington, 1981.
-   Arab Republic of Egypt: Issues of Trade Strategy and Investment Planning, Washington, 1983 (a).
-   Arab Republic of Egypt: Current Economic Situation and Growth Prospects, Washington, 1983 (b).
-   Arab Republic of Egypt: Current Economic Situation and Economic Reform Programme, Washington, 1986.
-   Second Agricultural Development Project, Annual Report, 5342a-EGT, Washington, 1985.
Ikram, K., Egypt: Economic Management in a Period of Transition, Washington:Johns Hopkins, 1980.
ILO, Rural Employment Problems in the UAR, Geneva:ILO, 1969.
Imam, S., An economic evaluation of farm management in Egypt, ADS Paper 117, Cairo, 1983.
-   and Khalil, M., Farm mechanization policy in Egypt, ADS Paper 118, Cairo, January 1983.

of the Pattern of Regional Specialisation in Egypt', Cairo, 1984.
Huntingdon, R., Mehanna, S. et al, The Introduction of Appropriate Technology to Upper Egyptian Agriculture, Cairo:American University, 1984.
Hussein, H.M., 'Pilot survey of family budgets in Egypt', International Labour Review, 78(3)September 1958.

Hussein, M., Class Conflict in Egypt, 1945-1971, New
    York:Monthly Review Press, 1973.
Ibrahim, S.E., 'Social mobility and income distribution in
    Egypt, 1952-1977', in Abdel Khalek and Tignor (1982) op
    cit., pp.375-434.
-   Internal migration in Egypt: a critical review, Research
    Monograph No.5, Population and Family Planning Board,
    1982.
IBRD, Arab Republic of Egypt: Economic Management in a Period
    of Transition, (6 vols), Washington, 1978.
-   Arab Republic of Egypt: Domestic Resource Mobilization
    and Growth Prospects for the 1980s, Washington, 1980.
-   Some Issues in Population and Human Resource Development,
    Washington, 1981.
-   Arab Republic of Egypt: Issues of Trade Strategy and
    Investment Planning, Washington, 1983 (a).
-   Arab Republic of Egypt: Current Economic Situation and
    Growth Prospects, Washington, 1983 (b).
-   Arab Republic of Egypt: Current Economic Situation and
    Economic Reform Programme. Washington, 1986.
-   Second Agricultural Development Project, Annual Report,
    5342a-EGT, Washington, 1985.
Ikram, K., Egypt: Economic Management in a Period of
    Transition, Washington:Johns Hopkins, 1980.
ILO, Rural Employment Problems in the UAR, Geneva:ILO, 1969.
Imam, S., An economic evaluation of farm management in Egypt,
    ADS Paper 117, Cairo, 1983.
-   and Khalil, M., Farm mechanization policy in Egypt, ADS
    Paper 118, Cairo, January 1983.
El Imam, M.M., 'A production function for Egyptian agriculture,
    1913-1955', Memo 259, INP, Cairo, 1962.
Institute of National Planning, UAR, Planning the Labour Force
    in the UAR, Cairo, November, 1966.
Ismail, S. Gardner, D.B. and Abdou, D., The Distribution of
    Consumption of Basic Food Commodities in the Urban and
    Rural Areas of Egypt, ADS Paper 59, Cairo, 1982.
Issawi, C., Egypt in Revolution: An Economic Analysis, Oxford
    University Press, 1963.
El-Issawy, I., 'Interconnections between income distribution
    and economic growth in the context of Egypt's economic
    development', in Abdel-Khalek and Tignor, (1982) op
    cit., pp.88-131.
-   Employment Inadequacy in Egypt, Geneva:ILO, 1983 (a).
-   Labour Force, Employment and Unemployment, Geneva:ILO,
    1983 (b).
de Janvry, A. Siam, G. and Gad, O., 'The impact of forced
    deliveries on Egyptian agriculture', American Journal
    of Agricultural Economics, 65, 1983, pp.493-501.
-   and Subbarao, K., Welfare Effects of Forced Deliveries
    and Area Eequirements in Egyptian Agriculture, ADS Paper
    162, Cairo, 1983.
-   and Subbarao, K., 'Wages, prices and farm mechanization

in Egypt: the need for an integrated policy', in
Richards and Martin (1983) op cit., pp.237-264.

Kakwani, N.C. and Podder, N., 'Efficient estimation of the
Lorenz Curve and associated inequality measures from
grouped observations', Econometrica, 44(1):1976,
pp.137-148.

Kelley, A. et al., Population and Development in Rural Egypt,
Durham, North Carolina:Duke University Press, 1982.
-     Khalifa, A.M. and El-Khorazaty, M.N., Population and
Development in Rural Egypt, Durham:Duke University
Press, 1982.

Khafagy, F., 'The socio-economic impact of emigration from a
Giza village', in Richards and Martin (1983) op cit.,
pp.135-158.
-     'The socio-economic impact of the spending of remittan-
ces by emigrant Egyptian labour', PhD, University
College London, 1984.

El-Kholy, O., 'Disparities of Egyptian personal income distribution as reflected by family budget data', L'Egypte
Contemporaire, 64, 1973, pp.33-56.
-     and Abbas, M., A Socio-Economic Survey of Small Farmers
Within the Domain of Selected Village Banks, Cairo, 1982
(mimeo).

Killingsworth, M.R., Labour Supply, Cambridge University
Press, 1983.

Knight, J.B. and Sabot, R.H., 'The returns to education:
increasing with experience or decreasing with expansion', Oxford Bulletin of Economics and Statistics,
43(1):1981, pp.51-72.

Korayem, K., The Impact of the Elimination of Food Subsidies
on the Cost of Living of Egypt's Urban Population,
World Employment Programme, Working Paper 91,
Geneva:ILO, 1980.
-     'The agricultural output pricing policy and the implicit
taxation of agricultural income', in Abdel-Khalek and
Tignor (1982) op cit., pp.165-197.
-     Government Policies and the Labour Market in Egypt, INP
Memo 1393, Cairo, 1984.

Koval, A.J. and Bahgat, A.A., 'Ten Horsepower Agriculture',
Cairo, 1980.

Krishna, R. and Chibber, A., Policy Modelling of a Dual Grain
Market: The Case of Wheat in India, Washington:IFPRI,
1983.

Kutcher, G.P., 'The agro-economic model', Water Resource
Development and Use Report 16, Cairo, 1980.
-     and Norton, R.D., Operation Research Methods in Agricultural Policy Analysis, Reprint Series 234,
Washington:World Bank, 1983.

Landes, D., Bankers and Pashas: International Finance and
Economic Imperialism in Egypt, Harvard University
Press, 1985

Lesch, A.M., Egyptian Labour Migration: Economic Trends and

Government Policies, UFSI Report No 38, Africa;
Indiana, 1985.
Levy, V., 'Cropping patterns, mechanization, child labour and
fertility behaviour in a farming economy: rural Egypt',
Economic Development and Cultural Change, 33(4):1985,
pp.777-792.
Loza, S.F., 'Differential age at marriage and fertility in
Egypt', in Determinants of Fertility in Some African
and Asian countries, CDC Research Monograph 10, Cairo,
1982.
Mabro, R., 'Industrial growth and agricultural underemployment
and the Lewis model: the Egyptian case', Journal of
Development Studies, 4:1967.
-    'Employment and wages in dual agriculture', Oxford
Economic Papers, 23(3):1971.
-    The Egyptian Economy, 1952-1970, Oxford University
Press, 1974.
-    and Radwan, S., The Industrialisation of Egypt,
1939-1973: Policy and Performance, Oxford University
Press, 1976.
Marei, S., 'The Agrarian Reforms in Egypt', International
Labour Review, 69(2):1954.
Marsot, A.L.S., Egypt in the Reign of Mohammed Ali, Cambridge
University Press, 1983.
-    A Short History of Modern Egypt, Cambridge University
Press, 1985.
Mazumdar, D., The Urban Labour Market and Income Distribution:
A Study of Malaysia, New York:Oxford University Press,
1981.
Mead, D.C., Growth and Structural Change in the Egyptian
Economy, Illinois:Richard Irwin, 1967.
Ministry of Agriculture, Egypt, Third Agricultural Census,
1950, Cairo, 1958.
-    Fourth Agricultural Census, 1961, Cairo, 1967.
-    Agricultural Economics Bulletin, Cairo, 1979.
Ministry of Health, Arab Republic of Egypt National Survey,
1978, Cairo:USAID, 1979.
Ministry of Planning, Egypt, 'The detailed frame of the five
year plan for economic and social development,
1982/3-1986/7', Cairo, 1982.
Mohammed, A.A. and El-Shenawy, M.A., Food Intake According to
Region and Landholding Size in Rural Egypt, ADS Paper
174, Cairo, 1983.
Mohie-eldin, A., 'Agricultural investment and employment in
Egypt since 1935', PhD, LSE, 1966.
-    The External Migration of Egyptian Labour, Cairo, 1980.
-    Employment Problems and Policies in Egypt, Beirut:ILO,
1975.
-    'Underemployment in Egyptian agriculture', in ILO/ECWA,
Manpower and Employment in Arab Countries: Some
Critical Issues, Geneva, 1975.
-    'The development of the share of agricultural wage

labour in the national income of Egypt', in Abdel-Khalek
and Tignor (1982) op cit., pp.236-267.

Mursy, M.K., L'Evolution Historique du Droit de Proprieté
Fonciere en Egypte, Cairo, 1935.

McInerney, J.P. and Donaldson, G.E., The consequences of farm
tractors in Pakistan, Staff Paper 210, Washington:World
Bank, 1975.

Nagi, M.H., Labour Force and Employment in Egypt: A
Demographic and Socio-Economic Analysis, New
York:Praeger Press, 1971.

-      'Internal migration and structural changes in Egypt',
Middle East Journal, 28(3):1974.

Nasr, M., 'Betriebliches produktionsverhalten im Rahmen des
Agyptischen Systems der Staatlichen Anbauplanung in der
Landwirtschaft', PhD, Gottingen University, 1983.

Nassar, S. and Imam, S., Alternative Agricultural Pricing
Policy in Egypt', ADS Paper 169, Cairo, 1983.

Nassef, A.F., Demographic Developments in Egypt, 1960-1976,
Gen 1983.

Nutting, Anthony, Nasser, New York:E.P. Dutton & Co, 1972.

O'Brien, P.K., 'Industrial development and the employment
problem in Egypt, 1945-1963, Middle East Economic
Papers, Beirut, 1962.
The Revolution in Egypt's Economic System, Oxford
University Press, 1962.

-      and Mabro, R., 'Structural change in the Egyptian
economy', in M.A. Cook (ed), Studies in the Economic
History of the Middle East, Oxford University Press,
1970.

Oweis, J.S., 'The impact of land reform on Egyptian
agriculture, 1952-1965', International Economic Review,
11(1):1960.

Owen, E.R.J., Cotton and the Egyptian Economy, 1820-1914,
Oxford University Press, 1969.

-      'The development of agricultural production in
Nineteenth Century Egypt: capitalism of what type?', in
Udovitch (1984) op cit., pp.523-546.

Papers on migration and mechanization in Egyptian agriculture,
ADS Paper 56, Cairo, 1982.

Perlmutter, A., Egypt, The Praetorian State, New Jersey, 1974.

Pesaran, M.H., 'On the general problem of model selection',
Review of Economic Studies, 41,2,126, 1974, pp.153-173.

-      and Deaton, A.S., 'Testing non-linear regression
models', Econometrica, 46(3):1978, pp.677-694.

Psacharapoulos, G., Returns to Education, San Francisco, 1973.

Radwan, S., Capital Formation in Egyptian Industry and
Agriculture, 1882-1962, London:Ithaca Press, 1974.

-      Agrarian Reform and Rural Poverty: Egypt, 1952-1975,
Geneva:ILO, 1977.

-      The Impact of Agrarian Reform on Rural Egypt, 1952-1975,
ILO/WEP Working Paper, 1977.

Raj, K.N., Employment Aspects of Planning in Underdeveloped

Countries, Cairo:National Bank of Egypt, 1955.
Raymond, A., 'The economic crisis of Egypt in the Eighteenth
    Century', in Udovitch (1984) op cit., pp.687-707.
Reiss, P. El Haddad, Z. El Yamani, A.T. and Lutfi, R.,
    'Agricultural mechanization and labour: a look at the
    demand and supply sides' Cairo, 1983.
 - Lutfi, R. El Din Nasr, N. and El Tunsi, A.,
    'Agricultural mechanization project villages profile',
    Cairo, 1982.
Rehnberg, R. and Ayad, G. et al., Farm record summary and
    Analysis: Kafr-el-Sheikh, EWUP Technical Report 76,
    Cairo, 1984.
Reynolds, L. (ed), Agriculture in Development Theory, Yale
    University Press, 1976.
Ricardo, D., Principles of Political Economy, Cambridge
    University Press, 1951.
Rice Mechanization Project, 'Egypt-Japan technical
    co-operation, annual Report 1982/3', Ministry of
    Agriculture, Cairo, 1983.
Richards, A.R., 'The agricultural crisis in Egypt', Journal of
    Development Studies, 16(3):1980, pp.303-321.
 - 'Mechanization in Egyptian agriculture', International
    Journal of Middle East Studies, 13(4):1981, pp.409-425.
 - Agricultural mechanization in Egypt: hopes and fears,
    ADS Paper 2, 1981.
 - 'Peasant differentiation and politics in contemporary
    Egypt', Peasant Studies, 9(3):1982, pp.145-161.
 - Egypt's Agricultural Development, 1800-1980: Technical and
    Social Change, Boulder:Westview Press, 1983.
 - and Martin, P.L., Rural social structure and the
    agricultural labour market: Sharqiyya evidence and
    policy implication, ADS Paper 8, Cairo, 1981.
 - and Martin, P.L. (eds), Migration, Mechanization and
    Agricultural Labour Markets in Egypt, Boulder:Westview
    Press, 1983.
 - and Martin, P.L., 'Labour shortages in Egyptian
    agriculture', in Richards and Martin (1983) op cit.,
    pp.21-44.
 - and Martin, P.L., 'The laissez-faire approach to
    international labour migration: the case of the Arab
    Middle East', Economic Development and Cultural Change,
    31(3):1983, pp.454-474.
Rivlin, H., The Agricultural Policy of Mohammed Ali in Egypt,
    Harvard University Press, 1961.
Rosenzweig, M.R., 'The demand for children in farm households',
    Journal of Political Economy, 85:1977, pp.123-146.
 - Rural wages, labour supply and land reform: a
    theoretical and empirical analysis, Programme in
    Development Studies Discussion Paper 20, Princeton
    University, 1976.
 - 'Determinants of wage rates and labour supply behaviour
    in the rural sector of a developing country', in

Binswanger, H.P. and Rosenzweig, M.R. Contractual Arrangements, Employment and Wages in Rural Labour Markets in Asia, Yale University Press, 1984.

Roumasset, J., Boussard, J-M. and Singh, I.J. (eds), Risk, Uncertainty and Agricultural Development, New York, 1979.

- and Smith, J., 'Population, technological change and the evolution of labour markets', Population and Development Review, 7(3):1981, pp.401-419.

Rudra, A., 'Farm size and yield per acre', Economic and Political Weekly, 3 (Special Number):1968, pp.1041-5.

Saab, G., The Egyptian Agrarian Reform, 1952-62, Oxford University Press, 1967.

Sabot, R.H. (ed), Migration and the Labour Market in Developing Countries, Boulder:Westview Press, 1982.

Sagi, E., 'An econometric study of some issues in the economic development of Egypt: agricultural supply, industrial growth and the burden of defence expenditures', PhD, University of Pennsylvania, 1980.

El Salmi, A., Public Sector Management: An Analysis of Decision-Making and Employment Policies and Practices in Egypt, Geneva:ILO, 1983.

El Sanhouty, S., 'Credit and agricultural development in Sharkiya Governorate', Ninth International Congress for Statistics, Social and Demographic Research, Ain Shams, University of Cairo, 1984.

Sanyal, B. et al, University Education and the Labour Market in Egypt, Oxford:Pergamon Press, 1983.

Sarris, A., Egyptian Food Security: An Optimization Approach, ADS Paper 96, Cairo, 1982.

Sayed, H.A. and Khorazaty, M.N., 'Levels and differentials of fertility in Egypt, Population Series 55, Cairo, 1980, pp.11-38.

Sayegh, F., 'The theoretical structure of Nasser's Arab socialism', in A. Hourani (ed), St Antony's Papers: Middle Eastern Affairs, 4, London:Allen & Unwin, 1965.

Schneider, R.R., 'Food subsidies: a multiple price model', IMF Staff Papers, 32(2):1985, pp.289-316.

Scobie, G.M., Government Policy and Food Imports: The Case of Wheat in Egypt, IFPRI Research Report 29, 1981.

- Food subsidies in Egypt: Their Impact on Foreign Exchange and Trade, IFPRI Research Report 40, 1983.

Schutjer, W.A., Stokes, C.S. and Poindexter, S.R., 'Farm size, land ownership and fertility in rural Egypt', Land Economics, 59(4): 1983, pp.393-403.

Sen, Abhijit, 'Market failure and control of labour power: towards an explanation of structure and change in Indian agriculture', Cambridge Journal of Economics, 5(3)&(4):1981, pp.201-228 and 327-350.

Sen, A.K., 'Size of holdings and productivity', Economic Weekly, 16, Annual Number, 1964.

- Employment, Technology and Development, Oxford

University Press, 1975.
- 'Economics and the family', Asian Development Review, 1(2):1983, pp.14-26.
El Shafei, A.N., 'The current labour force sample survey in UAR', International Labour Review, 82:1960.
Shafik, N.T., 'Analysis of the Egyptian Government Budget: Agriculture, Health and Education Sectors, Cairo, 1984 (mimeo).
Shami, M.G.A., 'Impact of cotton on the economic development of Egypt, 1952-1976', PhD, University of Wisconsin, 1979.
Shapouri, S. and Soliman, I., The Role of Meat in the Egyptian Economy, ADS Paper 119, Cairo, 1983.
Sharaf El-Din, H.A.F., Labour Productivity in Egyptian Industry, 1965-1975, Swansea:University of Wales, 1982.
Shaw, R.P., Mobilizing Human Resources in the Arab World, London:KPI, 1983.
El-Shenawy, M.A. and Abdou, A.I., Patterns of food Expenditure in Egypt, ADS Paper 160, Cairo, 1983.
Shepley, S., 'Egyptian cotton production economics and farmer response to government price intervention and meat import policies', Cairo, 1984.
- Gaiser, D.W. and El-Haddad, Z., 'Reducing maize losses through optimizing the date of planting', Cairo, 1983.
- Shoukry, M. and Wassa, Z.H.K., 'Crop enterprise budgets and mechanization impact on long birseem production', Cairo, 1983.
- Wissa, Z.H. and El-Haddad, Z., 'A methodology for evaluating economic and financial costs of tractor operations in Egypt', Cairo, 1982.
- Wissa, Z.H. and El Din Nasr, N., 'Partial economic analysis of mechanized wheat production in selected project villages', Cairo, 1984.
El Shinnawy, Haider, M., Skold, M. et al, Farm Record Summary and Analysis, El-Hammami (1978-1983), EWUP Technical Report 77, Cairo, 1984.
Soliman, I., 'Concentrated feed mix in Egypt: an analysis of government production and distribution policies and free market price patterns', Cairo, 1981.
- Food Security in Egypt: the Socio-economic Implications of Dietary Protein-energy Interrelationships, ADS Paper 97, Cairo, 1982.
- 'Milk response analysis under traditional mixed farming systems in Egypt', (unpublished), Cairo, 1984.
- Abdel-Azim, M. and Habib, F., Some Observations on Livestock Policies in Egypt, ADS Paper 135, Cairo, 1983.
- Ragab, A. and Mahdy, S., 'Milk disposal patterns and milk processing on traditional farms', Cairo, 1984.
- and Mahdy, S., 'Labour use patterns for livestock operations', Cairo, 1984.
- and Ragab, A., 'An economic study of livestock on traditional farms', Cairo, 1983.

-    and El Shahat, Z., _A Study of the Applicability of_
     Current Livestock Policies Among Producers in Sharkiya,
     ADS Paper 77, Cairo, 1982.
-    and El Shenawy, M., 'Livestock working power in Egyptian
     agriculture', Institute of Statistical Studies, 18th
     Annual Conference, 18,1, Cairo, 1983.
-    El Zaher, T. and Fitch, J., _Milk Production Systems in_
     Egypt and the Impact of Government Policies, ADS Paper
     121, Cairo, 1983.
Springborg, R., _Family, Power and Politics_, Pennsylvania
     University Press, 1982.
Squire, L., _Employment Policy in Developing Countries_, New
     York: Oxford University Press, 1981.
Standing, G. and Sheehan, G. (eds), _Labour Force Participation_
     in Low Income Countries, Geneva:ILO, 1978.
Starr, G., _Wages in the Egyptian Formal Sector_, Geneva:ILO,
     1983.
Stauth, G., 'Patterns of small peasant reproduction and its
     destruction: the case of the Fellaheen of the Nile
     Delta', _Arbeitspapiere_ 20, Bielefeld, 1982.
Sternberger, H., 'Defence expenditures in perspective', Cairo,
     1983 (mimeo).
Stiglitz, J.E., 'The efficiency wage hypothesis, surplus
     labour and the distribution of income in ldcs', _Oxford_
     Economic Papers, 28(2):1976, pp.185-207.
Taylor, E., 'Egyptian migration and peasant wives', in _MERIP_
     Report, 124, 14(5):1984, pp.3-10.
Taylor, L., _Macro Models for Developing Countries_, New
     York:Mcgraw Hill, 1979.
Thomson, A., 'Egypt: food security and food aid', _Food Policy_,
     18(3): 1983.
Tignor, R., 'Nationalism, economic planning and development
     projects in interwar Egypt', _International Journal of_
     African Historical Studies, 10(2):1977, pp.185-208.
-    'Equity in Egypt's recent past, 1945-1952', in
     Abdel-Khalek and Tignor (1982) op cit., pp.20-54.
-    _State, Rural Enterprise and Economic Change in Egypt,_
     _1918-52_, Princeton University Press, 1984.
El Tobgy, H.A., _Contemporary Egyptian Agriculture_, Cairo:Ford
     Foundation, 1976.
Turnham, D., _The Employment Problem in Less Developed_
     Countries, Paris:OECD, Paris, 1971.
Udovitch, A.L. (ed), _The Islamic Middle East, 700-1900:_
     Studies in Economic and Social History, Princeton
     University Press, 1984.
USAID, 'Status report on agricultural mechanization in Egypt ',
     (unpublished), Cairo, 1983.
-    'Egypt, FY 1986, country development strategy
     statement', Cairo, 1984.
USDA, 'Egypt: major constraints to increasing agricultural
     productivity', _Foreign Agriculture Report_ 120,
     Washington, 1977.

Vatikiotis, P.J., The Modern History of Egypt, London:Allen &
    Unwin, 1969.
-    Egypt Since the Revolution, London:Allen & Unwin, 1968.
Warriner, D., Land and Poverty in the Middle East, London:
    Frank Cass & Co., 1948.
Waterbury, J., Egypt - Burdens of the Past, Indiana University
    Press, 1978.
-    Hydropolitics of the Nile Valley, Syracuse University
    Press, 1979.
-    'Patterns of urban growth and income distribution in
    Egypt', in Abdel-Khalek and Tignor (1982) op cit.,
    pp.307-350.
-    The Egypt of Nasser and Sadat: The Political Economy of
    Two Regimes, Princeton University Press, 1983.
Wikan, U., Life Among the Poor in Cairo, London:Methuen, 1980.
Willcocks, W., Egyptian Irrigation, London:F. Spon, 1889.
Wilson, R.J.A., 'Egypt's export diversification: benefits and
    constraints', The Developing Economies, 22(1):1984,
    pp.86-101.
Wood, R.H., 'Tractor mechanization and employment on larger
    private Mexican farms', International Labour Review,
    22(2):1983, pp.211-225.
Youssef, I.A., 'Estimation of employment in the agricultural
    economy of Sharkiya Governorate', MSc, University of
    Zagazig, 1983.
Zaytoun, M.A., 'Income distribution in Egyptian agriculture
    and its main determinants', in Abdel-Khalek and Tignor
    (1982) op cit., pp.268-306.
Zimmerman, S.D., 'The women of Kafr-al-Bahr (Menoufiya): a
    research into the working conditions of women in an
    Egyptian village', Women and Development Series, Leiden
    University, 1982.